The Secret of Coexistence

The Secret of Coexistence

Jews And Arabs In Haifa During The British Mandate In Palestine, 1920-1948

Daphna Sharfman (editor)
Eli Nachmias, Johnny Mansour

BookSurge 2007

The Secret of Coexistence

Table of Contents

Acknowledgements

We would like to thank the people that assisted us in the research and publication of this book—Haifa's Mayor Yona Yahav and Professor Ya'akov Goldstein for writing the introduction and the preface of the book. Dr. Gabriel Alexander, director of K.K.L. Institute of History of the Zionism and Settlement; the former director of the Haifa City Archive, Dr. Zipora Har-Shefer and the archive staff Luba Ormanski, Liat Proser-Romano, Binyamin Ophir, Gershon Shai and Igor Volkovitski. Haim Sperber for his kind advice; Shalom Benoliel and Natalia Farber of the Ahva publishing house for their assistance; the Haifa History Society: Chairman David Hendel, attorney Eli Roman and Yair Safran; architect Ziva Kolodney, for providing historical sources and information on conservation in Haifa. Bracha Sela, Secretary General of Haifa Municipality, for her encouragement along the way, and Aviva Shpigelshtein, director of Haifa Arts Foundation. The book is published with the assistance of the Western Galilee College, Israel.

Daphna Sharfman
Haifa, 2007

Introduction

We Are All the Product of Haifa's "Melting-Pot"

Attorney Yona Yahav, Mayor of Haifa

I was born in Haifa about 60 years ago and grew up on Hilel street in Hadar HaCarmel neighborhood. Living in this street were Arabs, Jewish veterans and newcomers who arrived from Europe after surviving the Holocaust. We, the kids from the neighborhood, played and studied together, children of families who came from Germany and Poland, with Arab and Christian Muslim children. We are all the products of Haifa's "melting-pot."

Approximately 271,000 inhabitants are living in 100,000 households in Haifa. The city is built on a slope which stretches from the Carmel Mountain to Haifa's bay. The city is surrounded by thickets and long sandy beaches. There are two universities in Haifa with 35,000 students and about 8,000 academic staff members. There are also university hospitals, a high-tech center, scientific research and high-tech industries which are the largest in Israel. International companies such as Intel, General Motors, and Phillips operate alongside Israeli companies such as Zoran, El-op, etc. The research center of IBM, which is the largest outside of the United States, is located in Haifa. There is a deep-water harbor in Haifa and beside it a petro-chemical industry area and the refineries. In the last decade, approximately 70,000 new immigrants found new homes in Haifa, the majority of them from the former Soviet Union states.

I believe that peace will reside, and when it does, it will be designed according to the "Haifa Model." What is this "Haifa Model" which the authors of the book try to portray?

About 12% of Haifa's inhabitants are Arab, 65% of them are Christians, and the rest are Muslims. In the city council, 31 members operate in the wall-to-wall coalition. Three members are Arab; one of them is deputy-mayor. The Haifa municipality's treasurer is Arab and so are many senior officials. In the municipality of Haifa, about 20% of the workers are Arab. That is a higher percentage than their proportion in the population. Justice Salim Jubran was chosen to the Supreme Court recently, the first among Israel's Arabs. Many of the lawyers and Judges are Arab.

Approximately 20% of the students in the University of Haifa are Arab and there are Arab professors and lecturers in the academic staff. Sixteen percent of the doctors and nurses in Haifa's hospitals are Arab. The same goes for school teachers, merchants, store-owners and other occupations.

The integration of Haifa's Arabs in all the economic and social systems in the city helps them believe that they are equal partners in managing the city and establishing the city's goals. They also feel that they are partners in shaping their own future as an inseparable part of the city life. They do not consider themselves rejected or inferior and there is no "patronizing rule" in Haifa. This is the "Haifa Model" in a nutshell.

The writers of this book aim to portray the character of Haifa and the reasons for the "coexistence." In my opinion, there are many aspects in analyzing the unique reality of the shared life and the tolerance that characterized the city in the Mandate era. We can examine the different economic aspects of the segregated but also cooperative economies in Haifa; the unique coexistence between Arabs and Jews, including culture and entertainment patterns in British Mandatory Haifa; the diverse features of life in the Arab society in Haifa; the points of view are different and distinctive.

The findings of the book point to a unique model of Haifa, which was designed through the years and developed a style of its own that is basically dynamic. The thread passing through it is a solid spine of tolerance, coexistence, understanding and a will for a shared life between Arabs and Jews in this interesting and special city.

As mayor and resident of Haifa, I am very concerned with the question of what to do in order to preserve the unique reality of the shared life and tolerance. I believe that the solution lies in presenting challenges to the people of Haifa, challenges which each of them can identify with and support.

These challenges are found in the many fields of ecology, the improvement of the quality of life, and the preservation of the environment. The proximity to nature and the beautiful scenery (which always characterize the physical environment of our city) requires great responsibility in taking care of them; while at the same time developing the city in a considerate and high quality way as a center of high-tech industry and an attractive city for young people.

The "Haifa Model" has already broken out of the country's boundaries. There are imitations, and I am glad for it, although I should mention that the imitation does not always match and coincide with the Haifa original. However, I cannot write a "patent" on the Haifa lifestyle. All I want is the model to extend to the rest of the country and receive a position of respect. Nonetheless, the existing web should be strengthened; although it is stable, it needs "constant maintenance" of acknowledgement and positive reassurance. It is a pleasant duty for me to admit that I, as mayor of Haifa, have the responsibility of sailing the ship forward, preserving what was in the past and row towards a constant improvement of the existent; it needs to be remembered that the life of sanity and political tolerance that the inhabitants of Haifa chose willingly and knowingly for several generations, is bearing fruit. Proudly, I can bring you our message, from all of Haifa's inhabitants: "It is different in Haifa. Haifa is an island of sanity in a stormy ocean."

The authors of the book endeavor to portray the outlines of Haifa's history, while trying to trace the roots of the political and social state I described earlier. From the description and data given by the different essays included in the book, we detect that the uniqueness of Haifa is not expressed in some bombastic manifestation but in prosaic ones, such as leading a normal lives of integration between Jews and Arabs in schools, being neighbors, organization in the trade union in workplaces. It must be mentioned that all this was done not by legislation and not through instructions from above, but by the free will of the city's inhabitants for ages and until today.

In conclusion, I would like to thank the editor Dr. Daphna Sharfman, and the additional authors, Eli Nachmias and Dr. Johnny Mansour, for the thorough work they invested in writing and publishing this book. In my opinion, the city, which is third in its size in Israel, deserves more frequent and intensive research of its history; alongside an attempt to trace the "genetic code" of its unique creation and the essence of the common life of Jews and Arabs which were created in it. The authors will be blessed for their important contribution.

Yona Yahav

Mayor of Haifa

Preface

Theodore Hertzel describe in his utopian book *Altnoiland*, the way he viewed Haifa in his mind's eye, as he approached it from the direction of the sea:

> A beautiful city had been built close to the deep blue sea. Grandiose piers and dams lay in the water, and they showed immediately what Haifa had become: the safest and best port in the Mediterranean, vessels of all shapes and sizes and of all nations lay in peace here...

As he continued his visit from the harbor towards the streets, he described what he envisioned and referred to Haifa as "this wonderful city"...

Not only Hertzel predicted a bright future for Haifa in the beginning of the twentieth century. Abas effendi (Abd El Baha), leader of the Baha'is, also spoke in similar spirit, in 1914, when he observed the city:

> This great semicircular bay will be transformed into the finest harbor, wherein the ships of all nations will seek shelter and refuge...The mountain and the plain will be dotted with the most modern buildings and palaces... Wonderful gardens, orchards, groves, and parks will be laid out on all sides. At night the great city will be lighted by electricity. The entire harbor from Akka to Haifa will be one path of illumination.

Haifa is located on the shores of the only natural bay in the country, a city that combines in its boundaries the "ever-green"

Carmel Mountain with the sea. These special blessings gave it the natural beauty which so impressed and impresses whoever visits the city.

Even a hundred years ago, the great potential that the city's bay possessed could not have been disregarded. In the period when international seafaring switched to new and large steam ships, which required deep waters, the old and rocky harbor of Acre became irrelevant.

The British Mandate days in Palestine (Eretz-Israel), which lasted only 28 years from 1920-1948, were a determining time period when the new Hebrew settlement in the country was established in aspects of quantity, finance, and culture. From a meager settlement of only 55,000 people in 1918, the Jewish population grew to about 600,000 people on the Independence War eve.

The Jews established a comprehensive and thriving industry from a community that presented only buds of industry during the Ottoman Empire period. During the years in subject, the settlement institutions were developed, as well as the whole of the autarkic economy. A sort of "state within the state" was formed on this foundation, developing under the problematic, yet protective, umbrella of the British Mandate.

During the days of the British Mandate Haifa was nourished by the same processes that furthered Eretz-Israel in general and specifically the Jewish settlement. The quantity data by itself reflects the great leap that the city made in the discussed period. There occurred a growth of population from 24,470 people in the year 1922 to 145,430 people in 1946. The growth took place both among the Arab population and among the Jewish one. While the first grew due to the internal immigration of people coming from neighboring countries to find work in the prosperous country, the Jewish population grew owing to immigration from the Diaspora. Most of the quantity change in the Jewish community occurred between the years 1931-1946. By 1946 the number of Jews in Haifa was 74,230 compared to 70,910 Arabs.

The Jews obtained a majority of 54% to 46% Arabs on the eve of the Independence War. There was an equivalent in the financial field, especially in the Jewish sector, to the impressive quantity growth for both sectors.

Haifa was and is a mixed city with a cosmopolitan hue given by the harbor, and a mosaic of ethnic and religious groups. Other than the major division of Jews and Arabs, one can find in Haifa population from these different religious and ethnic groups: Greek-Orthodox, Greek-Catholics, Anglicans, Maronites, Latins, and Armenians. Prominent are the unique ethnic groups of the Baha'is and the Ahmadians. The Druze ethnic group, which resides near the city, also adds to this uniqueness. No other Israeli city, in the past or present, showed such multi-colored human variety.

Despite Haifa's being a mixed city, it can be determined that the Jews and the Arabs lived only seemingly together, but mostly apart. The different ethnic religious groups lived under the same urban umbrella, but all had separate autarkic social-religious and cultural frameworks in most aspects of life. The authors of the book are right in indicating that the linking points between the different communities were only in three fields: financial, urban and governmental.

In *The Secret of Coexistence,* the book presented to us, we find three essays discussing the ensemble of life in the city during the British Mandate. The authors made a correct choice by concentrating on this relatively short period of time, which contributed to a great extent to the building of the country and the building of the Arab community and the Jewish settlement, not to mention the building and prospering of Haifa.

Eli Nachmias's essay "Arabs and Jews in a Dynamic Job Market" is thorough and comprehensive. The writer debates, among other issues, the question whether what is commonly generalized as "coexistence" among the Arabs and Jews in the period he discusses actually existed, or was it a myth that had nothing to do with reality. The writer is inclined to the opinion that there was a circumstance, which he names "cohabitation," meaning a restricted cooperation in certain fields only.

Dr. Daphna Sharfman's essay "People, Places and Events in Haifa's History" is very interesting. In a way the essay resembles the research done by the late professor Shmuel Avizur, who concentrated mainly on everyday life, that is research of the material life in pre-state Palestine. Sharfman dedicates a great deal of attention and detail to the description of a variety of fields, such as tourism, immigration, transportation and roads, hotels, restaurants, culture-life, and women in the Arab society. She also refers to a series of personalities in the Arab and Jewish sectors in the city. The writer presents a great deal of data which contributes to our knowledge.

The last essay, "The Arabs in Haifa During the British Mandate" written by Dr. Johnny Mansour, is very important. By the nature of things, there is more research that deals with the Jewish and the British sectors, hence the importance of every research on the Arab sector.

This essay deals with the demographic slicing of the Arab population, its growth in the city, and its ethnic group division. The writer also offers his view of the social-educational activity in Haifa. Mansour believes that the Arab community did not stagnate during the days of the British Mandate. He is of the opinion that the Arab public in the city went through "a process of extreme change." From a society he refers to as "classic" to a modern society that adjusted itself to the new reality.

All the essays are well-constructed, thorough, detailed, and based on the given literature we possess dealing with national subjects and subjects specific to Haifa. This is a comprehensive book, worthy to be found on the bookshelf of anyone who takes an interest in Haifa's and Israel's history. There is no doubt that this book constitutes a new important layer to the research on the city.

Professor Ya'akov Goldstein

University of Haifa

Prologue

For two decades, in the period between the two world wars, Haifa was to play a central role; not only of local or regional significance, but with international dimensions...It is the locus of interplay of many different national cultures, interests and aspirations. Geographically it is where Europe, Africa and Asia come together...In Haifa the orient and the west were to meet...It was a collision point of imperial strategies, international financial interests, Zionist aspirations, and also the entrenched local concerns. [1]

Haifa is a fascinating, multi-faceted city; it is a new, mixed, and cosmopolitan city, a Mediterranean city. Haifa was created first and foremost by nature, given a sheltered bay, a bay which secured it as early as the beginning of the 20th century the precedence over the historical Acre.

Haifa was created by the British, who saw it as a most strategically important city in all Eretz-Israel (Palestine); they built a harbor, an airport, and public service institutions and transported the oil from Iraq to it. Haifa was created by its inhabitants, Jews and Arabs, who came from all parts of the area and the world, and built the city, each according to his vision, separately or in cooperation. The larger part of this creation was done during the period of the British Mandate (1920-1948) as the city's landscape, appearances, and myths were designed.

We are dealing with the creation of Haifa's "coexistence" experience at that period. Is this a concept of practical meaning and components, or is this a myth with no grasp of reality? We can claim that there are many ways of understanding social and political processes; at times it seems the past is practically "erased" and even more often than that, the past is reflected in the deceiving and some time misleading memories of plenty of personalities, of whom the researchers also nourish. Evolution and cultural continuation, verbal signals, style, and political expression, cannot be disregarded. They all can create more objective "truths" which help those who seek to reach a solution and understanding of the political, sociological, and historical truth.

The cosmopolitan charm of Haifa in the Mandate period

Hertzel described Haifa in his book *Altnoiland* as a "city of wonders" and predicted the development, modernization and cosmopolitanism that would come upon it.[2] Lawrence Oliphant portrays Haifa through his colorful images of the cosmopolitan air of the town in the outset of its growth.[3] The focus of the British development on Haifa brought many to the perception of the Mandate period as the "golden age" of the city.[4]

The literature notes that the Hellenistic period was the best era of cosmopolitanism and that it was characterized by creating a shared-economics market of Macedonia and the Persian world.[5] The term "cosmopolitan" is derived from the Greek perception of the cosmos and "polis," the Greek local-city-state.

The emphasis in "cosmopolitanism" is not put only on the financial aspect, but also on the political traditions, bureaucracy, music, culture, and even types of parliamentarianism. In order for cosmopolitanism to occur there must be willingness to live with a variety of cultures, economies, and politics, all the while fighting (either openly or in concealment) the anti-cosmopolitan phenomenon, such as xenophobia.[6]

Britannica Encyclopedia presents the through definition of cosmopolitanism: "a stoic philosophy adopted by the stoics as an opposition to traditional Greek differentiation, between Greeks and the Barbarians." According to this perception, the

Greeks viewed themselves as "cosmopolitan," stating that their polis (city -state) was the entire cosmos.[7]

Wikipedia mentioned the "signs or representations of many countries" that is "cosmopolitanism." The term "cosmopolitan" also refers to the individual who preserved his mother-country's roots, but managed to adopt appetite and taste for other cultures as well; this way, that same person is both local and global at the same time.[8] "cosmopolitanism" refers to these fields:

A. The creation of a shared economic market regardless of national considerations.

B. A readiness to live with a variety of cultures, economies, and politics.

C. Preservation of national, cultural roots, while recognizing a new integrative reality, which is a different creation and entity.

Lawrence Durrell renounces the rich Middle-Eastern variety in his book *The Alexanderia Quartet*.[9] The Greek poet Constantine Cavafy describes the city of Alexandria artistically, as a city full of cosmopolitan characteristics, in which ambivalence, unstable charm and conflicted identity bloom alongside the complexity of the immigrant's existence.[10]

Nathan Shaham adds the romantic outlook:

Haifa...a gate to the distance, an access to a faraway longing, a city in which every window opens towards mountain and sea, a city of rising chimneys and pine forests, it has somewhat of abroad in it, as the sun as it sets forever captures a ship that sail far away over a golden road which it casts from the horizon to the coast.[11]

The British, whose glorious empire encircled half of the globe, were necessarily cosmopolitan, their empire clerks and soldiers moving from one country to another, taking with them their customs and government far across the sea, but also blending well in the local atmosphere. Their Haifa was a vibrant city: there were orchestra bands, military officers clubs, and clubs run by wives of British soldiers who were stationed in Haifa. It seems the British in Haifa did not miss an opportunity to celebrate for one reason or another. For instance, on the 19th of October 1940, the dignitaries of the city were invited to a party with a British band in "Khayat Beach" to collect donations for London's mayor relief fund; the host for this occasion was the British police in Haifa.[12]

The British loved music very much and enjoyed a great many bands that played for them, in the Windsor Hotel,[13] or in the Panorama Garden club on Panorama street where they liked to dance to the beat of the swing, played by famose Joe Nadel's Swingers.[14]

German Jews contributed much to the international air; they excelled in their culinary perceptions alongside their love for classical music; the "Yekes" (Jews of German origin) began arriving in Haifa in the 30's, following Hitler's rise to power in Germany. They liked Haifa due to its European character, the combination of mountains and sea and a German speaking community. The Muller family established "Ata" textile factory, Drezner developed the local hotels industry, Sternheim founded a café and the doctors brought advanced medicine to the city. A culture of cafés, music life, and receptions blossomed in Haifa.[15]

Erel,[16] and Gelber,[17] underline the German Jews' economic-commercial-business establishment that managed to make a way into Haifa's economic systems in the mid 30's; according to Gelber, there were many complaints made by the old-timers in Haifa against the immigrants from Germany, who were blamed for the rising price of land in the city, along with creating a different atmosphere in Haifa's culture life.[18]

Meltzer notes in a humorous tone that the increase of the ethnic groups and the international atmosphere of the city made it a "city of spies." The existence of secret operations in Haifa was derived from the fact that it was highly important for the British, for their war efforts and especially for the oil industry. Being a port city and a natural entrance to the Galilee also made Haifa a twilight operations site.[19]

The Alexandrian atmosphere in Haifa manifested in the cafés and bars on Panorama street, in the fancy casino on Bat Galim seaside, where British officers and young Jewish women had a good time.[20]

Quite a few espionage affairs occurred in Haifa: Ya'akobah Cohen, the Palmach's Arab Department man, considered one of Israel's all-time greatest spies, operated in Haifa when he was sent by his commander Yitzhak Sadeh to work in Haifa's harbor and live with a group of Arab Hourani laborers 24 hours a day.[21]

During the 30's and 40's Ruth Zucker operated as a spy in the Shay Service (information service) of the Haganah; alongside her was Wolf Lazarus, originally from Berlin, who went to work in Haifa's harbor every morning disguised as an Arab.[22]

Cna'an describes in his book *The Fifth Column*, the adventures of the pro Nazi German-Templers in Haifa, who were arrested on the 2nd of September 1939, when the British surrounded the German Colony at six in the morning.[23]

Haifa as a mixed city

Haifa is a mixed city, a fact which comes up all through its history, sociology, and politics. Goren defines a mixed city in the context of mandatory Palestine, as occupied by two dominant population groups that differ from each other in their culture and religion and are in a process of national struggle between them. He adds that the focus on the demographic aspect was the basis for the definition of the British authorities of these cities as "Mixed Cities." In his opinion, the British definition expressed mainly a prominent demographic mark for Jews and Arabs living together while differentiating between them and the cities inhabited by a homogeneous population. However, he adds that the definition is too narrow and does not clarify the unique style and character of the mixed city during the British Mandate period. In accordance to that, he offers a few parameters to test the phenomenon:

1. Analyzing the heterogenic status of the population.
2. Investigating the different characteristics of the spread of the population in the urban space.
3. Examining patterns of shared occupations.
4. Examining the municipality's activity and its influence, as a mixed institution, on the urban development.
5. Researching the landscape design of the urban space which may also reflects the extent of the heterogeneous status of the city's population.[24]

The municipal authority of the mixed city had influenced the big conflict in the city very much, as it could bridge the gaps or worsen the dispute. The British preferred to base their Mandate rule on the local elites, which naturally chose to allow the current condition to continue, rather than let in western political reforms. However, Goren believes there is no way to perceive the shared lives in these cities as a stimulus for creating solutions on the national level, as the national interests have influence on the local level as well, and each problem is tested by the community first and foremost in view of the national policy. A condition like this creates tension inside the local level, as each group will do its utmost to prevent the other group from receiving privileges regarding city services.

This contrast can grow as the two communities differ in their cultural level and all change towards modernization is perceived as contribution to one community and the lack of it will be perceived as holding back progress. There is also a danger that the urban arena will be used for passing national-political messages, which could hurt its ability to cope with the municipal assignments.

The British preferred to manage a balanced policy to relieve the tension, especially in the cities where they had special interests, including Haifa, a very important city in strategic, economic terms, a transportation junction and the main harbor in the country. They preferred using the municipal establishment in favor of all sides, to maintain a moderate atmosphere while neutralizing the national conflict in the municipal system as much as possible.[25]

Ben-Artzi note the extension of Haifa's area of jurisdiction starting with its defining by the Mandate rule in 1924: In that time it encircled the historical space of the city on the coastline from Bat Galim to Shemen Beach, and on the mountain terrace from Hadar HaCarmel to Rushmia stream. In the beginning of the 30's, when the official outline plan of Haifa was prepared, a new municipal territory was established, which also encircled the areas of the northern Carmel and the center of Carmel, Ramat Hadar and its hillsides.

Ahuza's inhabitants' demand made in 1937 to establish a local council and not be included in the boundaries of Haifa, was contrary to the political interests of the Jewish representatives in the municipality and the Jewish Agency leadership who aspired to demonstrate the Jewish power in the city, also expecting the possible struggle over including it in the future partition plan of Palestine. In February 1940, the city's boundaries widened so that they included all of the settled Carmel areas, which were mostly Jewish.[26]

A unique urban character of a mixed city was created in the country, in which operated spontaneous and natural development powers, with competing national and political direction that result in development, combined with separation inside a united municipal territory. The geographical separation increased with the growth of the national conflict, but despite that, the urban operation framework was shared in the united municipality and in the every-day life, in the financial and business aspects.[27]

Bollens indicates several principals connected with designing an urban policy in the condition of ethnic conflict; let us mention a few of them:

1. Separation can give birth to animosity because instilling stereotypes is easier if you don't know the opposite side. The objective of the policy should not necessarily be integration then, but a society in which

differences can exist and the communities are free to establish contacts among themselves as they please.

2. An ethnic group that feels vulnerable and in danger of degradation in its status has psychological and objective needs that are related to residences and also financial opportunities.

3. A trustworthy and unusual political leadership that searches for ways to solve the differences. Good relations established between communities are usually very much in contrast to ordinary politics, based on representation of the interests of a certain defined population.

4. Politics of majority and minority is not suitable for a framework of mixed cities.

5. Creating the true peace between ethnic groups requires exposing personal and group traumas. The need to come in contact with the "other" distances the person away from the sense of security in his perception of the world and leads him to a path of defense and confusion when existing perceptions do not go hand in hand with reality. However, this way can lead to building a policy that side with ethnic adjustment and not assimilation.[28]

The book before us display Haifa in the Mandate period, presenting the historical view of the Jewish and Arab population that we hope to put together in a loyal and multi-faceted portrait. To encourage the combined discussion of the history of different communities living, then and now, in one city that belongs to them all.

Arabs and Jews in a Dynamic Job Market

Eli Nachmias

Preface

Eva Peled, a Jewish girl that survived the 25 November 1940 *Patria* ship disaster, and who lived on the Carmel Mountain in Ahuza area, was most likely not familiar with the phrase: "coexistence between Jews and Arabs in Haifa."[29] The same as Munira, an Arab Christian woman who was born in Haifa in 1915 and escaped from the city in 1948, after her wonderful childhood years (according to her testimony) in the great city.[30] Samia Abadnur also remembers Haifa and describes it as a "jewel of a city." Samia, who studied in the Notre Dame de Nazareth school, does not recall in her memoirs any connection or contact with the city's Jews, who were an undeniable demographic factor, at least in the 30's and 40's.[31]

Moshe (Musa) Botton tells us about his childhood in Haifa. Botton home was in Anaporte street (Nevi'im street today) number 10, a street that borders on the Arab area of Nisnas Valley. According to Botton, he spoke a Syrian-Lebanese Arabic tongue as a child; most of the apartments in the house in which he lived were owned by Jewish people. The daily contact with most of the Arab citizens was also limited.[32]

Mordehai Shreiber wrote in his memoirs of Haifa in the 40's:

> I remember how my mother and her women neighbors used to bargain in the Luntz and Sokolov streets corner with Arab peddlers from villages near Haifa, and exchanged with them brown sugar for rice. The peddlers had a unique talent for languages and spoke pretty good Yiddish, while the Jewish housewives spoke only basic Arabic.[33]

Mordehai Ron, in his memoirs of Haifa in the 20's and 30's, claims too that the connections between Jews and Arabs (if there were any) were economic relations for the most part.[34] Here we see that the phrase "coexistence," which is customary in our language today, was created and formed in those years, starting from the 20's. The question is to what extent the history "creators" of those years aim in their actions and decisions to form the nowadays term of "coexistence"?

Sharon Rotbard claimed that the city is built just like history—always by the victor, and always according to the victor's narration. Whoever rules the actual space, rules the cultural space as well, the opposite is also true—whoever rules the cultural space rules the actual space, and that is because in order to change a city and to write history, a lot of strength is needed, and strength is never divided equally.[35]

In the following essay we will try to examine and characterize (maybe even refute) truths and myths, such as the nature and essence of Haifa's coexistence, the formation and characteristics of the "civil economy" in "Red Haifa," and most of all, Haifa's sudden evolution from a godforsaken town to a heavy industrial city, and the beginning of its demise already during the British Mandate period.

Background: economic and social life in Haifa at the end of the Ottoman period and the beginning of British Mandate

Haifa has a poor history compared to other old cities in Eretz-Israel. There is no mention of it in the Holy Scriptures, although events took place around it, which were important to the Jewish Peoples' life in biblical times. Although the Carmel Mountain, which is a part of Haifa, is sacred to the Jews, Christians, Muslims, and Baha'is; in its caves were found remainders of the oldest habitat of the prehistoric man. The Greek philosopher, Pythagoras, passed through Haifa on his way to Egypt; the prophet Elijah worked miracles on Mount Carmel; Jesus Christ's family stopped there on their way back from Egypt; the crusaders mounted up to the Carmel in 1150 and the Druze settled on this mountain in the 16th century; the German Templers built their colony in 1868 at the foot of the mountain, and in 1891 Baha u'lla'h set his tent there and made it a holy place for the Baha'i ever since; the Ahmads (a Muslim cult), also have settled in Haifa.[36]

Despite these historical facts, it seems that the city of Haifa has suffered much historical disregard and anonymity. For instance, not many know that Leopald Trepper, who led the famose "Red Orchestra" spy ring in the Second World War, stayed in Haifa in the years 1926-1927 as secretary of the Haifa branch of the Communist Party and was arrested by the British,[37] or that General Montgomery, the legendary victor of the "El Alamein" battle, came to Haifa in October 1938, and also stayed there for medical care in May-June 1939,[38] that Adolph Aichman visited Haifa on the 2.10.37 as part of a wide-ranging journey of the Middle-East.[39]

The city's varied demography, society, and geography, have led Haifa, in our opinion, to be perceived only partially. The city's long-years description as "Red Haifa," resulting from the labor movement domination, has made academic study focus on the part of the movement in Haifa, including personalities in it such as Aba Hushi, the well-known mayor of Haifa. Among these researchers and writers were De Prise, Medding, Nachamias, Zaltz, and Eshel.[40]

As a result of Haifa's image as a social-political site in which the Haifa Workers Council was very dominant (Mapah-Haifa Workers Council), the workers movement economy was also highlighted: The factories of the union organized in the "Workers' Company," collective factories, housing factories, health services organization, etc. Therefore, it wouldn't be wrong to claim that the Haifa "generators of economy" such as the industrialists' union, the trade bureau, the small industry, the different craft organizations, and the like were hardly ever researched in depth; there were, however, some publications by different personalities who tend to evaluate their organization through a personal prism. Economic organizations also have published several books in the anniversary of their establishment.[41]

We can assume that the geographical distance between Haifa and Jerusalem, which was the formal and administrative capital of the mandatory government, assisted with the sort of process of political, social, and even economic segregation; therefore, we can point out that a unique social and political phenomena formulated in Haifa alongside an economy that did not grow in a routine-linear way, but as a complex process of many integrated social-political-economic variables acting simultaneously. For this reason, in order to understand the economy and the society in mandatory Haifa, we need to define a row of independent variables alongside mediating variables, which can explain the Haifa's economy, cosmopolitan character, special relations (the well-known "coexistence") between Jews and Arabs, and the celebrated Haifa tolerance.

There are two types of independent variables—ecological and social-political. Among the ecological variables we will include the demographic aspect—the presence of a largely heterogeneous population, cosmopolitan in part and not just Arab and Jewish, the formation of an industrial and transport monopoly in Haifa, economy-employment variables, geographic variables, (such as the topographic structure of Haifa next to the fact that it is built in a gradual process of neighborhood by neighborhood, without any suitable transportation connection in the Mandate period), and special population groups variables, such as Haifa being surrounded by kibbutzim established by the labor movement.

Of the social-political variables, which characterized Haifa's space during the British Mandate period, we must enumerate the tendency for political and social separation-segregation of at least an important part of the Haifa essence; that is, the workers movement that crystallized a dominant ideology and influenced the personal, educational, and communal services of Haifa's Jewish citizens. Therefore, we will present for the reader the fundamental nature of Haifa's civilian middle class economy which was not a part of the workers movement; along with the effort to understand the reciprocal relations that used to exsist between the diverse demographic components that functioned in Haifa during the Mandate period. We will also try to examine it as a period of economic and social growth, which had much effect on the formation and design of governing and organizing patterns that left marks for years to come, even after the end of the British rule.

We aim to present Haifa from a comprehensive point of view as opposed to a partial one; to observe the sum of all components of the Haifa society in the British Mandate period especially including the ethnic, political, and economic mechanism; there will be a special emphasis put on the formation of a "civil society," parallel to the organization of the workers culture, which was powerful and mighty.

Let us point out again, that as opposed to the city's image as having syndicalistic features, a cosmopolitan period had passed over the industrial city, which was impossible to erase at once; that contrary to the belief that demographic crowding, as was in Haifa, is enough to cause a political or economic "explosion," we find coexistence manifested in shared economic endeavors along the establishment of political and economic relations in the Haifa municipality, which serves as a political regulator and "filter" for the establishment of Jewish-Arab relations in Mandatory Haifa.

General Allenby occupied at first the south of Eretz-Israel and its coastal plane, but Jerusalem and the north were still under Turkish rule. In the record of Apek Bank (an Anglo-Palestinian company), which later became Leumi Bank, it is told that by the end of 1917 the Haifa branch of Apek Bank was cut from the British controlled part of the country and continued to operate under the Turkish rule for another year, until Eretz-Israel was completely conquered by the British. Because of that, a big sum of Turkish money, in cash, was left in the funds of the Haifa branch. The bank managers estimated that the Turks were in for a big defeat and the entire empire might crash, and they decided to make quick use of the money and to buy the lands of Mount Carmel.[42]

Indeed, Haifa's development during the 18th century and the beginning of the 19th century was slow but constant. Alex Carmel notes decisively that the opinion that "till the beginning of the 20th century Haifa was a poor and polluted fishermen town and its population was a mere few hundreds," should not be accepted; Carmel states that even a superficial examination will prove that this statement has no basis. It is sufficient to just take a look at Sir Lawrence Oliphant's notes to understand that Haifa was not a product of the 20th century alone, since even in the early 80's of the 19th century its development caught up with Acre's, and it became the main urban center of the northern part of the country.[43]

The engineer Nahum Wilbush recounts in his memoirs that when he arrived in Haifa in 1903, it was a small town in the initial stages of its development. Haifa belonged to the Turkish Beirut's district, and the Kiamakam (governor) had chosen Acre, the area's major city, for his office.[44]

Carmel noted that:

On the eve of the First World War, and at the end of 400 years of Turkish rule in the country, Haifa's status was already known and secure. Its population was already over twenty thousand, and was going up constantly. The import-export trade was on an upscale, and so ensured the cosmopolitan character of the Bay City.[45]

In Wilbush's opinion, the German-Templers contributed to the prosperous period of Haifa, in the end of the Ottoman empire, during which the population of Haifa grew at a six times quicker pace than any other city in Eretz-Israel (in the years 1870-1922), from 4,200 to 24,634. By 1869, the building of what is now called the "German Colony," began and, at the end of the 80's, the foundation of the first neighborhood of the Carmel Center of our days was placed. The Turks made an important contribution to the vision of Haifa as the "future city," according to Hertzel in *Altnoiland*, since they made Haifa the only connection between the Hijazi railways and the Mediterranean.[46]

Moreover, like the rest of the citizens of the northern part of the country, the citizen of Haifa too, had to wait almost a whole year until the British broke through the Turkish front, north to Jaffa. A first attempt to conquer Haifa was made on the 22nd of September 1918. General King, commander of the British army, faced a strong Turkish resistance. On the eve of the 23rd of September 1918, many of the city's people gathered in the big mosque square in Haifa to hear King's speech. Hassan Shukri, the mayor, gave the British commander his sword, as a symbol of surrender. Four hundred and two years of Ottoman rule in Haifa came to an end.[47]

Haifa's growth pace was clearly increasing at the beginning of the 20th century. Even though the Jews were a small part of the country's population, their part in the urban settlement was significant. Moreover, as for the economic modernization, the Jews' contribution and the immigrants' in particular was highly apparent especially in fields like investment import where their contribution was even more crucial in the beginning of the last century. However, most of the small Jewish community was integrated closely in the general urban economy of Eretz-Israel.[48]

Carmel describes Haifa's status at the end of the Turkish rule:

> In 1914, Haifa was still a small city, and in the judgment of a stranger—not much more than a town. However, everyone felt the same about the future that this vibrant and developing place beheld. When the Turkish rule was

over, the foundation of Haifa, on which it has grown and prospered up till today, has already been placed.[49]

Haifa was described here as being a mixed, cosmopolitan city, but was mandatory Haifa really characterized by these features between the years 1918-1948?

At the outset of this complex question, we will refer to the demographic aspect of Haifa. Gad Gilbar weighs the population development in the main cities of Jerusalem, Haifa, and Jaffa, in 1860-1946.[50] He notes that in comparison to Jaffa and Jerusalem, the percentage growth rate of Haifa's population—490.2 in general and 1091.5 for Jews, is the largest for Jews, Muslims, and Christians. Haifa was a major demographic attraction for the three religions. This is in comparison to Jerusalem (an increase of 192.4% for Jews in the years 1922-46) or Jaffa (increase of 505.9% in 1922-46); the same was true for Muslims and Christians.

Suad Kraman, a member of one of Haifa's most prominent families, speaks of Haifa's cosmopolitan character and its being a magnet for immigrants from all of Eretz-Israel-Palestine. In her reference to Haifa's Jews, before 1948, she says:

> In Haifa, a new, mixed, organized, modern city, they proved their competence. Haifa was a city in which everyone was a foreigner. The Arabs that came to Haifa, they too came from diverse places, and when the city grew, the Jews grew with it and claimed a stake there. [51]

Joseph Klausner, who visited the city in 1915, wrote of its foreignness, but also of the charm of Haifa. Klausner is enthused by the sights of Haifa and the Carmel, but his soul was upset by Haifa's being, for him, "a German and Christian city," Klausner refers, in particular, to the massive settlement of the German-Templers in Haifa.[52]

David Hacohen, one of the directors of Sollel-Boneh, the union's construction company, and a member of the Haifa city council at that time, described the civilized and varied character of Haifa:

Haifa was very lucky to have developed in such a quick pace. It is possible to regard its quickened growth to its unique strategic spot; in 1905 the Haifa-Damascus Hijaz railway was built which gave it a big commerce leap, and in 1918, with the British take-over, the city became the capital of the north. However, I believe that this exceptional combination of dynamic Jews from all classes, the Ashkenazi's and Sephardi, workers and capitalists, traders and professionals, bankers and clerks, intellectuals and business people—all of them together—nurtured the economic factories, the industry, shops, and the education institutes of the city. [53]

Referring to the cosmopolitan side of Haifa, David Hacohen describes in his memoirs the senior officials (Jews and Arabs) of the Mandate government which were of a special status and influence on the whole of Haifa's existence.[54]

Shabtai Levi, who was mayor from 1940-1951, tells that Haifa was the only city in Eretz-Israel where true harmonic relations prevailed between Jews, Muslims, and Christians; the political work concentrated, according to Levi, in Haifa's city council.[55]

Focusing on the economic side of Haifa, as a vital foundation for an economic-cosmopolitan society in the city, Ben-Artzi claims that during the British Mandate period, Haifa adopted a unique style compared to other cities in Eretz-Israel. Processes that originated at the end of the 19th century ripened in this period on the one hand, and on the other, new enterprises began that brought to the realization of the developing potential of the city and its geographic and economic prosperity.

Many think that the Mandate period was the "golden age" of the city, after which was the so-called withdrawal. This feeling is not justified in realistic senses, but it is true in the sense of the urban atmosphere and pace, which changed with the Mandate period. [56]

Ben-Artzi notes that the Mandate government made another contribution to Haifa by making it a district city and also an independent sub-district. This decision was in fact an official approval for the line of historic and geographic processes. The district officers and the government offices that managed the daily life, settled in Haifa. Hence, different offices and business were attracted to the city and people from all over the north surged to it.[57] Ben-Artzi thinks that the city formulated a unique character derived from the human texture and the functioning mosaic of the city, a "cosmopolitan international atmosphere." International shipping, oil pipes from Iraq, railway lines to Egypt, international airport—all these gave the city an unlimited sense of activity and possibilities, and the presence of people from different ethnic groups and nations added a cultural and social touch to these spatial connections. The harbor and the passenger ships traffic, the foreign sailors, the consulates, taxi lines to Beirut, settlements of the Jewish immigrants from central Europe—all these created a unique social and cultural touch. Cafés, night clubs, and the multi national character of the cultural activity enhanced the city's cosmopolitan atmosphere that did not characterize Tel Aviv or Jerusalem.[58]

The days of the Second World War increased, undoubtedly, the aspect of "self involvement" of the city; it was disconnected from Europe, and during the war days, a unique cultural scene had formed there; the casino in Bat Galim, for instance, was a lively place in the British Mandate years. The large café that operated inside it drew English officers, Jews, and Arabs and quite a few beautiful women. The casino contributed a lot to the international cultural character of Haifa.[59]

Out of many memoirs written by British soldiers we chose Patrick White's, who served in Haifa at the Second World War period:

> I was stationed in Haifa, Palestine, in 1943 as an anti-aircraft gun soldier...But there was hardly any aerial activity...In

Haifa I found remainders of the cabaret culture I so loved in Germany before the war...I noticed a certain colorful but depressing collage in Haifa-murders that were committed by the Stern gang, adultery between the Allied forces soldiers and their Jewish lovers, bribery...Night after night the cabaret operated under the windows of the hotel we were staying at. In the morning we would hear a concerto from Warsaw played on a piano, while we ate the vegetables for breakfast...The next night, in a different club in Haifa, we heard another diva sing the song '...You walked out of a dream.' [60]

When we defined the concept "cosmopolitan," its meaning and features, we claimed it was composed of an economic reality of a shared economy market in which most of the components of the community take part; of a willingness to accept and cooperate with a cultural, and economic diversity, while creating a new synthetic existence; all this along with conserving the national cultural roots, and accepting integrative reality, which is in fact a new entity. If we project these features on Haifa, it seems that most of them, if not all, had existed during the British Mandate period.[61] The British, due to interests of their own, caused the formation of a new, powerful economic entity. Immigrants came to the city in large quantities, from different cities and countries; slowly but surely a new cultural existence was created with the formation of a culture and an administrative status characteristic to this process.

Tom Segev, who studied the demographic data of Haifa, found that during the years 1929-1935, one of two citizens of Haifa was new and foreign in the city.[62] Haifa went through a revolution. At the end of the 20's, it was the most important industrial city and one of ten factories in Eretz-Israel was located in it; 16% of all industry workers, Jews, and Arabs, were employed in Haifa in those years.[63]

The Jewish immigrant, the Arabs that just arrived from their villages, the English, together with the old German-Templers, the Ahmands and the Christians, experienced together a practice of displacement and maturity; experienced a sense of living on a kind of European island in the heart of the Levant, but spiced with the Levantine characteristic and touch that were significant, and that was very probably the charm of cosmopolitan Haifa.

How did Haifa, a small, godforsaken town, become a heavy industry city in Eretz-Israel

Most of the literature that analyzes the fundamental and pragmatic reasons for the emphasis on developing Haifa by the British during the Mandate period—maintain that with the end of the First World War, the British empire ruled, for the first time in it's history, over a territorial continuity that extended from the eastern basin of the Mediterranean to the Persian gulf. On top of forming a wide terrestrial defense belt stretching from north-east to the Suez Canal, the new situation also allowed Britain to prepare a secured land transport track on the way to India, which could reduce the importance of the canal and take advantage of the oil reserves in Mesopotamia. These two options involved building an imperial transfer port to the east basin bays of the Mediterranean, a port which would serve as a bridge head to the new track and an outlet for the oil line from Mesopotamia; the British finally chose the bay of Haifa as an appropriate location for these objectives.[64] Fine notes that in 1924, the fundamental decision making phase in consolidating the British policy in the matter of Haifa harbor was concluded.[65]

Naor and Giladi add that Haifa's development began as early as the end of the 19th century, regardless of the British strategic decision to build up the harbor. They maintain that the Jewish settlement in Haifa developed at the end of the 19th century citing the fact that mostly business people came to the city, who were drawn to it as result of the trade growth extent, that was going through its harbor; the harbor that gradually replaced Acre's as the important hub in the northern part of the country.[66] The first British High Commissioner, Herbert

Samuel, predicted the British tendency to develop Haifa in the future in his visit to Haifa in December 1924:

> Everything that you can see in the development of Haifa up till now is only the beginning of a much bigger advancement that the city will undergo.[67]

The engineer Nahum Wilbush, one of the founding fathers of the industry in Haifa, refers to the pre-British period and notices three events that pushed Haifa ahead and upgraded it from a small town to the large city of today: The Templers arrival in Haifa; the Hijaz railway track constructed in 1903-5 by the German engineer Meisner Pasha under the command of the sultan Abd El Hamid; the second immigration of Jews to Eretz-Israel (1903-1914), and to Haifa in particular.[68]

Ladislas Farago presents pragmatic assumptions for the British preference of Haifa over many other cities in the Middle East; he claims that prominent Jewish leaders in England persuaded the British business people to invest in Haifa. Farago also assumes that in time of emergency, when Britain would lose control over Suez Canal, an alternative canal could be dug from Gaza harbor to the red sea in Aqaba, and so he states that Haifa would replace Alexandria as a British harbor city.[69]

Indeed, it seems that Haifa, the Carmel city, had become the symbol of the renewing Eretz-Israel. The Second World War period was a time of a great deal of economic activity and the city became the capital of the north. Army camps were built near Haifa, roads paved, and the railway track was extended north through Rosh Hanikrah (Ras El Nakura). A tunnel was quarried in the rocks, through which the mandatory military train went between Haifa and Beirut; the deep water harbor of Haifa which was inaugurated in 1933, was the only active harbor in Eretz-Israel during the Second World War; in it's construction thousands of acres of sea water were reclaimed and docks and new streets were built and paved instead in the Port street and Kingsway (Ha'azmaut street of today). At the rear of the harbor a new international transport junction was developed including extensions to Iraq and Egypt; Haifa harbor also functioned as an outset harbor for raw oil that arrived from Iraq. The crude oil products were purified in the refineries in Haifa; the Eretz-Israeli citrus and potash export also used the harbor.[70]

Herbert Sidebotham stresses the importance of Haifa harbor development and add that Haifa was preferred over Tel Aviv because of it's location, the natural harbor, the British-future plan options for Haifa, the nearby bay area and Haifa's slow quantity increase, at 1937; Sidebotham further adds that the new harbor, built in 1933, is the only safe harbor along the Levantine coast, from Turkey to Alexandria. He believes that Haifa, as a planned city at the time of his writing, would become the industry and commerce center of Palestine, since it is located at the meeting point of east and west.[71]

Six years earlier (1931), in a previous book, which is actually a memo (British Interests in Palestine), Sidebotham makes basic assumptions as to the British interests in all of Palestine and Haifa in particular; he claims that Palestine and Haifa are needed for the defense of the Suez Canal, the indispensable connection Britain has with India. He further assumes that there is much strategic importance to the aerial connection between Palestine and India.[72]

Shimon Stern also believes that the mandatory government had a special interest in Haifa because of its strategic importance. He emphasizes that the British interest in Haifa as an important strategic site came long before their occupation of Eretz-Israel. As early as 1861-1865 they had already planned for the first time a railway track leading from Haifa to Baghdad. This plan was not executed, in fact, but renewed after the signing of the Sikes-Picot agreement that gave the British permission to constract this track.

In the 30's, this plan was exchanged for an alternative idea of a paved road along the same route, which was not executed as well. However, the British perceived Haifa as the main gate from the Mediterranean to countries under their authority: Eretz-Israel, Trans-Jordan, and Iraq; emphasized by the geographical location of Haifa in the entrance to Yizrael Valley, which is one of the more comfortable paths from the Levant coast to the inner desert area.[73] Consequently, the British built in Haifa a deep water harbor, strengthened the railway junction in the city, built an airport, and chose Haifa as a terminal for the Iraqi oil line; they also located there the Eretz-Israeli customs administration; due to Haifa's strategic importance, many army camps were built in it.

An even more dramatic emphasis on Haifa's new positioning starting in the mid-thirties, gives *The New Palestine Guide* in its 1936-7 edition:

> Haifa is currently the main aerial connection between Palestine and England, Iraq, Persia and Europe; in Haifa also important international concerns operate, such as the imperial chemical industries, 'Shell' and the Iraqi oil company.[74]

Zohar Alufi adds new aspects to the British outlook of Haifa as a strategic asset; she stresses elements from the report of the royal commission of 1937 (the Peel Commission), which refer to mixed cities like Haifa. The commission believed that the success of the implementation of the partition plan and especially ensuring the rights of the minorities is highly depends on the mixed cities—Tiberias, Safed, Acre and Haifa—staying under Mandatory rule for a definite period of time therefore, the commission recommended that free passing of trade between the Arab state and Haifa would be ensured in the agreement for a Jewish state there.[75]

On July 20, 1937, a discussion was held in the House of Lords on the "Peel Commission" report. Lord Meltzet mentioned that Britain had important interests in Haifa, especially in the harbor. He thought that the government could get prerogatives in Haifa through one of two ways: first, to have full control of the city, second, to give it to the Jews and sign a contract ensuring the interests of the harbor.

The Air Minister, Lord Swinton, noted that Haifa was more than a harbor and an origin for the oil pipes; it was also the origin of an extensive "Hinterland" in the Middle East. That is why the British government did not want to make a final decision about Haifa.[76] In his memoirs, Ben Gurion emphasizes Haifa's central position:

> There could not be a Jewish state without Haifa, and I can not think of any other local asset in the country, more important than Haifa. Our battle of Haifa will not be an easy one; this is an interests' junction of the whole near east and the British Empire. We will give England all the rights it needs, but we will keep this treasure of Eretz-Israel's. No other port in the country deserves this name, even after we can board passengers in Tel-Aviv—we should not forget that this is a port for the southern part of the country only. The port of Eretz-Israel and the Jewish state can only be that of Haifa. [77]

Looking for more approaches of the status and analysis of Haifa in the British's point of view, it is possible to mention that most of the researchers see the bay of Haifa and its geo-political status as good enough reason for the city's designation by the British as a future accelerated development area. Among them are Naor and Giladi,[78] Shorrer,[79] Smith,[80] Yaffe,[81] Barslavski,[82] and Freidman.[83] Bernstein summarizes the essence of economic and demographic characteristics that caused and accelerated the development of Haifa. In her opinion as well, the geographic and strategic location of Haifa were doubtless the crucial factors in the development of the city that became the center of economic development and as a result, an important center of immigration and demographic growth. The importance of the city to the mandatory government in Eretz-Israel and to the British Empire generally attracted Jewish investors, in particular into industrial factories that needed the proximity of a harbor in order to import raw materials, and railway tracks to transport products.[84]

Sherman stresses that in the 40's the British thought that Haifa would replace Alexandria as the main British stronghold in the eastern Mediterranean and that their long-term interests could be realized even if there is a Jewish resistance to that cause.[85] Gross also agreed, as he assumed that the primary goal of the economic policy of Eretz-Israel's government was to promote the British Empire's strategic interests. Close to the end of the First World War, Britain's military and navy commands did not, in fact, express any special interest in developing Eretz-Israel in general and the Haifa harbor in particular, and explicitly denied their strategic value (only the Air Ministry approach was different from the beginning); but this stance can be explained by the fear of budgetary expenses. By 1923, there was already a change in the military approach to the subject, which had very much to do with the formation of the plans to transport oil from Iraq to the Mediterranean coasts, as well as the need to defend the imperial routes to India. Gross argue that the top importance of the strategic consideration was indeed manifested by the British government's willingness to invest money in Eretz-Israel; this strategic consideration was of course paramount during the First World War, and, later, during the Second World War.[86]

Bigger[87] also confirms Gross's claims and adds that beyond economic, military, and strategic advantages to the preference of Haifa over other cities in the Mediterranean basin, there were also biblical and theological reasons as for the importance of Yizrael Valley and the proximity of Meggido, the location of the Armageddon-the last battle according to the Christian tradition, to Haifa.

To wrap up this discussion of Haifa's change from a small town to a strategic industry city in Eretz-Israel, we will present the main characteristics and reasons for this trend:

A. Geo-political and strategic rationale that derive from Haifa's location.

B. Economic reasons that derive from the physical location of the city.

Beyond that, we bring additional explanation:

A. Pressures of the economic and political bodies tied with the Jews on the British government, to prefer Haifa as the "future city."

B. The British perception of Haifa as a city that might stay under their control after the end of the Mandate.

C. Haifa being almost a blank blackboard in the beginning of the 20's, demographically and economically speaking; this basic fact allowed the British to design the city in the way they pleased, while regulating the civilian powers that formed in the city; this manipulative ability allowed them to build a city, not always by pure urban-economic logic. When the British forces were to leave Eretz-Israel in 1948, General Hugh Stockwell, commander of the northern area, took decisive steps meant to secure the future of the post Mandate's demise British enclave in the bay of Haifa.[88] That is, the British had a future plan for Haifa, as opposed to other cities in Eretz-Israel.

Haifa between right and left—the formation of the dumbfounded bourgeois of Haifa

In the introduction to this essay we noted the small volume of research on the subject of bourgeois and/or middle class and civilian circles; much in contrast to the development of extensive research of the workers' movement, including what is phrased in the political jargon as: "Red Haifa."

A middle class or a typical bourgeois did develop in Haifa; it was expressed by the penetration of Jewish capital into Haifa's economy, the capital accumulation by Jews, the development of unique factories, and organizations that represented merchants, tradesmen, contractors and others. We would survey and analyze these organizations, in purpose of interweaving them in the wide economic context of Haifa, including the active, dominant, and affecting labor economy.

The phrase *bourgeois* has multiple meanings; it expresses ownership of property and its social influence and also origin, lifestyle, status and a bourgeois culture as a social experience, derived from the variables we noted.

Amir Ben Porat writes on Eretz-Israeli bourgeois before and after the founding of the state:

> The central streams of the Eretz-Israel's historiography glorified, not without reason, the share of the workers' movement in the founding of the state, and tend to downsize the bourgeois' contributation for all its different sections. [89]

In this article, we chose to combine the different terms that mark "bourgeois," "middle class" and "civil circles," mainly for methodological efficacy; however, we will mention already at this point, that there are some differences between the terms. The traditional bourgeois, that is the small and medium bourgeois who we nowadays call "middle class," still exists; it did change its shape and form, but it is present now practically everywhere in the world.[90] The background that was needed for the formation of a new middle class existed already in the second half of the 19th century and was expressed for the most part by the free-professionals whose property was actually knowledge: lawyers, accountants, doctors, clergy, teachers, engineers, professors, etc. Ben Porat assume that the property on one hand, and the bourgeois culture on the other, present two important terms to examine the progress of the bourgeois in Eretz-Israel.[91]

The Jewish Labor movements' ("The Bund") negative attitude towards the prominent Jewish bourgeois had begun already in the Diaspora; the accusations that "The Bund" hurled, as early as the 19th century, at "Hovevei Zion" (Zion lovers) are presented here:

> It is our bad luck, us, the Jewish proletariat, to be used by the lowest and most loathsome bourgeois in the world.

Not only have our political rights been taken from us (as was done to the Russian proletariat), but our civil rights as well.[92]

The name "civil circles" was given to several social, economic, and political organizations that began to form in Eretz-Israel at the time of the British occupation in the First World War, and existed during the 20's and 30's. The first of these organizations was "The Citizen" party, founded by Meir Dizengof and S. Ben Zion (this one probably originated the nickname "civil circles" for all these organizations), were placed in the center of the political sphere of the Jewish Eretz-Israeli settlement; that is to the right of the labor movement and to the left of the Jewish orthodox movement, the "Mizrahi," and also the Revisionist movement; but, unlike the consolidation of the left and the right in the political life of the settlement, the center was fragmented and split; the center organizations were mostly without wide political awareness, and their activity was usually limited to a few defined fields. The major attempt to organize them was the foundation of "The Federation of the General Zionists." Other attempts were the founding of "The National Civil Association," and Farmers Organizations. [93]

Moshe Lisak is also of the opinion that the "civil" bloc in the settlements period was more heterogeneous from the get-go, and the political groups that composed it were not really stable and institutionalized. Groups among the "civil" bloc were not typical political groups but economic ones that were very ambivalent about their job description in the political plane.[94]

The "Farmers' Union" was out of the ordinary in the "civil" bloc; they were a homogeneous social group, focused mainly on local economic interests; the urban professional-economic bodies of the civil bloc could not reach political unification despite different attempts (by Meir Dizengof and Bezalel Yaffe in 1925, for instance).[95]

As for the ideological approach of the Eretz-Israeli bourgeois, the principle of equal division of reward given for work was totally invalid among the rivals of the workers movement. The "civil circles," opposed the monopolization of the national resources, which had to do with the strong dispute that was going on at the time (the 30's and 40's mainly) over the importance of the national capital in strengthening the settlements' economy. The civil camp resisted the diminution of the middle class's prestige—like merchants, craftsmen, farmers, manufacturers, and different employees, who were not part of an organized frame and did not participate in the ideological Hebrew work conquest operation.[96]

Among the many organizations and groups of the civil circles, the professional-economic bodies were the most common, but they were a part of an unstable and un-systematic frame, did not function on a national base lack organizational connection.[97]

Sa'adia Paz writes of the beginning of the "middle class" in Haifa. He notes the arrival of poor young people, mostly men, from Jerusalem and Tel Aviv to Haifa at the beginning of the 20th century.

> These young men, could not pay the military ransom (instead of military service), to the Turks, and so they went to Haifa, where they wouldn't be known...There they changed their names from fear of bad omens...These guys did pretty good business with the German and Austrian military, Allies of the Turks, who were at the country back then. They even bought lands on Mount Carmel and its slope from the Germans; that is how the Jewish middle class in Haifa was born. [98]

In the fourth immigration in the 20's many people from the lower middle class came to Haifa and they did not fit in the workers camp or the working settlement. Together with the fifth immigration of the 30's (which mostly included natives of Germany) an attempt at the settling of the middle class in Haifa's area was made; that is how settlements, like Kfar Gideon, Ramat Hashavim, Ramat Hadar, and Kfar Bialik in the Haifa area were set up.[99] We should mention that the first initiative to found a Modern Hebrew suburb near Haifa was made by "Agudat Ahim" (brothers union), which was established in Haifa at the end of 1906. At the head of it stood Shabtai Levi, the manager of the lands department of Yc"a company, and the merchant Moshe Levin; the "Ahuzat Beit Haifa" group got together in the years 1909-1912 to acquire real estate around the Technion in Hadar HaCarmel; "Agudat Nahala," founded in Haifa at the beginning of 1913, bought lands about 800 meters north of the Technion. After the First World War, the Hadar HaCarmel neighborhood was built on these grounds.[100]

However, the construction work was not all the civil circles' aspect in Haifa. The private initiative and private capital made an important contribution in the 20's to the Hebrew industry growth in Haifa; at the end of 1925 "Nesher" factory for cement was established near Haifa; Yc"a helped found a row of modern factories in the Haifa area, like the "Eretz-Israel salt company" in Atlit, which began it's activity as early as 1922; "The Big Tahanot" (flour mills) and the oil products factory "Shemen" began operateing in 1925. The first power station, opened in 1922, also contributed to the further development of Haifa.

Apart from the organized economy and industry (the "Workers Company"), civil organizations existed in Haifa that represented the industrialists, craftsmen, merchants, lawyers, and many other free-professionals. Sectored organizations were also established, according to ethnic groups; for instance, the Romania natives association was formed in 1928.

The chief representative organizations were the industrialists' union, the craftsmen, and tiny industry unions, and the Jewish merchants' union in Haifa. The first Jewish merchants' meeting in Haifa was held on 16 August 1919; Nathan Keiserman was the head of the association in Haifa, and Ya'akov Zilberman (Caspi) served as secretary. The Jewish merchants in Haifa refused to accept the candidacy of an Arab named Wadiea' al-Bustani, as a second secretary for the association, according to the British High Commissioner's explicit request. M.G Levin also told the Arab merchants that there were 60

Jewish merchants in the gathering who knew that Wadiea' Bustani "hates them." The Arab members (the Arab merchants in Haifa that is) informed Levin that they didn't need a second Arab secretary.[101] On the 7.2.1919 the chairman and the secretary informed the merchants union in Jaffa that:

> A union of the Hebrew merchants in Haifa was established, and its goal is to unite all the Hebrew merchants in our city and since we know that you by now have a union according to regulations, we ask you to provide all the material regarding this, so we can match our work together.[102]

But apparently the dispute between the Arab and the Jewish merchants continued. According to their record from 13.11.1919, it turns out that the Jewish merchants objected to their low representation in the shared bureau for Arabs and Jews. The members in the shared bureau were 58 Jewish merchants, 40 Christian and 25 Muslims.[103] On the 14.6.1921, the mandatory government recognized the establishment of a "Jewish commerce bureau," which was the first in the country.[104]

Later the Jewish commerce bureau changed its name to the "Hebrew commerce and industry in Haifa bureau." As for the political character of the organization, it is possible to note decisively (based on its records), that the bureau stances were in most cases un-political and it preferred to ignore political issues, while making intermediate decisions, neither here nor there.

A confirmation of this claim can be found in Yigal Drori's research concerning the beginning of the economic organizations in Eretz-Israel in the 20's who asserts that:

> The middle class in the cities, who constituted the larger part of the Jewish population in Eretz-Israel already in the first years after the First World War, was mostly without any awareness of organization on ideological basis, and also: naturally the first organizing attempts of the middle class focused primarily on professional routes and not ideological stances.[105]

The Haifa commerce bureau maintained correct ties with the workers movements' leaders, as manifested by the extensive correspondence found in the archives of the bureau. Another professional union was the Haifa Journalists' Union, founded in 1940. The founders of the organization included representatives of *Ha'aretz*, *Yedioth aharonot*, *Davar*, *Haboker*, and *Hamashkif*. The English language *Palestine Post* journalists also participated in the founders meetings. In the early 40's they were held in the "Café Lebanon" in Jaffa street in downtown Haifa.[106]

The Industrialists' Union in Haifa was established more than 70 years ago by the founders of industry in mandatory Haifa.[107] The "Association of Industry Owners and Employers in Tel-Aviv-Jaffa" was founded as result of the unwillingness of the British to impose protective tariffs in order to protect local manufacturing.[108]

The "General Merchants and the Middle Class Union" (which name was shortened in the 50's to the "General Merchants' Union") also operated in Haifa. The Merchants' Union was founded in Tel Aviv by a group of merchants led by Yehoshua Shedov, for the purpose of representing the retail commerce shop owners to the British Mandate. The Haifa branch was founded in the 30's.[109] The Craftsman Union was also founded in the 20's and operated with greater vigor in the 30's.[110] The organizations function in a purely professional way, and the craftsmen's organization kept firm political ties with the leadership of the workers' movement in Haifa. The general secretaries of this organization were members of the labor party—Mapai and Mapah political bodies.

Features of the Haifa "bourgeois" in the Mandate period

In the preface to this sub-chapter we mentioned that the term "bourgeois" usually includes, lifestyle, origin, status, and also a "bourgeois" culture as a social experience; as we try to project these variables on the research of the events in Haifa, they seem to be expressed in the forthcoming characteristics:

A. The "bourgeois" or the "civil circles" led separate lifestyles from the prevailing "worker" lifestyle that was manifested in pastime and enterntainment patterns; the cosmopolitan way of life in Haifa was partially lived by the men and women, who were mostly industrialists, engineers, doctors, lawyers, etc.

B. The "bourgeois" were part of the primary objectives of Zionism; that is, building a national home for the Jewish people in Eretz-Israel, and voluntarily joining the public effort towards that goal.[111] The coordination meetings of the different Jewish public organizations also served as background to the contacts between the "civil circles" and the workers movements and others.

C. Reciprocal-relations between the Haifa "bourgeois" were also created during the common meetings between owners of factories and stores, engineers, professors, and lawyers. At times, especially as result of absorption problems of many newcomers, some of the lawyers, engineers and the like, found their place in lower employment frameworks that did not match their accustomed social status.

D. The relative weakness of the secondary "civil" centers caused a modest level of establishment of the "bourgeois" organizations in Haifa; their activity was not systematic and institutionalized, unlike the workers' movement institution. The inclination to organize on the basis of narrow, particular interests caused a reduction of the ideological aspect as an existence center of these organizations, as well.[112] As an example it could be mentioned that only in 1941 the three commerce departments of Tel Aviv, Jerusalem, and Haifa were united.

E. In the mid 20's and more so in the 30's, the workers' movement and the general union changed their attitude towards the "bourgeois"; the workers' movement showed great interest in the development of industry and the private capital flow to the country. We should stress that everything was done under the condition of organized work through the workers' union.[113] Due to that, the "class struggle" generally, and particularly in Haifa, came to a stop. Other than that, the union needed public (and private) capital for investments in its factories of the "Workers' Company." Aba Hushi, secretary of Mapah in the 30's and 40's, did not yield however to the industrialists in the matter of the workers' salary; the post war period increased Mapah's fear of harm to their salary; in the annual convention of the industry owners' union in Haifa, the industry and commerce department manager of the Jewish agency, Dr. Shmorak and the chairman of the union in Haifa, Yosef Miller, both supported the deduction of workers' salary. This demand was promptly pushed aside by Mapah's trade union people.[114] However, generally the conflict between the "classes" was limited to the field of workers' wages and the trade union only.

F. In the Mandate period, the urban bourgeois took second place in the local political hierarchy in Haifa, after the workers. Since the conclusion of the First World War the bourgeois economy prospered. Aside from factories, production plants, and real estate, a developed economic infrastructure was established in Haifa, which included workshops, commerce services such as general services, private medicine, private ownership education ("The Reali" school, for instance), ownership of houses for rent, etc. The organizational division was vast and nearly every "free profession" made an effort to establish a framework for itself. The framework was usually unstable, for example, the architects and engineers' union in Haifa, which was founded in the mid-30's. Nevertheless, the Haifa "bourgeois" was still considered a secondary body, and its social, economic, and public weight did not come to a dominant expression in the Haifa existence.

Between Jews and Arabs in Haifa — characteristics of segregate economies and their interface

The pre-First-World-War feudal Arab society had contact with the Jewish immigrants right after their arrival. After the War and with the beginning of the British Mandate rule, a new chapter began for the Jews and the Arabs, written by the two sectors that continued to sustain neighborly, trade, and conflict relations. At the basis of these relations was the contest over the ultimate control of Palestine.[115] The establishment of a wide economic infrastructure mainly by the British government who planned to develope Haifa had accelerated the integration of the Arab community into the urban economy. As soon as 1928 the city was recognized as the major economic center of Eretz-Israel. It served as a central location for government and international factories in which thousands of Arab workers were employed. Most of them worked in army camps, the mandatory railway, the harbor, Haifa's municipality, and oil companies. Others found their livelihood in Arab industry and craft, trade, clerical work, services, and even non-Arab industry. Generally speaking, at the end of the British Mandate, the Arab community in Haifa was in a constant prospering state.[116]

Analyzing an industry and handcraft census conducted in Eretz-Israel in May 1928 (by the trade and industry wing in the custom department of Palestine-Eretz-Israel government), Bigger notes that already in 1928 Haifa was the big industrial center of Eretz-Israel. That year, it comprised more than 9% of the country's factories, and 16% of all industry employees in Eretz-Israel worked in the city. Approximately a quarter of the industrial output value was produced in the city, and more than

35% of capital that was invested in industry in Eretz-Israel was invested in Haifa.[117] We should also point out that the Israeli professional literature that deals with the industry and trade development in the British Mandate period discuss mainly the macro-economic processes, as the focus on the Haifa arena was minimal; more so, as we are dealing with the Arab settlements' economy in the British Mandate period. In this sub-chapter we will try to examine, and characterize the development of the two different economies in Haifa—the Arab and the Jewish. To conclude, we will examine the possible reciprocal relations between the two segregate economies.

A: Arab economy grows and adjusts in mandatory Haifa

The Jewish pioneers who landed on the coasts of Haifa in the 20's saw it as a city immersed in slumber. That is the opinion of Bernstein, who further claims that the relatively small Haifa Arab settlement began to develop in 1831, when Ibrahim Pasha, son of Egyptian ruler Muhamed Ali, captured Haifa from the Turks. As the years went by, with the conquering of the city by the British, a demographic growth occurred in it, along with the geographic expansion.[118] Despite this accelerated development, the Arab settlement feared the organizational power of a Jewish labor, which had just immigrated to Haifa.[119] It should be mentioned that the economic resources of the Arab settlement at the time (early 20's) were considerable and were not inferior to the economic abilities of the Jewish immigrants. On the contrary, Kimmerling and Migdal note that life in cities like Jaffa, Haifa, and Gaza resembled similar lives in major Mediterranean cities like Marseille, Athens, Beirut, and Alexandria—more than in the Palestinian Hinterland.[120]

The Mandate government did not believe it was its duty to develop local industry or encourage potential investors. In fact there were not any allocations of direct support of local industry, whether old or new, in the mandatory government budgets.[121] At the beginning of the British Mandate period there was no actual modern industry to be found in Eretz-Israel, in neither the Arab nor the Jewish sectors. That is why, even though the Mandate's government did not encourage industries directly, it did make a few important steps in the 20's, which provided partial support to Arab and Jewish industries; like the cancellation of the customs on raw materials, abolition of taxes on equipment and machinery, and of export tax and a few customs on competing import.[122]

Regarding more specifically the general industrial extent in Haifa in the 20's, it is possible to rely on the first industrial survey conducted in 1928 (published in 1929). According to this survey, in 1928 there were 321 economic organizations in Haifa that employed 2,808 men and women; their financial output (in 1927) was 1,002,616 pounds sterling; the capital invested that year amounted to 1,228,370 pounds sterling. For comparisons' sake, the financial output in Jerusalem reached 474,709 pounds sterling, while the capital invested in Jerusalem was 356,507 pounds sterling; in (Jewish) Tel Aviv 2,800 men and women were employed in 284 factories and there was an output of 538,083 pounds sterling.[123]

In the beginning of the economic development in Eretz-Israel, the Arab industry lacked capital, credit sources, and professional workers. In both of these fields, the Arab industry (in Haifa too) used outside help, especially when it needed expert workers.[124] The carton industry, for instance, was first established in Haifa with Jewish women workers; the same occurred in the "Wagner" factory in Haifa (in the metal industry branch) or the Jewish factory for rice cleaning in Haifa, which employed 60 Arab workers. With the founding of a similar Arab factory in 1937, the workers transferred to it; the soaps and oils factory that belonged to the Templer Shtruba, and was founded in 1899, employed 20 workers; after the First World War, that factory developed and employed tens of Arab workers. While before the war the tobacco and cigarette industry did not exist in Eretz-Israel, by 1923, there were already eleven of those factories, mostly Arab; four of them were in Haifa and the

monthly salary in the city reached 2.1—3.2 Eretz-Israeli pounds
in average, compared to 1.4-1.8 in Jerusalem and Nablus area.
The biggest of the cigarette factories was in Haifa, the Greek
Sarkidis factory, which employed less than 10 workers. In 1925, a
large cigarette factory was established in Haifa—Kraman, Dick,
and Salty's plant, which employed 50 workers. In 1926, another
cigarette factory, which employed 30 workers, was founded in
Haifa—Salum, Negia, and Khoury's.

In 1927, the "British-American Tobacco Trust" (which
established the "Misparo" factory in Jaffa in 1921), bought
"Kraman, Dick, and Salty" in Haifa, and decided to concentrate
the entire cigarette manufacturing for the Arab market in
it. Later on, the "Trust" bought the majority of the cigarette
factories and employed more than 500 workers.

Until 1928, there were not any Arab factories active in the
carton boxes manufacturing department. For their packaging
needs, the Arab factories used boxes brought from abroad or
from Jewish factories that developed between 1921 and 1923.
By 1928-9, three Arab factories were established, two of which
were in Haifa. In Jabar's big carton boxes factory in Haifa, were
employed between 50 to 100 Arab women workers. In the nails
production department, Kraman bought a Jewish nail factory
in 1933 and started manufacturing metal nets as well. In 1937,
a rice-cleaning factory was established as aforesaid, and it
employed a few tens of workers and its private capital reached
25,000 Eretz-Israeli pounds. This factory suffered from the lack
of raw materials for its production.

Haifa's Arabs ruled the construction business; they knew
construction stone masonry, and they knew how to make cement,
mortar and plaster, and of course, more professional works in
the construction field. Only Arabs did the Haifa Arabs' building
construction. In the days of the fourth immigration (1925), the
number of the Jewish tenants who were looking for apartments
and had to live in Arab houses in their neighborhoods, increased.
The apartment rents rocketed, and that poured much capital
to Arab contractors and entrepreneurs in Haifa. Apartment
leasing was seasonal and depended on the general reciprocal

relations between Arabs and Jews and also on the development pace of Jewish neighborhoods in Haifa.

Abramovitz and Glaft wrote that trade was focused mainly in the Haifa markets. Near the markets developed bigger shops; in 1921 there were 3272 of these shops in all of Eretz-Israel; in 1935, 5361 shops; the 2089 shops that were added were spread across Haifa, Jerusalem, Jaffa, Tel Aviv, Tiberias, and Safed.[125] Concerning the Eretz-Israeli export, the larger part of the Arabs sectors' firms focused on traditional export branches such as soap, souvenirs, religious objects, citrus crops, etc. Eretz-Israel's Arabs sent their citrus through Jaffa harbor more than through Haifa's, because of its distance from their orchards. However, the country's main crops trade center was in Haifa.[126] As an indication, it is possible to note that by 1927, out of 38 Arab importers of crops, 20 had their offices in Haifa, 12 in Jaffa, and 6 in Jerusalem; out of 41 exporters of crops, 21 were located in Haifa.[127]

As to the Arab banks in Eretz-Israel, the "Anglo-Egyptian" bank merged with "Barclays Bank" in 1925; by 1930 this bank had branches in Jerusalem, Jaffa, Tel Aviv, Nazareth, and Haifa. "Ottoman" bank also opened a branch in Haifa. In 1930, there was an attempt to establish an independent Arab bank chain. In November 1930, an "Arabic trade convention" was held in Haifa, and it was decided to issue 30,000 stock shares. Finally, in 1932, an "Arab Bank" branch opened in Haifa.

Mahmoud Yazbak stresses yet again the claim that before the First World War there was a significant number of Muslim and Christian Arabs, who served as merchants, entrepreneurs, and land and property owners, who conducted import and export businesses with European countries. The Jewish population did increase dramatically between 1918 and 1948, but the Arab population of Haifa also grew impressively, from 34,148 citizens to more than 50,000 in 1938.[128] Yazbak's central claim is that, other than the successful cigarette industry, Haifa Arab entrepreneurs' attempts to develop industries in fields of oils, shoes, beds, ceramics, pipe production and ice factories, etc., failed due to a lack of financial support.[129] May Seikaly, in her book on the transformation of the Arab-Palestinian society in Haifa 1918-1939,[130] accepts Yazbak's claims and adds that the Haifa Industry was a Jewish protectionist monopoly.[131] Seikaly also describes the Haifa-Arab industry and trade; she claims that industries such as the rice grinding factory and the cigarette factory were meant first and foremost to provide the needs of the Arab population of the city. Medium and small magnitude Arab entrepreneurs suffered from a lack of investment capital and from an inability to market their products to a relatively wide market. Indeed, after 1933, there was an expansion of trade in Haifa, and the city's Arabs too developed shops and factories to produce ceramics, nails, pipes, and cables, but this production provided the internal-Arab market and not external markets.[132]

Yizhak Klein also claims that the economic life of the Arabic community in Haifa was greatly affected by the new conditions and the development processes that the British government and the Jewish settlement in Haifa that grew at the time brought with them.[133] Klein sees the essence of the Haifa economy this way:

1. Employment places in Haifa—about 2,000 workers (mostly Arabs) were employed in the building of the deep-water harbor of Haifa. The harbor also provided work for Arab import and export agents. In the building of the mandatory railway tracks to Rosh Hanikra, 1445 Arab workers were employed. Ninety-eight percent of the I.P.C. workers were Arab; the Haifa municipality employed 600 Arab workers and laborers. Out of 3000 laborers who worked for private Arab employers, about a third worked with rock masonry, about a fifth with driving, a fifth with hotels and restaurants; 8% were in the tobacco industry, 5% in the metal industry, and 5% in laundries. In addition, Arab laborers also worked in Jews' workshops, in canning factories, coloring places, driving, and tiles factories. Their number was estimated in 1946 in Haifa and in Jaffa, at 2000-2500 laborers.

2. Trade—Haifa as a harbor city, excelled in fishing and

the fishing trade. In the Mandate period, there were four fish markets. Every market had its permanent fishermen working for it and also fish vendors in specific stands. Haifa was also a market for the suburbia around it including agricultural products. In the 40's, the cooperative movement expanded in the Arab settlement. In 1940, a supermarket for the Haifa municipality's laborers was opened. In 1941-1943 the "Palestinian laborers union" built three grocery stores in Haifa; by 1938, the slaughterhouse laborers' cooperative was founded. The Arab merchants of Haifa were united in the trade department led by Rashid el Haj' Ibrahim. The department handled issues of trade, taxes, excises, price rates and rent.[134]

3. The Arab industry in Haifa—the industry's level was not very high, although in comparison with the rest of the country, in Haifa exsisted an Arab industry concentration that can be defined as light industry. The capital invested in it was not large and it concentrated in tapestry industry (Syrian and Egyptian capital); toy, cosmetics and drugs; welding, garages, and carpentry workshops; tobacco industry and two carton factories.[135]

4. The services—the Arabs of Haifa had a major part in it. Haifa's central location as a junction, and its natural panorama were utilized by the tourist industry. Hotels and restaurants were built in the city. For example, the famous businessman Charles Bothagy founded the "Windsor" hotel with his partners. A few transport companies operated in the city, among them one owned by Boullus Perah, of the leaders of the "Laborers Congress"; these transport companies were organized in a union led by the lawyer Hana Asfour. Another important services department was the banking sector.

Concerning the important families in mandatory Haifa, the ruling families' affect on the Arab public life was much less than in other Arab cities; the reason for that is probably the young age of the developing city. The prominant families were:[136]

1. **Halil family**—owned many assets. Among their

sons: Ali Halil, landowner and a member of the Haifa municipality, and Ahmed Halil, magistrate's court judge.

2. **Shukri family**—a respectable and influential family, whose power faded after the death of Hassan Bei Shukri, who was the mayor of Haifa.

3. **Ta'ha family**—a respectable and rich family. Its head, Haj Halil Ta'ha was murdered in 1936, as was his son, Dr. Ta'ha.

4. **El Haj' family**—Abd Rahman el Haj', who was mayor of Haifa in the 20's, head of the Islamic union, head of the district wakf committee etc., was from this family.

5. **El Maadi family**—originally from Ag'azem (between Haifa and Atlit), owned lands, property, and businesses.

6. **Sahioun family**—very rich family, involved in many economic fields. The most remarkable in the family were Elias Sahioun, Ibrahim Sahioun, and lawyer Joseph Sahioun.

7. **Khayat family**—Victor Khayat was one of the prominant and richest merchants in Haifa; Francis Khayat was a justice in the mandatory Supreme Court.

8. **Touma family**—a rich merchants family; among the sons was Emil Touma, of the leaders of the Eretz-Israeli Communist party and later a Knesset member in Israel.[137]

Other remarkable personalities in the Arab economy in Haifa were **Emil al Bustani**, publisher and engineer, owner of a trading and contracting company; **Emil Theophil Bothagy**, a Christian merchant that had import business and was the representative of a few European companies, owner of branches and shops in all of Eretz-Israel, chairman of the merchants union in Haifa (1936); **George Khoury**, an Independent lawyer in Haifa and owner of businesses; at the end of the Second World

War he also served as secretary for the Haifa branch of "The Palestinian Arab Party" and was a member of the Haifa "Arab Front"; **Naguieb Nassar**, stood at the head of "the economic Arab union" in Haifa in 1922-1923 and was one of the first Arab journalists in Haifa (*El Carmel*), was an entrepreneur in the land acquiring field; **Jad Suidan**, businessman, one of the richest men in Haifa, a member of the trade bureau in the city and elected as their representative in the country's bureaus convention in 1943; he was also vice president of the Haifa branch of the "Palestinian Arab Party" in 1944; **Salah A-Din Abasi**, a lawyer, supporter of the "Al Istiklal" party, member of the administrators council of the "Nation's Fund" (1944), **Abd el-Hadi Amin a** landowner from Haifa, was a member of the Ottoman parliament, and of the "Supreme Muslim Council"; sold some of his lands to the Jewish National Fund; **Camal Abd A-Rahman** was active in the trade and financial life of Haifa in the 40's, he was a member of Haifa's trade bureau presidency, and by 1947 a member of the administrators' council of "Treasury House"; **Taher Kraman** was among the rich merchants and business owners in Haifa, he was a partner in the "Kraman, Dick, and Salty" a cigarette factory in Haifa. He bought Bedouins' land near Haifa. During the Second World War he was vice mayor of Haifa.[138]

B: The Jewish economy in mandatory Haifa: characteristics of a foreign, technological, varied and hegemonic economy

The records of Haifa's laborers council (Mapah), point out that between the years 1910-1913, the laboreres were employed in: "Atid" factory (later "Shemen") composed of 33 laborers, including 3 clerks; "Apek" (Anglo-Palestine Bank) composed of 10 clerks; "Ottoman" bank with 2 clerks; the railway made up of 10 laborers; schools and kindergartens with 15 teachers; the construction work in the Technion and in the "Hareali" school was at its beginning and few masons, mostly Yemenites and Sepharadim who were brought from Jerusalem, were working there.[139] In 1914, with the beginning of the First World

War, the work in Haifa stopped, including in the Technion and in "Atid" factory and the employment situation was dire. After much effort, Mapah managed to reach an agreement with "Hachsharat Hayeshuv" (Zionist Settlement Company) with the participation of Apek, for paving some of the roads in Hadar HaCarmel. All of Haifa's laborers worked there, their numbers reaching about 100 and the daily payment was about four "bishlikim" (20 grushim).

Between the years 1917-1918, the "Carmel" (carpentry) and "Amal" (for fixing machinery and foundries) cooperatives were established.[140] In 1920 the "Hashomer Hazair" (young guard) regiment in Haifa, got coal-unloading work in the Haifa harbor. In 1922, the "Valley Group" arrived in Haifa from Seg'ara in the lower Galilee and started working in the houses construction in Hadar HaCarmel area. During the 20's, the big factories began to grow and evolve: "Shemen," "Nesher," "Htahanot Hagdolot," (mills) and the electricity company. The laborers who worked in the construction of these factories, later on worked in them.

In 1923, a strike broke out in the "Brothers Rosenfeld" printing house. It was one of the first strikes conducted by Mapah in Haifa; this strike failed; the police arrested the leaders of Mapah, and "Brothers Rosenfeld" continued to employ strike breakers.[141]

In the beginning of 1924, "Solel-Boneh" (the public work company) started to work in Haifa. That year was characterized by economic prosperity brought by the fourth immigration. In the summer of 1925, the "Nirenstein strike" broke out; he was a contractor who built two houses on Hatavor street, and employed laborers who were not organized in Mapah. Following his complain to the police 10 Mapah activists were arrested. Due to the riots at the construction site, 43 additional members were arrested. In the end, Mapah succeeded in imposing its will in the field of the trade union.[142]

The formation of work-relations patterns started in mandatory Haifa, they were characterized by a tough and syndicalist "trade-union" approach, with the much disciplined worker culture. These political processes were accompanied by a strengthening of the workers' movement, through building an independent worker economy for all its factories, especially in the field of heavy industry in the Haifa's area.

The union industry was an important layer of the industry in Haifa. Together with "Solel-Boneh," additional factories were developed, such as: "Even and Sid" (rock and whitewash), established in 1935 as a company, was based on a cooperative group of eight members, which organized in Haifa in 1922 under the name "Sid Kav ve Naki." The entire construction department got renewed momentum as a result of "Solel-Boneh" falling apart in 1927 and the founding of the contractual office in Haifa in April 1928, following the third union conventions' decision (July 1927), to set up local contractual offices as replacements for "Solel-Boneh." In 1924, 11 industry and craft factories were founded, and in 1925, additional 29 factories. At the beginning of that year, there were 547 industry and craft factories in the country and they employed 4,770 workers. There were only 59 factories in Haifa that employed 500 workers, but in 1925 there occurred an apparent increase in the city's industry development.

That year, in Haifa were added the biggest number of factories, countrywide. The industry in Tel Aviv increased by 75%, in Jerusalem by 152% and in Haifa by 163%.[143] The increase in industry and craft factories in 1925 can be attributed to the fourth immigration, which brought many middle class people to Haifa.

From the early 30's until the end of Second World War, there was an accelerated economic development, with exchanges of high and low tides. The economic development that began with the start of the fifth immigration reached its peak in 1935. The decline that began at the end of the same year increased with the eruption of the violent incidents, and reached the heights of unemployment in 1938; that is how the construction business, for example, suffered a major crisis that came to actual expression in Haifa as well.

The union economy kept on growing, even though it also

had its seasonal crisis as occurred in the entire mandatory economy. Factories that belonged to the union economy of Haifa were "Fenicia," flat glass; "Volcan," metal casting; "Nesher" (which was acquired in 1946 by the "Workers Company"); "Solel-Boneh"; "Even Vesid" (rock and whitewash), "Herut" (freedom); and "Hamegaper."[144]

We can stress the prominence of the union industry in Haifa, however, the private initiative had existed already in the early stages of the development of modern Haifa, and it started to grow in coincident with the development of "the Workers Company" factories. Mapah regarded the private industry with awe and reverence, understanding that it constituted workplaces and livelihoods for the large labor public in Haifa. Mapah was strict about the basic requirements in the field of trade union like the right to organize and establish a workers' committee, sign collective work agreements, but it was well understood that it should not damage the employment of the workers who were organized in Mapah. The reciprocal relations between the strong Mapah and the private employers and industrialists were mostly symbiotic; neither side wanted the other to be diminished or fall apart.

As mentioned above, the Haifa industry began to come into being in the beginning of the 20th century. As early as 1906, Joseph Miller, born in Jaffa, opened an import agency in Nazareth Street in Haifa (Kibbutz Galuyot today). Through the agency he established, he helped build the Hijaz railway (the construction began in 1906). In 1928, Miller established an oxygen plant in Nazareth Street.[145] The engineer Nahum Wilbush tells about the first buds of Haifa's industry. He recounts the founding of "Atid" that was established in 1906 by Shmuel Pevsner and Wilbush himself. They decided to set up "Atid" in Haifa because of the proximity to the sea and the harbor (raw material import), and because of the city's closeness to agencies and banks. A hundred workers and clerks worked in "Atid" factory. During the same time, an Anglo-Palestine bank branch (Apek) was opened in Haifa under the management of Nathan Keiserman.[146]

According to the statistical data on the industry in Eretz-Israel in 1926, it turns out that by the number of factories, Tel Aviv was in the first place (51% of all factories), followed by Jerusalem (25%) and Haifa came in third place (10%); however, according to invested capital in the industry, Haifa was in first place. Forty four percent of the capital invested in Eretz-Israel's industries was invested in Haifa's factories, as result of the large industry concentration in Haifa in contrast to the tiny industry in Tel Aviv and Jerusalem. According to data from 1926, in every factory there was an average investment of 13,000 pounds in Haifa, 1,700 pounds in Tel Aviv, and 1,600 pounds investment in Jerusalem. [147] The Second World War acted as a catalyst for the acceleration of the industrial development in order to contribute to the war effort of the Allies. [148]

As for trade, hotels, and services in mandatory Haifa, Jewish entrepreneurs, alongside local Arab entrepreneurship, contributed to the development of these fields. There were 13 hotels recommended by Ze'ev Vilnai and Eliezer Boneh in the Haifa part of a 1935 Eretz-Israel guide.[149] Among these hotels we should mention "Villa Migdal," hotel on Ahad Ha'am street (18 rooms), "Zaltzman hotel" on Mount Carmel (30 rooms), "Teltesh House" on Mount Carmel (30 rooms), "Wallstein House" on Mount Carmel (19 rooms), "Hertzelia Hotel" on Allenby street (10 rooms), "Zaltzman hotel" on Hertzel street (11 rooms), "Windsor hotel" in the German Colony (40 rooms), "Eden hotel" on Hatechnicom street, "Spector hotel" on Mount Carmel, "Zion hotel" (30 rooms), "Mendelwitz hotel" on Mount Carmel (10 rooms), and "Carlton hotel" in the German Colony (13 rooms).

Apart from these hotels, Jewish owners operated cheaper hotels and guesthouses. In Hadar Hacarmel were the "Bezalel hotel," "Geula hotel," "Stern hotel," "San Remo hotel," "Mizpeh hotel," "Emek hotel," "Tarshish hotel," and in the downtown area were the "Efron hotel," "Bezalel hotel," "Yarden hotel," and "Dresner hotel."

The prominent cafés in Haifa by 1935 were "Vienna Café" on Nordau street, "Kompanitz Café" on Hertzel street, "Astoria Café" in Hadar HaCarmel opposite the Technion, "Tnuva Café" in Hadar HaCarmel and in the old trade center; and "Europe Café" in the new trade center; "Gil Café" on Arlozorov street, "Spinney's Café" in the German Colony, "Nordau Café" on Nordau street, the vegetarian "Pure Café" in Hadar HaCarmel.[150]

Ten banks operated in Haifa in 1935; these banks had branches in the downtown city area and/or in Hadar HaCarmel: "Barclays bank" (trade center on Jaffa street), "Apek" (trade center on Jaffa street), "Union bank of Hollandia" (new trade center), "Ottoman bank" (Khamra square), "Eretz-Israel Mercantile bank" (on Jaffa street), "Templer-Gezelshpat bank," a German bank (on Jaffa street), "Loan and Savings bank" (trade center), "Folk Credit bank" (trade center).[151] The trade and industry office in Haifa noted the activity of these other banks: "Apothikai bank," "Eretz-Israel-South Africa Company," and "Banco Di Roma."[152]

Movie theaters in Haifa in 1935 included "Ein Dor" (on Jaffa street), "Gan Ha'ir" (Jaffa street), "Bitan Ha'ir" (in the German Colony), "Aviv" (on Jaffa street), "Amphitheatre" (on Hahalutz street), "Hertzeliya" (Anaporte street), and the "Maccabbi" stadium (Hertzel street).[153]

Forty five shipping companies' agencies operated in Haifa in 1935; among them were "Aharon Rosenfeld," "Dizengoff and co.," "Caspi and co.," "Pardes Company," "Alonzo and son," "Haifa boating agency," "Hiti and Faga'lla," "Brothers Green," "Henry Hild and co." Flight company agencies also operated in Haifa, including Flight lines of the British Empire, K.L.M and the Egyptian airlines company that operated in Haifa through the "Herman Tiz traveling agency in Haifa."[154]

In 1941, the Palestine (Eretz-Israel) governments' industry exhibition took place in Cairo;[155] among Haifa-based companies that exhibited their products were many Jewish factories, but only three Arab factories: "United Arab company for tobacco and cigarettes" Ltd., "Eastern rice mill" Ltd., and "Kraman,

Dick, and Salty" of cigarette and tobacco. It seems that the comparison between the Jewish and Arab factory exhibition speaks for itself.

John Hope Simpson detailed, in a memorandum to the British Parliament in 1930, his conception of "the immigration, the settlement, and the developing of the country."[156] He describes the Palestinian industry's characteristics in the mid-20's, and stresses the dominance of the Jewish industry already in that stage. [157] He notes:

> Of the industry institutes that operate in Eretz-Israel, there are 1236 factories with the comprehensive capital of over a million pounds, which existed even before the war. Since the war and up to the industry census date, the number of factories added is 2269, or it grew in 183% and the capital grew in two and a half million pounds or in 250%. This is an apparent increase and due almost entirely as result of the involvement of the Jewish capital and the Jewish immigration.[158]

Bernstein[159] and Even Shoshan[160] consent to that opinion, as are Horowitz and Lisak, analyzing the formation of a Jewish economic prominence. They consider, among others, the Arab's economy as a mainly agrarian one, and also stress the Hebrew ideology dimension, against a lack of institution for the Arab sector.[161] Smith emphasizes the difference of production methods between the Arab-Palestinians and the Europeans, including Jews; the latter bring land processing methods and industrial production more advanced than those used by the Palestinians.[162] David Horowitz also mentions that the development of Eretz-Israel's industry was very much the product of Jewish enterprise. The development of the Jewish industry is described in the Jewish agency's census this way: while in 1921-1922 there were 1850 factories, with invested capital of 600,000 pounds, by 1937 there were 5606 factories, with invested capital of 11,637,000 pounds.[163]

Yehoshua Zimmen, while analyzing the Mandate period data, refers specifically to Haifa, and notes:

> Haifa evolved from a small insignificant town...And became a big and populated city, the main harbor city of the country. Approximately 60 years ago, there were only 5,000 people in Haifa...Today (1946) there are 120,000 people...This is one of the most glorious pages in the history of the Hebrew settlement of the country. [164]

We notice the formation of a segregated Jewish economy that is more technological, different from the traditional Eretz-Israeli economy; a varied and advanced economy, accompanied by significant capital investments and as result, the formation of hegemonic economy.

C: Selective reciprocal relations beyond the restrains of a segregated economy in Haifa

In Eretz-Israel under the British Mandate the two communities maintained limited economic relations and political contacts that were mediated by the government.[165] Gross claims that:

> The creation of mandatory Eretz-Israel in the years 1919-1922 as a political and administrative, separate-territorial unit, was also the creation of Eretz-Israel as an independent economically united unit, although in the economic field there was no absolute separation from the neighboring countries...In this way, the framework was created for the economic development of the two separate national communities that came into being in Eretz-Israel under the Mandate rule, and very much with its help. The economic policy of the Mandate government determined in many areas the association between the Jewish and the Arab economy in Eretz-Israel...At the same time, the Zionist movement and the organized settlement did not settle for the services and the investments that the government provided for the Jewish sector, and financed and managed an additional separate system for the Zionist-public sector. [166]

The professional division of the Jewish and the Arab sectors, teach us of the low employment differentiation among the Arab sector compared to the Jewish one. Polak notes that in a 1931 census, the Jewish settlement included 174,610 people: 66,683 providers, 11,754 dependant workers, who do not earn enough for a complete livelihood, and 96,173 dependants who do not work. The data reflects the enormous growth of the Hebrew economy in the years 1932-1939, which is the outcome of the growth in the number of providers by twice and a half as much in only seven years. Polak believes that this process occurred as result of a large flow of workers and capital that came to the country at the time. This economic growth did not stop during the the Second World War, but that was not the case for the Arab economy in Palestine.[167]

As for mandatory Haifa, two features characterized the Jewish settlement: the internal unification and the organizational ability. Life in a mixed city required mediation over inside conflicts and standing united against the British on the one hand, and against the Arab settlement on the other. The Technion constituted a central stage for consolidating the Hebrew spirit of the city, along with its role as a local technology promoter, a technology that had an almost monopolizing character in Eretz-Israel.[168]

Despite the dominance of the local workers' movement, a middle class developed in Haifa comprised mainly of merchants and service employees. There was also a narrower high class that included merchants, industrialists, and senior officials.[169] The same occurred in the the Arab sector. In this case, the question is: apart from the formation of the two segregated economic poles, did one of them benefit more from the accomplishments of the other, in the few interface points between them?

Most of the researchers of the period in general and of the Haifa economy in particular, are of the opinion that the fruits of the Jewish economy's progress, brought a certain prosperity to the Arab economy in Haifa; that is, the opinion of Boneh, who claims that examining the income balance of every sector from the other in Eretz-Israel, proves that the Arab sector benefited more from the limited cooperation. Specifically, Boneh states that in 1935-6, the Arabs' incomes from Jewish sources was 3,500,000 pounds; and in addition, the Arabs received about a million and a half Eretz-Israeli pounds from the government's money, an income that come mainly from the Jews.[170] In Haifa, as in the rest of the country, the Eretz-Israeli industry lies mostly in the Hebrew economy fields, and its share in the general economy is estimated at approximately 80%...And in 90% of all capital invested and in 83% of output value.[171]

The departing consul of Holland in Jerusalem wrote in earlier years (1930), in a report to his government:

> The Arabs are without a doubt qualified people, but it cannot be expected that from their inferior situation in Palestine they will grow to the levels of the Jewish population, they will finally accept the fact that their progress is tightly tied with the progress of the Jewish settlement.[172]

Horowitz detects a tight connection and correlation between the growth of the Jewish economy and the beginning of the Arab economy's prosperity; due to the Jewish prosperity, the salaried Arab laborers class also developed. The work opportunities in the cities drew farmers from the villages next to Arabs from neighboring countries, to work in Eretz-Israel; on top of that, an Arab middle class was created and it was manifested in the rising number of merchants, industry owners, government clerks, free-professional workers and municipality clerks. The rising of this middle class was connected to capital flow from the Jewish economy to the Arab one due to land selling to the Jews. This land selling, in the years 1920-1940 reached a total of about 8,900,000 pounds.[173] Let us examine the nature of the two-way segregation along with the possible interface points between the two Haifa economies—the Arab and the Jewish:

1. There is no dispute over the fact that we are dealing with two segregated economies; we accept the

approach of Horowitz and Lisak in this matter.[174] The two economies in Eretz-Israel had autarkic characteristics, and they also tried to avoid the economic contacts that would lead to economic exchange, and all this out of national viewpoints of particular contradictory interests.

2.   Bernstein is of the opinion that the main tendencies in Haifa's work arena were similar to the Palestinian work arena that was manifested in the separatism of the Jewish community, in the formation and creation of a split labor market and a firm connection between economic variables and national-political variables.[175] We tend to accept this description by Bernstein, with one reservation: the separatist policy began in the Jewish economy, but with time it expanded to the Arab economy as well, and led to an even more advanced phenomena of economic segregation—a real voluntary economic segregation.

3.   We will further mention, that, in spite of the relative advantage (capital and technological) of the Jewish economy in Haifa, there was still a relative advantage for the Arab sector in work that did not demand much sophistication, in light of a cheap Arab work force that operated in the country and did not allow Jewish economic penetration to works like tiny soap industries, toy manufacturing, souvenirs, olive oil, oil products, etc.[176] In other words, there was no intense competition between the two sectors, to say the least, due to the lack of contracting points of similar production on the one hand, and the slower development of the Arab industry on the other.

Yazbak stresses in this context that despite the demographic growth of Haifa's Arabs between 1918 and 1947, the process of losing the majority, the social status and the economic power of the city's Arabs still occurred; Yazbak believes that the reasons for that derived from the cooperation between the mandatory government and the Jewish Agency and the leadership of Haifa's Jews; Haifa was chosen by the Zionists as the future industrial center of Palestine. According to Yazbak, the main reciprocal relations between the Jewish and the Arab economies in Haifa were manifested by employment and exploitation of cheap Arab laborers by Jewish employers. [177] However, he agrees with the claim that the flow of Arab and Jewish immigrants to Haifa caused Arab merchants to change and vary their economic activities, which bore fruit not only among Arab clients, but among Jewish and British as well. [178]

4.   The meeting points and the reciprocal relations between the Arab and the Jewish economies came to practical expressions in these topics:

A.   The municipality: elitism in the disguise of practicality.

B.   The administration of the British Mandate government.

C.   The general economic cooperation.

D.   Cooperation in the trade union field.

A. The municipality: elitism in the disguise of practicality

There is a wide and detailed research of the history of municipal government in Eretz-Israel,[179] but there is not much research, or even descriptive literature of the local government in Haifa.[180] However, all of the period's researchers accept Rubinstein's claim that the mixed municipalities in Eretz-Israel at the Mandate period constituted the only official political table around which the Arabs and the Jews sat together. As such, the relations between Jews and Arabs in the councils were affected directly by the relations between the two national ethnic groups.[181] Local (and self) rule was an important method of ensuring the realization of the Zionist movement's national objectives; the Jewish sector also perceived the municipal field as an important method of developing a modern society in Eretz-Israel.[182]

Therefore, the Jewish sector looked forward to the issuing of the mandatory municipalities' order from 1934; as prior to that, with the British occupation, all the former Ottoman laws were valid. Thus until 1934, the Ottoman municipalities' law from 1877 was in power, according to it, there were 22 municipalities in mandatory Eretz-Israel, including Jerusalem, Jaffa, and Haifa. Haifa was among the very few mixed cities that functioned at the time: Jerusalem, Haifa, Jaffa, Tiberias, and Safed.[183]

As result of the "Peel Commission" recommendations of 1936, the local councils' order was re-legislated in 1941, and that greatly extended their authority. The appointment of head of the municipality was still the British's prerogative. In Haifa, the mayor had been for many years, until 1940, the Muslim Hassan Bei Shukri, who maintained fair relations with the Jews, and after his death in 1940, when the population wheel in Haifa turned over and the Jews became the majority, his Jewish deputy, Shabtai Levi, was appointed mayor.[184]

It is interesting to mention the conflict of opinions that appear in memoirs, books, written testimonies, archives etc., between the Arab viewpoint of the relationship in the Haifa municipality, and the Jewish viewpoint; David Hacohen, a member of the Haifa city council (appointed in January 1927 as one of the two representatives of the Jewish community in Haifa, together with Shabtai Levi, out of 11 members of the city's council), praises his close friendship with Hassan Bei Shukri, Mayor of Haifa.[185] Abraham Halfon (who was the first Jewish municipal secretary of Haifa) also refers to Hassan Bei Shukri's humanity and to his good relations with the Jews.[186] Shabtai Levi draws attention to the patterns of municipal cooperation between Jews and Arabs:

> I believe that despite the limited activity of Haifa's municipality in its first days, it had political value even then. It was the only body where the local leaders managed

to maintain harmonious relations among Jews, Muslims and Christians. It should be noted that we always worked in an atmosphere of peace, and that the council accepted most of the decisions unanimously.[187]

We may add that Rubinstein explicitly says:

...In the Haifa municipality the tangible relations between Jews and Arabs were better than in other places. That may have been paradoxically resulting from the fact that the Jewish community in the city was for the most part new in the country and its contacts with the Arabs were not connected to common lives for many generations; the Jews did not experience the transition process from an inferior and tolerated community to an equal one, in terms of its political weight, as was in the other mixed cities. [188]

The Arab viewpoint of the reciprocal relations in the Haifa municipality is actually different. Yazbak claims for example that the municipal elections in Haifa in 1927 reflected for the first time the effect of the Jewish population on the political daelings within the Arab leadership. That happened when the united Jewish voters presented demands in exchange for their support of Arab candidates, Hassan Shukri and his list won their trust and Shukri was elected Mayor of Haifa.[189] Seikaly is of the opinion that the Jews benefited more than the Arab residents of Haifa from the municipality's activities. Evidence of that was seen in the investments made for the development of new neighborhoods (which usually housed Jews) in Haifa, and also investments in infrastructure, water, medicine, etc.[190]

Here again, we detect the opposing approaches as for the Jews and Arabs' function in Haifa's municipality. We will emphasize, again, that at the same time that the Jewish community perceived the municipal unit as a progressive factor, the Arab community (despite the majority it had in the city's council for many years) did not perceive the municipality as an egalitarian factor. Ben-Artzi and Goren claim that Haifa society generally operated as one unit, especially in the economic and municipal fields; however, the separation between the Arabs and the Jews was revealed in times of inter-community violent outbursts.[191]

This approach is mentioned in non-Arab or Jewish sources as well. For instance in E.S.C.O, the foundation for Palestine in a publication from 1947. Referring to Haifa, it says: "despite the political antagonism, Jews and Arabs worked normally together in practical matters of mutual interests." [192]

Goren examines the secrets of the cooperation between Jews and Arabs in Haifa municipality in the shadow of confrontation, and his conclusions are:

1. Abd el Rahman el Haj's period of service as a mayor (1920 till 1927) was comparable to that of his associates in other mixed municipalities in Eretz-Israel. In his opinion the municipality was an Arab establishment in the full sense of the word; therefore, it operated out of an Arab dominance approach.

2. Hassan Bei Shukri was mayor from 9.6.1927 until his death, in 28.1.1940. Goren believes that Shukri gradually designed a new conception of a municipal administration in Haifa. First of all, he changed the approach of an exclusively Arab municipality. Second, he tried to involve Haifa's Jews in the municipality's activities, while neutralizing the ethnic group-political element as a main source for conflict.[193]

The Haifa municipality's conduct under Shukri's tenure from 1927 was considered efficient and financially viable. Interesting to point out that Haifa's municipality practically did not have any deficits for many years; quite the opposite, almost every year the municipality ended the financial year with noteworthy balances. For instance, 1935 ended with a balance of

18,220 Palestinian pounds[194] even though it expanded its budget in the 30's and the 40's.

The number of workers in Haifa's municipality in 1945-6 was around 1,100. That is the division of the workers according to Haifa's ethnic groups and the division of the total sum of their monthly salaries in Eretz-Israeli pounds:

68 Muslim clerks 1,650 pounds.
86 Christian clerks 2,220 pounds.
138 Jewish clerks 4,200 pounds.
484 Muslim laborers 5,850 pounds.
120 Christian laborers 1,550 pounds.
195 Jewish laborers 3,600 pounds.[195]

Conclusions:

1. Analyzing the Haifa municipality's conduct over the years, teaches us of a common ground pattern, in both the Jewish and Arab sectors. The Arab sector perceived the municipality of Haifa as an Arab tool and mechanism in its essence. However, the Arab elite have chosen to ignore the huge advantages that the municipality gave the Jewish population, which distanced itself with the years from the city's center and Hadar HaCarmel and built several segragated and separated neighborhoods, including Ahuzat (estate) Herbert Samuel, and Neve Sha'a'nan. The Jews who continued to grant advantages, here and there, to the Arab sector welcomed this Arab policy, of course.

2. Beginning from the 20th century, eight city councils served the Haifa municipality (including the un-completed council in 1948). Here is the division of the council members according to the Jewish and Arab division:[196]
    In 1900-1914 there were 7 council members, all Arab, the same was in 1914-1925; in 1925-1927—7 council members, 5 Arabs, 2 Jews; in 1927-1934—11 council

members, 9 Arabs, 2 Jews; in 1934-1936 — 12 council members, 8 Arabs, 4 Jews; in 1936-1940 — 9 council members, 5 Arabs, 4 Jews; in 1940-1948 — 10 council members, 6 Arabs, 4 Jews; in 1948-1950 — 6 council members, 2 Arabs, 4 Jews.

The data speaks for itself. Even when the number of Jews evened (or surpassed) the number of Arabs in Haifa, the number of Jewish council members was drastically lower than their share in the population. The explanation for that lies in aforementioned point number 1; the Jewish ethnic group perceived the Haifa municipality instrumentally, as a tool for realizing part of the object of establishing a Jewish state in Eretz-Israel.

3. The people that were in office at the high level of Haifa's municipality (especially the city's council members), belonged to the city elites, both in the Arab and in the Jewish sectors. These elites preferred to maintain the status quo, not to cause any shocks, and of course not to hurt their own economic interests. This argument partly explains the molded way in which the municipality conducted itself even during the riots and violence between Jews and Arabs.

4. We have already note that Seikaly, Yazbak, Vashitz and others described the falling apart of the Arab society in Haifa. The disintegration and the splits aforementioned were also drowned out in the municipal structure, and in fact neutralized it from becoming a structure and a tool that would be used for the ideological and violent effort of the Arab settlement against the Jewish one in Haifa.

5. In both the Arab and the Jewish side, the Haifa municipality constituted an electoral zone for candidates that would represent the civilian sector

of Haifa's citizens; on the Jewish side, the powerful Mapah of "Red Haifa" perceived the municipality as a target for future political domination, and indeed Aba Hushi won the municipal elections at the end of 1950, when he stood at the head of the "union" in Haifa.

The day to day Jewish municipal activity was conducted in the Hadar HaCarmel committee, controlled by the "civilian circles" in Haifa, but also in the neighborhood committees of the Jewish neighborhoods in Haifa, meaning that the city council, even though it was the supreme municipal institution of the city, was not an electoral power center.

Therefore, when we examine the Jewish representation in Haifa's city council, we can notice personalities representing sectors that did not exactly belong to the inner circles of Mapah. For instance, former senior officials, merchants, managers in the union economy, etc. The same goes for Haifa's Arab sectors' panel of city council members.[197] It introduces again the claim that the Hebrew community committee in Haifa[198] alongside the activity of Hadar HaCarmel committee and other neighborhoods' committees[199] filled an active municipal duty (welfare services, kosher services, securing water supply, etc.) We can comprehend the relatively low part of Haifa's municipality in the power texture of the Jewish sector. We believe the same was true for the Arab sector.

B. The administration of the British Mandate government

Lesch notes that at the end of the 20's, a significant number of young Muslim-Arabs, who were educated in government or private schools, were planning governmental, professional, or economic careers.[200] The Jews also perceived the Eretz-Israeli administration as an important source for potential employment that the Jewish community should not ignore.

Colonel Kish writes in his memoirs that when he met with Israel Lipshitz, secretary of the Jewish community in Haifa, the conversation revolved around Lipshitz's claim that Jews were not employed in the railway's administration, and that the Jewish clerks who worked in the mandatory railway were slowly getting driven out.[201] This example clearly illustrates the insistence of the Jewish sector to get the best representation in the British administration in Eretz-Israel; the Jewish agency approved the Mandate's policy as a nominal implementation of the British obligation in Eretz-Israel.[202] In this basic rule, the Jewish agency demanded to recieve proper representation in the government's administration, for all its different and varied offices.

Reuveni sharpens this approach by claiming that the official Jewish demand for "benefiting from the government services" was partly aimed at government and municipal employment, whether in the permanent clerical sphere or in the different public works, including contracting work.[203] Of course, there was an inter-ethnic group contest over public employment, when every once in a while as a need to employ or fire employees came up, the two ethnic groups fought for what they believed was their appropriate representation.

Data from the 1922 population census shows that in the local clerical work in Eretz-Israel, there were 45% Christians, about 20% Jews and approximately 25% Muslims; in the junior division (that is the plain workers), there were 68.7% Muslims, and the rest Jews and Christians. Later, the Jewish representation in the low employment ranks excelled. In 1947, the division of the higher-ranking workers in the Mandate government indicates a reduction of the Christian factor from 45% to 42.9%, while the Jews and Muslims stood at approximately 28% each. The Jews' part in the senior personnel was close to their share in the population; the Muslims' part was about half of their share, and the Christian-Arabs' part was, as it was in the past, five times bigger than their share in the population (about 8%).[204]

C. The general economic cooperation

The interface points where the daily economic reciprocal and exchange relations were conducted between the Jewish and the Arab sectors in Haifa in shops, trade houses, trade services, etc. were straightforward and clear; the reciprocal relations existed out of comfort and economic need, although they went through a process of differentiation when the geographical gaps in Haifa widened, with the Jewish expansion to new neighborhoods.

Research that was completed about 1936 indicated that there was a sort of "payment balance" between the Jewish sector and the Arab sector. Derived from this research is the fact that the extent of the trade was relatively small. The Jews bought land and merchandise from the Arabs, and paid rent and salary to Arab laborers. The Arabs bought from the Jews about half the value of their sales to them, usually only industrial and electricity products. The explanation for the reduction of trade between the economies lies in national reasons and not economic ones. The period of riots in the 30's caused a greater disconnection between the economies.[205] The "payment balance" was frequently in favor of the Arab sector, and a surplus of money would pass to it from the Jewish settlement.[206]

Vashitz, who surveys the reciprocal relations between Arabs and Jews in the civil society of Haifa, notes that:

> As for the political relations between the two sectors, Haifa was not different from any other part of the country. However, it was different in all the civil society fields.[207]

Haifa had one harbor, one main business center, and one oil economy, and there was hegemony of the governmental sector in the city's economy. All this did not enable in Vashitz's opinion, an existence of two separate closed societies. He gives an example by showing that non-cooperation in the municipal field would have results contrary to the common interest of promoting and developing the city.[208]

Arabs and Jews met in their daily lives also as representatives of common interests, personal or collective. Because of that, two separate political systems evolved in Haifa, the same as the rest of the country, and one system of civil society. In the permanent trade relations, there was great significance to the personal plane. Vashitz mentions that in this field as well, appreciation of the personality of the economic partner often determined more than his national affiliation.

We will present some remarkable people from Haifa presented in *Palestine Personalia*, at the end of 1947.[209]

1. **Reuven Aharoni**, supervisor of lands in the mandatory Department of the Interior.

2. **Yakutiel Baharav**, secretary of the Eretz-Israel electricity company.

3. **Muhamad Abas Barday Bei**, district judge in Haifa and Nablus.

4. **David Bar Rav Hai**, lawyer and deputy chair of the Jewish community in Haifa from 1931.

5. **Ya'akov Bergman**, Haifa district officer, was responsible for rural matters of the Jewish sector.

6. **Teresa Mater**, gynecologist, owner of a private maternity hospital.

7. **Rafik Beidun Bei**, district officer, was in charge of Arab matters.

8. **Yosef Ardstein**, the manager of the "Yehuda" insurance company branch.

9. **Ya'akov Caspi**, an insurance agent, ships agent, and vice president of the Haifa trade department.

10. **Hanna Asfour**, lawyer, member of Haifa city council.

D. Cooperation in the trade union field

By the end of 1923, Symes, the District Commissioner of Haifa district, reported that the Arab press emphasized the "Economic Zionism" as a means for the Jews to take over Palestine.[210] It seems that this Arab estimate had its basis. At first, until 1927, the question of Hebrew labor and the competition between Arabs and Jews over the work had mainly been an ideological one. Since the mid-20's, the dilemma became first and foremost economic and political: how to secure the workplaces in the private Jewish economy for the Jews, in order to receive as many immigrants as possible and widen the Zionist hold in the country.

Shapira claims that according to the then common perception by the heads of the labor movement, the workers were responsible for the Zionist realization, because of the so-called objective identification between their interests as laborers and their Zionist interests.[211] In a different essay Shapira sharpens her explanation, and claims that the idea of Hebrew labor, originated in the time of the second immigration, was accepted even by the farmers and became an inalienable asset of the Zionist ideology.

The victory of Hebrew labor's ideology did not come because all were convinced in the righteousness of the socialist-moral claim of the second immigration's people, a claim that a Jewish settlement should not be built on the Arab sweat; not because of fear of the formation of a working Arab class and against it an exploiting Jewish class, too. The political reality of distancing and alienation between the two nations, which dictated national seclusion for security reasons, actually served as a foundation for proving, in retrospect, the validation of the Hebrew labor idea.[212]

There was somewhat of a tragedy and historical irony that the Socialist foundations in the national Jewish movement that aspired to change the world including the social agenda, found themselves, in light of the unique Eretz-Israeli reality, at the frontline against the Arab laborer, and this happened at the time of the Hebrew labor crisis. This predicament dictated ambivalent attitude towards the Arab laborer from the get-go.[213]

Since 1932, the extremity of the Arabs in their struggle against the Jews and the government policies that dealt with them grew. The Arabs' battle focused, in addition to the major battle over immigration, also against selling lands to Jews and the Hebrew labor policy.[214] The work relations field, which ideologically speaking was a topic of most important discrepancy in the Jewish settlement, was only one of the fields where existed reciprocal relations between the Jewish and the Arab economy. On the political plane as in the ecological, cultural, and economic ones, the society in mandatory Eretz-Israel was fundamentally a dual society characterized by the limited contacts between the two national groups, affected by the developments in the political conflict between them.[215]

Nevertheless, despite the inclination of the Jewish settlement to create a dual society, practical attempts were made in Haifa to establish common frames for Jews and Arabs, especially in the trade union field. In the third union convention (1927), a decision was made "to encourage the cooperation between the Jewish and the Arab laborers in common essential matters, and to establish for this need, the Eretz-Israel laborers' Alliance." This activity was meant to take place in cities with mixed population. The Haifa "Eretz-Israel laborers' Alliance" branch, which began to operate in 1929, got a boost with the election of Aba Hushi as secretary of the city's laborers council. For Aba Hushi the activity among Haifa's Arabs was a challenge which he took very seriously.[216]

In a booklet published in honor of 20 years of Haifa's union (1941), the cooperation processes ("The shared organization") between Jews and Arabs in Haifa were described, in the field of work-relations. In 1924, the union railway workers' committee appointed a special secretary to deal with organizing the railway, post, and telegraph Arab laborers. The new secretary tried to involve first of all one of the Arab laborers in the organization's activity, and only after he found the first one, Abraham Asmar, did the organizational activity actually began.

After a month, it was possible to meet tens of Arabs in this association, they would come every night to read a newspaper, participate in the meetings and the talks about their problems, and listen to a lecture on the workers movement. The activity encircled hundreds of Arab laborers. In the years 1925, 1926, and 1927 the Arab workers took part in the general gatherings, and their representatives were also among the speakers. The artistic program was also in Arabic and Hebrew. The Arab members participated in all the consultations of the railway workers' union and especially in the discussion if their union should be affiliated with the general workers movement or become international and also completely independent.

The success of the activity among the railway workers made a buzz among the Arab laborers in Haifa, and once in a while Arab laborers from different workplaces would ask the union to help them get organized and rectify their difficult working conditions, which was referred to by them, as work "Min el Parshi eila el Warsi" (from bed to the workshop) and again. A special club opened in Haifa in 1925 for the Arab workers, for all their different professions. The club was in the churches street in the city.[217]

This colorful and detailed description ends with a sort of— hint, that "undermining" from non-Jewish causes that took things badly—caused the stopping of the Arab and Jewish cooperation movement. Moreover, because of the riots of 1929, the activity of the Arab laborers club stopped for a short while.[218]

Amnon Lin, the union Arab department's manager-to-be (and Aba Hushi's son-in-law), also notes that "Eretz-Israel's laborers Alliance" became, right after it was born, something completely different than what was officially decided it would be. It operated small, but when the violent incidents erupted by 1936-1939 there was a steep reduction in its activity.[219] Haifa's centrality in the activity of "Eretz-Israel's laborers Alliance" did not go hand in hand with the fact that the Arab public in Haifa was continually under pressures to conduct militant activity for a significant part of the Mandate period. Haifa was also the base of the religion and terror leader, Sheik Izz al-Din al Qassam. Lin claims that in many aspects, Haifa's laborers council behaved in the second half of the British Mandate period, as if the power in the city and the area was in its hands. Aba Hushi was in charge of the activity among the city and the area's Arabs, and his key man in the field was Shlomo Alfia. This man, a native of Syria, understood and knew well the Arab society. He operated the "Alliance" club downtown, established an employment office for Arab laborers, and even linked it to sports teams considered extensions of the union sport club "Hapoel." On the 1st of May celebrations, the "Alliance" members marched with flags held up, challenging not only the nationalists, but the Haifa Communists, who did not forego their battle with the "Alliance."[220]

The reciprocal relations between Jews and Arabs came to an actual expression in mixed workplaces like "Nesher-Portland" factory; Bernstein brings her conclusions referring to the 1932 strike in "Nesher":

> If it seemed that the conditions of a mixed city like Haifa and a mixed workplace as "Nesher" could prepare the ground for the establishment of a relationship of sharing instead of competition and isolation, why, my conclusion is different—it was actually the mixture of working in the same workplace, the mutual exposure, the ease of access and the visibility that sharpened the competition and thwarted, in an obvious or not obvious way, sooner or later, the cooperation points.[221]

Schwartz also joins this view while referring to the strikes in "Nesher" from a class viewpoint.[222] De Prise, who researched "Nesher's" laborers of the 20's, reaches the conclusion that this workplace was a battle grounds between the Communists and Mapah, and that eventually the "Nesher" workers, who cut their ties with Mapah for a while, returned to it, when Jewish laborers got fired while Arab laborers continued to work in the factory.[223]

Aba Hushi, the powerful general secretary of Mapah who was greatly responsible for the formation of the reciprocal relations between Arabs and Jews in Haifa, analyzes in his article, from 30.11.1932, the three types of Arab workers in Haifa: (1) urban laborers, citizens of Haifa, laborers' or craftsmen's sons; these are professionals, living organized lives; (2) laborers who lived in close and remote villages, who came to Haifa to work;

these are farmers flowing to the city and cause the reduction of the work salary; (3) the Horan people and also others from Egypt and Syria, who lower the salary even more; their needs are small, and they are the target of hatred and disrespect from Haifa's Arabs.[224] In his book on the "Eretz-Israel's laborers' Alliance," published in 1943, he expresses his view formulated following the attempt to operate "Eretz-Israel's laborers' Alliance" since 1929. His approach is clearly ideological; he presents a realistic, ideological infrastructure for the cooperation between the two nations in Eretz-Israel and in Haifa particularly. He actually does the work needed for establishing a practical frame of alliance between Jews and Arabs, which center is in Haifa. He places special emphasis on developing a social life and personal connections between Jews and Arabs.[225]

The economic sectors in which a union activity is held in Haifa are: government, military and navy work, international factories, the contractors and the workers in these sectors, the mixed municipality, and also among the Arab industry and craft factories.[226]

As an example of the cooperation between Arabs and Jews in a big governmental workplace, Aba Hushi brings the big strike in the Iraqi oil company in Haifa in 1935 that took place from 22.2.1935 until 10.3.1935. Eight hundred laborers, coming from a demographic ensemble that was colorful professionally and nationally, worked in this company. The strike was conducted by the "Eretz-Israel's Laborers' Alliance" and the "Palestinian-Arab Laborers' Union," since the workers were organized in these two unions. The strike erupted on the workers' demand to cancel the announcement regarding the reduction of the salary of workers who would transfer from the construction department to the permanent work in the factory; the laborers also demanded an 8-hour work day for drivers. Additionally, they demanded 25% increase for overtime, a 7-day notice in case of dismissal, etc. The union invested more than 1,000 pounds in assistance to the strikers. The Palestinian union tried to separate the professional from the non-professional laborers. The strike incorporated about

600 workers of all professions. The oil company's management began to negotiate with the workers.

Fahari Nashashibi, the nephew of the mayor of Jerusalem Ragebe Nashashibi, appeared suddenly in Haifa and started to negotiate with the management above the demands of the workers, representing the Palestinian union. Nashashibi signed a contract with the company's management, that have agreed to establish a special workers union for its laborers (company union); some of the workers returned to work, and after a few days so did the rest. That is how the strike ended, in Hushi's opinion, in professional, organizational and moral failure, that take place after much mental, organizational and financial effort were invested in it by the "Eretz-Israel's laborers Alliance" and the union.[227]

We notice that in Haifa an important attempt was made to establish cooperation between Jews and Arabs. The attempt flowed to the field of work relations and the professional union relations, as on one hand, the Arab laborers worked in workplaces that were run and controlled by Jews, and on the other hand, Arabs worked in shared workplaces for Jews and Arabs. We have already shown that most of the researchers saw in this cooperation between Arabs and Jews a sporadic matter that was doomed to fail from the beginning. Gorney is of the opinion that the approach aforementioned originated in the will to create class solidarity in the 20's, a dream that faded in the 30's.[228]

In our interview with Amnon Lin, who participated in the activity of "Eretz-Israel's laborers' Alliance" in an earlier stage, he talked about the motives that drove Hushi to operate "against all odds" in his attempt to tighten the ties between Jews and Arabs in Haifa. According to Lin, Hushi was a member of "Hashomer Ha'zair" (the Young Guard), a left wing of the Labor movement, and the ideological theme (especially the international cooperation) was important to him; that is why he vigorously tried to tighten the ties with the Arabs' workers movement. However, Hushi was a pragmatist, and in the 40's even more of a national activist. He then opposed—so says Lin—the welcoming of the Arabs to the union in the 30's, because he feared that the extreme authorities in the Arab world would neutralize any chance of establishing the "Eretz-Israel's laborers' Alliance." Hushi operated gradually, as he believed that eventually Eretz-Israel's Arabs would join the union as full members. Hushi even tried to penetrate the camp of his rival the Jerusalem Mufti in 1936-8. His contact was Fahri Abd el Hadi from Araba near Jenin. "What interested Hushi was mainly the work market field and the work relations," claims Amnon Lin, and adds that as an organization meant to provide support for the union and the Jewish settlement when needed, the "Eretz-Israel's laborers' Alliance" no doubt failed the aforementioned test; the "Alliance" Arabs did not dare face the Arab rescue army in the War of Independence and Haifa's Arabs even fled the city despite Aba Hushi's efforts to keep them in Haifa.[229]

The union and Mapah included, conducted an ambivalent and even two-faced policy in their attitude towards the Arab workers and laborers; on the one hand, they tried to organize them and mobilize them as an organization appended to the union, and on the other hand, they joined the common (and legitimate) slogans in the Jewish sector about "Hebrew labor" and the need for a paramount coalesce of Jews in the workplaces. We find many proofs for this approach presence in the Haifa arena in the Mapah archives, in which there are hundreds of documents inducing the secretaries of the trade unions of Mapah to make an effort for the admittance of as many Jewish workers, even on the account of Arab workers. This central approach of "Hebrew labor" was expressed in a document from 6.6.1934, addressed to the union employment bureau in Haifa from the union's national executive committee. In this letter, the executive committee directs Mapah to:

> Immediately order the secretaries of the trade unions
> to provide the maximum assistance they can for the rail

laborers' center in their effort to admit immediately some 50-60 Jewish laborers for different jobs which have significance for the railway and our stand in it.[230]

Mapah's leadership shows interest in the employment ensemble of the Arab workers in Haifa. This interest came to expression in a frequent study of the professional framework of the Arab workers in the city, alongside an attempt to penetrate new professions.[231]

It seems that the Jewish and the Arab sectors in Haifa had different expectations from the "shared organization," which hit the highest point in the establishment of "Eretz-Israel's laborers' Alliance." The Arab workers that organized in the "Alliance" expected mainly proper trade union representation, a prevention of disgraceful exploitation, reduction of work hours, social security and medical insurance. The city's Arabs did not expect (or want) cultural, educational, sports, and political involvement. Mapah insisted on providing those rights further than their professional expectations. However, the Arabs in Haifa copied (in the form of autonomous professional organization) the union's actions, but on the other hand, they incited against it.

The Jewish sector, on the other hand, wanted the first step of the "shared organization" as a class solidarity expression, but this approach was deleted in the beginning of the 30's and the cooperation resulted mainly from political interest. Hushi and his colleagues in Haifa formed also an important layer of reciprocal relations between Jews and Arabs in the security field. In the end, Hushi's policy bore fruit, at least in the first years of Israel's existence, especially the reciprocal relations with the Druze and their huge significance both in the War of Independence and later on.

Summary: could the two walk hand in hand — the Haifa's coexistence — myth or reality?

The patterns of reciprocal relations between Jews and

Arabs in Haifa were different from parallel patterns in other mixed cities in Eretz-Israel; in the research literature that came later on (after the establishment of the state), these reciprocal relations were called "coexistence." Not many wondered about the theoretical and practical meaning of the concept, as there was no research in Israel about its history, foundations and origins. We are of the opinion that this is an illusive concept, which has two or even three meanings, understood to a certain extent differently by each side involved in the spinning of the Haifa's reciprocal relations.

In an international sense, the concept of "coexistence" meant a narrative of modernism, primarily reflected in a coexistence of differences[232]; in daily Palestinian-Eretz-Israeli life, coexistence was generally perceived as conducting discussion, conciliation, coming to terms with the other side and even a possibility of a shared life based on mutual respect.[233]

Ofir refers indirectly to the concept of coexistence:

Realistic self-awareness, essential to the actual existence of the entire national collective. From this self-aware viewpoint, the particularistic ideology, which places values such as peace, tolerance, and respect of man at the top of the list, is perceived as universal matter, and is separated from the political system, which is in fact nothing more than an essential tool for realizing the ideology and not a power struggle ring on its own.[234]

Herzberg assumes that the reciprocal relations between Jews and Arabs were entirely economic and that during most of the Mandate period the Jews and Arabs were preoccupied in a dispute over their historical rights, and the coexistence relations, for all their different colors, could not have existed at all.[235]

We tend to accept the slightly simplistic but realistic approach, which maintains that the mandatory coexistence derived from a narrative of modernity, that encompassed Haifa in the Mandate period as a cosmopolitan city, alongside there being together in groups and individuals with significant differences, recognizing the existence of the other, while leading a joint life, deriving from different reasons on each side.

The Jews perceived Haifa's Arabs through an instrumental perception that strived to achieve political, technological, social, and educational advantages; this by trying to quiet down the erupting and bubbling national conflict, as much as possible to gain precious time. The "Eretz-Israel's laborers Alliance" was a sort of tool made to subside potential conflicts between Jews and Arabs in the city. The Jewish establishment perceived the "Alliance" in entirely instrumental way, while Hushi tried to achieve political power and security, using an organization which was considered at times an ephemeral. In this context, we tend to accept Bernstein's conclusion that when it was not possible to separate the job markets (the Jewish and the Arab), the Jewish labor leaders tended to operate co-optation and manipulation processes, preferring these rather than cooperation.[236] How can the certain coexistence that did exist in the cosmopolitan city be explained then? The explanation lies in the cooperation between the Arab and Jewish elites in the economic plane, especially in the high level of the Haifa municipality.

The reciprocal relations were conducted on different planes: Haifa's municipality and its management; the hospitals where Jewish and Arab doctors worked; courts in which Jewish and Arab judges served; the law field in which formal ties between Jews and Arabs lawyers existed; the mandatory government offices where senior clerks from both ethnic groups worked, etc.

The changes generated by the Mandate government and the Zionist enterprise further accelerated the social separation and differentiation process. The development of an urban bourgeois class comprised of Christian and Muslim entrepreneurs increased the inclination of the urban, traditional, and new elite groups to come to terms with the British administration patterns out of fear for their own economic interests, despite the frustration and the complaints voiced over the Zionist policy of the Mandate government.[237] We have already claimed that the aforementioned elites were composed mainly of business people, land merchants, contractors, and others who preferred "industrial quiet" that offered them economic stability and relative growth, over unstable relations that could have hurt their economic interests.

David Hacohen tells of his desire to raise the low salary of the Arab laborer in the municipality. When he introduced the subject in a city council meeting, Ibrahim Sahioun, a council member, mocked him by saying that the members of the city council should strive to lower the salary, not raise it. Michail Touma, another member of the council, joined him and called Hacohen "Bolshevik!"[238]

Yazbak noted that only by 1936, as result of a lack in sewer workers, at time of the Arab strike, did the municipality of Haifa raise the daily salary of the laborers to 200 Eretz-Israeli mils a day.[239]

We can conclude that at the same time that the interests of Haifa's Arab laborers were anchored in the will to benefit from the services of the trade union of Mapah (which also included accessible and reasonable medical treatment), the interests of the national circles were completely opposite. This process may explain the cooperation of part of the Arab workers in Haifa with the "Alliance" despite major pressures of the national factors in the city. That is, while the Jews perceived the "Alliance" as a tool, which was supposed to reduce the inherent conflict between Arabs and Jews in the city, it was perceived differently by the Arabs who saw it as a technological progress opportunity for the improvement of their work conditions. Vashitz believes that this duality created a split between the loyalties of the individual Arab to his family's economic existence, and his national loyalty. For many, a sort of fragile coexistence was created between the economic usefulness to the national interest, which meant that the duality existed in the business, the municipal, and the trade-union world.[240]

The Arab municipal elites and the business people certainly supported the cooperation between the Arabs members of the

"Alliance" and the union, as it facilitated the development of economic processes and economic growth. But knowing this, despite all the Arab laborers achieved through the cooperation with Mapah, they stayed loyal to their national aspirations that surpassed the benefit of cooperation with the union.[241]

We have examined records of Haifa city council meetings from the 20's to the 40's to observe, albeit from a sampling, what matters usually came up in its daily agenda.

The city council's meeting of 1.6.1925 discussed the lighting of Haifa's municipality building.[242] On 8.7.1925, they discussed extending roads tender; made a decision on the concessionaire who would win the tender of feeding the municipality animals; selling the municipality's horse; paying rent to Aziz Khayat.[243] On 16.7.1929, a strategic decision was made—to build a new residence for the municipality.[244]

On 12.12.1929, it was decided to renovate Jaffa road and construct new roads in Hadar HaCarmel and in the Carmel.[245] On 1.5.1930, a financial report of 1930 was handed to the council members, and so it was decided to hire an additional worker in the city engineer's department.[246] On 2.6.1931, it was decided to buy donkeys for Haifa's municipality and to add a segment to Allenby road.[247] On 25.4.1932, the city council discussed a proposal to purchase a machine for asphalt spraying, and giving compensation money to cops who would get fired because of the urban police affiliating with the Mandate police.[248]

The first meeting of the new city council was held on 4.10.1934. Fifty Eretz-Israeli pounds were than budgeted for establishing a monument for King Feisel. A committee for naming the streets was chosen; Ibrahim Sahioun and Shabtai Levi were elected to serve as members of the local city building committee.[249] On 24.1.1935, the city council raised the salary of the senior clerks; a letter from Haifa District Commissioner was read, (number 283/1/22) including a request to legislate a municipal bylaw to prohibit "setting up tents in Haifa."[250]

We surveyed approximately 200 records, and they reflect a more or less organized decision making process, next to practical discussions in which Arabs and Jews both take part. The turnover among the members of the city council over the years was low, and the records show that a deep acquaintance developed between the personalities, and sometimes formed long lasting and meaningful friendships.

Fundamental conflicts between Arab and Jewish city council members are not reflected, except for matters of work relations (see quotations by David Hacohen above) and in the matter of enforcing plan and construction laws. This data confirms our claim that the Haifa municipality was a sort of "clearing-house" of economic interests exchange between the elites of the Arab sector and the Jewish sector.

The gap between the elites to the "grassroots" grew wider, as on each side, the main political actors almost did not perceive their municipal representation as a strategic factor to take into consideration; so it was with the nationalistic Arabs and powerful Mapah. The "civil circles" in Haifa, however, saw the municipal representation as an important economic extension to their businesses.

The concept of Haifa "coexistence," was dictated to some extent by the cosmopolitan character of Haifa, which came to actual realization in symbiotic relations between the two ethnic groups. These were more of an economic "give and take," while recognizing that the two sides would gain more from economic, security and political stability, than from deep conflict that might cause splits that they would be unable to reconcile. However, no significant quality groups who strived to realize "coexistence" and placed values of peace, tolerance and respect at the top were created on either side in Haifa. This clearly means that Haifa "coexistence" was mainly tactical and was meant to help achieve short-term objectives or to save time (on the Jews' part).

As an attempt to define this political situation, we may offer to adopt the concept of "cohabitation," which means cooperation between two sides merely in order to achieve specific objectives, without forming an institutionalized cooperative or a coalition.[251] We should point out then that the Palestinian literature, which describes the Arabs' lives in mandatory Haifa, does not even refer to the concept of "coexistence." The reason is that the reciprocal relations between Arabs and Jews in mandatory Haifa were perceived by both as an inevitability and as a symbiotic need that there is no way to deny and there was utility in it. However, despite the economic advantages of the symbiosis between Jews and Arabs in Haifa, the Arabs feared the Jewish dominance on the economic side as well.[252] This concept of "coexistence" exists mainly in the Israeli research literature and and in the discourse of Haifa and Israeli Politicians after the establishment of the state in 1948.

People, Places and Events in Haifa's History

Daphna Sharfman

Introduction

This chapter portrays the daily life of Jews, Arabs, and British, like a documentary film that present images, scenes, well-known and daily events joint with personal stories and recollections. It offers many subjective, emotional points of view not included in the official history of the major establishments in the city like the British administration, the municipality, and the labor council.

We would like to convey the story of Haifa's local culture and places of leisure, tourism and hotels, international transport, including airlines, trains, and shipping lines, local transportation and commerce, also the ceremonies and significant events, the Haifa's elites, British, Jews, and Arabs, the silent movie under the stars and world famous concerts, daily life as it really was.

Haifa at the beginning of the twentieth century

The British army crushed the Turkish front north of Tel Aviv and Jaffa on the 20th of September 1918 and started to flow rapidly northward, passed the mountains to the valley of Yizrael and occupied the town of Nazareth, H.Q. of the Turkish army. On the 23rd of September, following an intense battle in the eastern side of the town, battalions of Indian and Australians soldiers took over Haifa.[253]

Haifa was a small town with an Arab majority; the Jewish minority adopted a similar life style to that of the dominant Arab society. Yet, the education system and as expected, the religious institutions, were separate.

The Ottoman authorities posted high quality officials in Haifa that expanded public service in education, agriculture, maritime trade and commerce, and also initiated the participation of the public representatives in the city council of Haifa. The level of sanitation and hygiene in Haifa had advanced slowly; since the beginning of the century, there were some improvement of the dismal conditions that the European tourists had outlined some twenty years previously. In spite of that, the municipality failed to control the epidemic of cholera that broke in the city in 1911. Many of the inhabitants escaped to the Carmel Mountain and resided there until the plague was over.[254]

The new German Templers' settlment sprawled on a quarter of the city territory was planned and maintained exemplarily by the residents. They also preferred the services of the foreign post offices (the Austrian, French or Russian) to that of the Turkish post. The hospitals in the city were all foreign: German, English, and Jewish.

The city developed rapidly during the last 50 years of Turkish control, chiefly since the start of the 20th century, the population in 1911 numbered about 20,000 people. In the first four years of British rule, the number of Jews was doubled and rose to 6000 out of about 25,000. Relations between Jews and Arabs were tense, but not as much as between the Christians and Muslims. The animosity was expressed in different acts of violence and assassination. The Muslims usually enjoyed the sympathy of the authorities and while initiating most of the provocation received light penalties, if at all.

Muslims and Jews of oriental origins enjoyed good relations in general. The Muslims could visit the Jewish homes without having to worry that they may be served pork; or they bought merchandise sold by a Jewish trader whom they trusted. Most of the Jews dwelled in the Jewish borough of "Ard al Yahud" but, in reality, the houses of the Jews and the Arabs were closely attached to each other. Relations evolved at times to friendship, reciprocal visits in the period of holidays and mourning, and even exchanges of presents.

The residents of the German Colony dissociated themselves from the local people, evoking resentment among the population. With the outbreak of the First World War, the conflict among the monks in the different monasteries, chiefly the French Carmelite monastery in Stella Maris, adopted a political tone reflecting the war between France and Germany. [255]

The foreign population of Haifa was cosmopolitan: among them several hundred Italians, Greeks, French, Turks, citizens of Malta, Armenians, and others, most of them were independent merchants or commercial representatives from Europe; others were officials working in the management of the railway and professionals. Persians of the Baha'i denomination settled in Haifa at the beginning of the century. When they first arrived in the country in 1868, led by Baha u'lla'h ("The brightness of god"), they settled in Acre. By the end of the 19th century the remains of their founder, Mirza Ali Mohamed, were brought to the city and were buried on the Carmel in 1909.

Baha u'lla'h died in Acre in 1892 and his son Abbas effendi (Abdu'l-Baha), continued to proliferate his doctrine throughout the world and in particular in the United States. He settled in Haifa in 1908, living in a house on the Persians street until his death in 1921. Abdu'l–Baha was an admired person in the city and was described as "a figure of such esteem that Haifa never had before." [256]

In 1914 he stood on the balcony of Pilgrim House next to the Shrine of the Bab and looked into the future:

> The great vessels of all peoples will come to this port, bringing on their decks thousands and thousands of men and women from every part of the globe...The flowers of civilization and culture from all nations will be brought here to blend their fragrance together and blaze the way for the brotherhood of man. [257]

A well-known Arab author from Haifa described his authority in a poetic style:

> In those days, Baha Abbas was still alive, and like his name, he had magnificence and splendor. In the afternoon he would leave his house in the same hour, his disciples following him in a row, two steps behind, their hands interlaced and their heads are bent before his glory in a great apprehension. When he stopped walking, they also stopped, waiting for him to speak, as he only spoke when he stopped walking and would not turn his head towards them...A thread of grace was bestowed on the new neighborhood and its residents, small as grand, coming from the grace and glory of Abbas. People gave way to the procession, showing respect and admiration. [258]

The famous English orientalist Gertrude Bell arrived in Haifa in March 1902 and spent several months in the city. At first she resided on Mount Carmel, a distance of half an hour ride from the city center. In her diary entry from 26 March she wrote that there must be something in the air of Mount Carmel favorable to mental derangement of a special kind—at any rate if you want to commence prophet you take a little house in Haifa, you could scarcely begin in any other way.

She looked for her Arabic teacher Abu Nimrud all over the city and found him in his shop in the marketplace. Later, she visited Husein effendi, a son in law of her friend Abbas effendi, leader of the Baha'is. Her Arabic teacher wanted her to move to the city; she went to inspect two hotels and chose one of them, situated in a charming garden, where she moved a few days later. Her hotel was kept by Syrians and she was happy to hear and speak only Arabic. In her sitting room she put her books and pots of mimosa, jasmine, and wild flowers. [259]

The presence of varied communities and nations in Haifa, the passenger traffic in the harbor and the railway station gave Haifa a cosmopolitan ambience that charmed its visitors: Carmel brings the depiction of an English resident, Frances Newton, on the city that combine the European suits with the tarbush and akal of the local farmer, the pilgrim to Mecca alongside Christian reverends in their long ceremonial dress. Haifa was a new city that had not yet experienced the established, even restrictive, bonds existing among senior families in the old, traditional cities. [260]

Haifa was already acknowledged towards the end of the 19th century as the ascending city in the region, the key for Syria and an essential the base to protect the Suez Canal. In the Sikes-Piccot agreement, signed on the 16th of May 1916, that planned the distribution of the disintegrating Ottoman Empire between Britain and France, Britain handed Syria to the French, claiming for herself only the control of the Haifa bay.[261]

The regular maritime transportation to Haifa was maintained by many companies for passengers and cargo, headed by the Austrian "Lloyd," "The Russian Company of Steam Commerce," the Egyptian "Hadivil Mile Line," and the French "Messageries Maritimes." Ships coming from Germany, England, Belgium, Holland, and Turkey also visited Haifa at random. They were represented by consular agents of their origin country. Consuls of western European countries, the Austro-Hungarian Empire, Russia, and the United States, lived in Haifa. Shabtai Levi commented that amongst the honorary consuls, the American consul was a German by the name of Stroba, the Russian consul was a German named Schmidt, and the British consul, Pietro Avllala, was an Arab from Sidon. France and Germany were the only states represented by official consuls.

> ...I had good relations with these representatives, since the political sting was not dominant in that happy era in which neither we nor them had any political conceptions. In good conscience we sat with the gentlemen to a game of bridge or whist. [262]

Levi also mentioned the town crier, taditionally nominated by the municipality and the government to communicate to the public various announcements, as did also private companies such as shipping companies. The official town crier tolled his bell and proclaimed ships' departures or arrivals in the harbor, public auctions and the like. He continued his employment after the British occupation, but by then, restricted to the proclamation of events like the cinema and circuses. [263]

Economic activity was hampered during the war, while men were forcely mobilized to the Turkish army and thousands left the country to evade it. The French and English education institutes were closed for about four years. Hundreds or even thousands of people died in the typhoid epidemic. Towards 1917, the majority of the inhabitants were already desperately poor, many died of hunger, and the authorities persecuted the people under the protection of the French consulate. The cancellation of the capitulations abolished the rights of the Jews to conduct legal affairs in European courts, but the communal organization, with the assistance of a Jewish American fund, managed to overcome to some degree the famine and to keep the schools open. [264]

The first years of the British Mandate: railways, roads, and one telephone...

> With the conclusion of the war, Haifa suddenly found a new life, effervescent and lively; new and pretty buildings were built, new streets were constructed and paved, and stone staircases went from the city up to the Carmel Mountain... The influence of the British occupation was strongly felt all over the country and Haifa was the pulse of the whole country. [265]

Haifa was no longer isolated and became a junction of many routes: the first British train entered Haifa station on the 23rd of December 1918 and the city was linked to the railway system. The main lines were to Egypt and Syria, between Jerusalem to Cairo in the south and Damascus and Amman in the north.

In June 1919, the direct rail line from Haifa to Jerusalem opened to civilians. The train included two-second class and first class compartments and, by October, a third class was added.

When the line from Haifa to Acre was opened in February 1920 it offered scheduled service. [266]

The passengers departed from Haifa's east terminal at six o'clock in the morning and traveled south to Zamarin (Zichron Ya'akov) and to Hudieda (Hadera); the train then turned to Tulkarem, Kalkilia, and Rosh Haaine, and terminated its long journey in western Kantara by six in the evening. The trip to Damascus also took twelve hours and passed by Afula, Bith Shaan, Zemach and Daraa.[267] Later on, a special wagon was connected to the train, called "The High Commissioner wagon"; it was used by him for visits and trips in the country.[268]

In the first period, when Haifa East was the only station, the passengers from Egypt descended from the train that continued to Syria and took a taxi to Beirut.[269] Opposite the railway station were a number of Jewish hotels and shops including the main warehouses of "Spinney's,"[270] inside the station were several cafés frequented by passengers like merchants of crops, Arab effendis wearing tarbushes, Arab fishermen who sold their catch and even more picturesque characters:

> Among the crowd were conspicuous men of the Trans-Jordanian military dressed in their flamboyant costume with wide red sash and black hat (kolpak), Sheiks dress in brown robes made from camel hair decorated by embroidery of gold, to their waist a wide sash containing a gilded dagger, a revolver on their hip and across their chest cartridges of hunting gun. On their shoulder they kept a glossy double barrel gun...[271]

The state of the roads was not yet advanced, although it seemed in those days as an improvement compared with the muddy, unpaved roads that existed at the beginning of the century. The new paved roads of 138 kilometers reached from Haifa to Jerusalem by the valley of Yizrael, Afula, and Nablus. The Haifa-Jenin road was 50 kilometers long and contributed to a shortening of the travel.[272] The road to Tel Aviv was in a bad state during most of the thirties, and still unpaved. Its deplorable condition made the travelers take the road to Jerusalem, and then, via Tulkarem, to Tel Aviv and Jaffa. The traffic to Damascus was easier, via the Haifa-Tiberias road of 66 kilometers and from there the road continued to Damascus for the length of 195 kilometers. The public transport reached Damascus and Beirut and continued to Baghdad.

Since 1935 line B4 of "Egged" company (the Jewish buses cooperative), traveled the long route of Haifa-Tiberias-Mafraqe (Jordan) Rotba (Iraq) to Baghdad.[273] Egged built a central station in the Haifa port area, where passengers took the buses to Tel Aviv and Jerusalem. The Arabs had their special service to Nazareth, Acre, Shfaramm and villages in the countryside.[274]

A competing line was started some years earlier by the Nairn brothers, two former soldiers from New Zealand who, after the war, opened a service of cars between Haifa and Beirut, in the absence of a railway. When the competition in the line increased they decided in 1923 to offer an alternative to the expedition that was necessary in order to reach Baghdad—by ship via the Suez Canal, from Eden to Basra and then by land to Baghdad. They opened buses service that crossed the desert that separated Damascus from Baghdad in three days instead of a fortnight. The service operated for ten years facing varied dangers like armed robbers, sand storms, lack of water and other nuisances.[275]

The service of another form of communication, the telephone, was still scarce in the city. As late as the thirties there was just one public telephone, next to the post office in Hahalutz street. The conversations on the phone were not protected in particular from the listening ear of the police...[276]

Tourists and immigrants

Development of tourism in Haifa, as in Palestine in its entirety, suffered as result of the security problem that made it difficult for the tourist industry in Haifa to benefit from the new port that was inaugurated on 31st October 1933.

Tourists or immigrants that wished to take a comfortable trip to Palestine could sail in Hebrew ships like the *Tel Aviv* of twenty thousand tons that operated in the thirties by the "Eretz-Israel for Shipping" company on the Haifa-Trieste line, which offered to its passengers only one cabins class. [277]

The Hebrew lines operating in that period sailed from Haifa to Alexandria, to Beirut and Famagusta in north Cyprus, Rhodes, Istanbul and Piraeus, and even went as far as Italy to the ports of Brindisi, Naples and Genoa.[278] Departures from Haifa in later years sailed to different destinations throughout Europe and even to New York. [279]

Jews and Arabs cooperated in the efforts to encourage the tourism to Palestine in the framework of the "Association for the Development of Tourism in Palestine" that was founded in 1932. The association published posters, guidebooks and a calendar; they were circulated throughout the British Empire and in the neighboring states of Syria, Lebanon and Egypt. Illuminated signs were set opposite luxury hotels like the Shepheard's and the Continental in Cairo. By 1935 merely 90,936 tourists visited Palestine according to data given by the immigration department, about six thousand less than in the previous year.[280]

But the dark clouds were already gathering, the chairman of the association, D.G. Salameh, the director of Cook's agency in Jerusalem, surveyed in his speech the decrease in tourism from the United States resulting from the economic crisis there and the apprehension from a journey in the Mediterranean, resulted of the civil war that he opted to nickname "the trouble in Spain." [281]

As the situation deteriorated, Salame reported a year later of the cessation of the cruise tourism with the departure of *Rome* from Haifa's port in July 1938. He expressed his hopes that business would improve in the course of 1939, after the London Conference found a solution to the situation in Palestine, and the leaders of England and Europe brought about a settlement that would forego threats of war "at least for a decade."[282]

The immigration department of the Jewish Agency, working together with the Association of German Immigrants, received the immigrants that came mainly from Germany. Following the shutdown of the Jaffa port to Jews since the riots started in 1936; all the immigrants came through Haifa.[283] Taking care of their personal belongings usually caused countless problems, as they arrived separately in big wooden boxes called "lifts," whereas the east European immigrants always carried their few personal belongings with them.

The newcomers were also compelled to face developing tensions with the veterans in Haifa, mostly from east European origin, which blamed them of luxurious living, leading to the rise of prices and the cost of living. [284]

The association in Haifa prepared special leaflets for the immigrants who arrived in the country as refugees having no information about their future life and prospects. The leaflets detailed the currency rates, the tariffs of the trip in taxicabs, buses and trains, the tariffs of telegrams and telephone and also included a list of hotels in Haifa and their telephone numbers.[285] The immigrants usually stayed in pensions like the "Strand" in Vine street, or "Haiman" in Haalutz street, until they managed to find an apartment for rent. They could cook in their rooms or visit the nearby sympathetic workers' restaurant that sold clean, cheap food, including "take away" in the immigrants' own pots. Two families used to share an apartment, including the bathroom and the use of the kitchen. [286]

The airfield of Haifa was in the valley of Zvulon to the north of the city. It was a minor airfield during the thirties, but the British planned to enlarge it to an important terminal in the air travel between the west and the east.[287] The aerial connection with Palestine was indirect; the new route from Cairo to Baghdad established in 1924 included a landing in Gaza. But Gaza was too distant and the international airport in Lod was opened only in 1939. In the meantime, Haifa was viewed as the appropriate solution. Two questions were raised in the correspondence of the Air Ministry, the Colonial Office, and the Palestine authorities in the course of 1929: whether the airfield was essential to civilian usage and, in particular, for the aerial line to India, and whether it was vital for military purposes, for the defense of the city and the port. In addition was the prospect of having a base for flying boats that landed at times in the bay of Haifa and the Sea of Galilee. It was resolved to retain a piece of land for this purpose and the airfield was ultimately completed by 1935. In August 1937, the civilian aerial service in Palestine was opened by the Palestinian Airline with regular flights between Lod and Haifa.[288]

The Polish airline "Lot" used two 17-seats D.C.2 airplanes for its international service. By 1937, the flights departed three times per week according to the following itinerary: the flight took off by 8 A.M. from Lod, landing in Rhodes by 11.30, and later in Athens, Thessalonica and Sofia, arriving in Bucharest by 18.50. The next day the flight departed in 7.00 A.M., landing in Chernovitch and Lvov and ultimately arriving in Warsaw by 10.50 A.M. The price for the full itinerary was the huge sum of 30 Palestinian pounds. The passengers were cautioned that they must arrive in time in the airfield in order "not to stop the service on account of the passengers that are late to come, and that do not dedicate time for the formalities that are necessary for the trip."[289]

There was a discernible improvement after the war; the list of flights from Haifa for the 9th of July 1947, for example, included flights to Nicosia, Cairo, and Beirut-Damascus; a weekly flight to Amman took off on Tuesdays. They were operated by the Middle East airline, the Egyptian airline, and the Arab airline.[290] International flights departed from Lod, operated by companies like "B.O.A.C.," "T.W.A.," "Air France," and "K.L.M."

A minority of the Jewish Inhabitants of Haifa traveled abroad to visit relatives and for business; a short time before the war, the Jewish National Committee warned them of taking such trips. The Community Committee in Haifa also appointed a committee to grant permits in special cases. They sent an angry letter to the National Committee Executive in Jerusalem and demanded an urgent effort to restrict travel, indicating to what extent the high-ranking officials tended to disregard their own instructions, and to continue to travel abroad. [291]

The committee in Haifa received many requests for travel permits but refused to grant most of them. The owner of a ladies hats shop in Hadar HaCarmel wrote to the committee on the 20th of August 1939 and informed it that, as in every year, she had to travel to Paris to provide a selection of hats for the winter season, and requested a permit for one month which was denied.[292]

A young woman planning to travel to Poland "in the business of marriage" wrote a handwritten application in late August 1939, just before the outbreak of the war, stating that all the expenses were to be paid by her parents in Poland. In the margin of the letter was written: "she did not appear."[293]

Hotels and pensions

Hotels in Haifa were located throughout downtown, the German Colony, and on the Carmel. "Hertzelia" hotel in Allenby road was opened in the 20's; it offered its guests hot and cold water in the rooms and was patronized by prominent Jewish visitors in Haifa.[294] Among them was Michael Polack who founded in 1925 the cement factory "Nesher" near Haifa. Polack was a partner of the Baron Rothschild in an oil products plant in Russia and the baron appointed him as a member of the directorate of "Picaa," the Eretz-Israeli land company. Polack was also a well known generous contributor to charity and attracted to the hotel public figures that solicited his friendship.[295]

Hotel "Savoy" opened on the corner of Jaffa and Banks street and published itself as the leading hotel in the city.[296] In Hadar HaCarmel hotel "Zion," was one of the central hotels in town as it was situated opposite the new city hall inaugurated in 1942.

Immigrant's hotels were inexpensive and plain; the

immigrants usually stayed there on their first days in the country, like hotel "Aliya" close to Hahaluz street, or the "Strand" on Vine street.[297] Downtown was the proletarian hotel of the Effron family, where Jewish leaders likes Ben Zvi and Ben Gurion stayed during their visits to Haifa in the 20's.[298]

"Windsor" and "Eppinger" opened in the German Colony; Hotel Eppinger highlighted in its publicity the pampering of its guests, "A restaurant and a quality of service that are well known." During the Second World War it advertised that it was under Swiss management, owing to the understandable absence of the German owners of the hotel. [299]

Towards the end of the war, the government decided to return the hotel to its owners and it served as a lodge for the high-ranking officials and police and army officers. The Haganah command in Haifa saw it as a provocation against the Jewish community and devised a plan to harass the hotel owners and force them to leave the country. The Haganah planned to put there several assault grenades to intimidate its lodgers without inflicting casualties. A Haganah woman, dressed as a prostitute, put grenades on the balcony and in the toilets. The detonation wounded one Englishman that sat in the café; the Haganah explained the reason for the operation in a proclamation and advised the British against visiting the hotel.[300]

Hotels that also acted as sanatoriums were built on the Carmel, like pension "Zaltzman," also called the new "Hertzelia hotel" that was inaugurated by 1923 at the Carmel Center. Additional hotels that opened in the area later in the thirties were the "Heart of the Carmel," the "Carmel Palace," and the sanatorium "Bodenhaimer."[301]

Hotel "Teltsh," also called "Meggido" built in 1934-1935, was a special hotel with particular design and far reaching reputation. It was designed by Leopold Krakawer and was described as having absolute perfection between proportions and harmony, including aspects of international architecture, like the style of La Corbusier and the Bauhaus and local contributions that connected the building to the local landscape.[302] The hotel awarded its guests high standards of amenity and service and was well known in the entire Middle East. Foreign diplomats, Arab Sheiks, tourists, and the elite of local society were among its guests. It served as an appropriate destination to those seeking tranquility and composure, sun, fresh air and spectacular views, combined with the atmosphere of an international venue that demonstrated the changing character of Haifa.[303] Mount Carmel was a major center for the summer holiday, and includes many first-rate hotels, pensions, sports and amusements, forests and good tracks for long distance walks. [304]

The British administration decided to reinforce its supervision of the hotels' services during wartime, a policy that fostered antagonism and grievances among the hotels owners in Haifa. The management of the Organization of Hotels, Restaurants and Cafés in Haifa and its surroundings wrote a letter to the chief secretary of the Mandate government, Mac Pearson, complaining against discrimination of the modest hotels compared to the more lucrative ones. [305]

But the administration was apparently adamant to retain the level of service even at the time of war. The letter of the aid to the supervisor of provisions in the district of Haifa, dispatched to the president of the hotels organization in Haifa, did not leave room for any doubt. He authorized the hotels' owners to charge for laundry but warned them bluntly that in fixing the tariffs it was worthwhile that they would take into consideration the legal clauses against profiteering. He also emphasized that breakfast for the hotel guests should be an English breakfast, including tea or coffee; hotels were not allowed to charge for hot showers, only for a proper bath...[306]

In July 1944, the Jewish Orthodox "Organization for the Sabbath in Eretz- Israel" wrote to Mayor Shabtai Levi calling on him to prohibit the playing of music during the Sabbath, and not to enable "irresponsible people to interfere with the character of the Sabbath merely for money."[307] This appeal won the vigorous backing of the chief Palestine Rabbis Herzog and Uziel in their telegram to Mayor Levi from 24 July.[308]

Markets, restaurants, and cafés

Haifa, a meeting place of nations and and populations, enjoyed an abundance of cafés and restaurants, oriental and European, some in plain style and low-priced workers' cafés and others, that generally served the British, especially the military men, were high-class establishments. The British wanted to benefit from the special beauty that Haifa had to offer and to enjoy it in romantic and dizzy social events:

> At the foot of Mount Carmel, just below the beautiful Baha'i gardens, the British officer's banquets were held outdoors, under the silvery leafed olive trees. The tall Egyptian servant, in his snowy white galabia, red sash and red tarbush standing at attention behind each officer, looked more like the master than a servant. Accompaniment for the banquet, the music of the band of the Seaforth Highlanders reverberated through our Colony and provided a beautiful concert for us.[309]

Mustafa el Haj's small shop on the northward end of Khamra square, downtown, was very famous during the twenties. He sold exotic drinks like "Sus," Tamar Hindi and ice cream. The Jewish customers frequented his shop in big numbers, especially on Saturday night.[310]

Café "Kathca" on the sea front, near the railway, was a known gathering place of merchants, tourists, and citizens of Haifa. It was a special venue for the Jewish stevedores who immigrated in the 30's from Thessalonica, recruited by Haifa's labor council to help establish the Jewish influence in the new harbor. Next to it was café "Gale Yam" (waves of the sea), where they used to present a tall platter of pastries put in three stories and the customer paid according to the number of the cakes he ate.[311]

Rachel Bell-Turkasma loved to visit the Arab market, the smell of the spices, the shoe stores, and the churches. As she went eastward, there was the smell of the fish, the odor of the sea. Carmel Avenue, the main street of the German Colony, leads to the sea and a beach where people bathed and sailed in boats.

> In the cafés on the beach ladies with straw hats used to sit calmly drinking coffee, peculiar women, with blond hair, without veils and tanned.[312]

Ruth Zuker immigrated to Haifa from Germany by 1934, and was to take part in many dramatic espionage activities; she described the intriguing life in these days:

> I found my way encircled by people that were running around; automobiles that frequently blew their horns, and donkeys laden of merchandize. I was attracted by the vendor of Tamar Hindi that vocally proclaimed the beverage, while clicking his copper bells. A camel passed among the crowd every now and then with colorful harnesses. I stood for a long time by the corner of the street in the dust and heath charmed by the oriental magic.[313]

Ruth Sharfman that immigrated in 1935 aged 14, remembered fondly the Arab vendors carrying their merchandise from the market on the back of a donkey up the road to Hadar HaCarmel, selling fresh fish and glasses of Tamar Hindi to their Jewish customers.[314]

In the marketplace was the prison for Arab convicts. The photographer, Zvi Faigine, was invited once to photograph an execution of an Arab criminal.[315]

The Khamra family lived in Khamra square in a two floors house of 250 square meters. Next to the house were narrow alleys, the Al Jerina mosque and center, cafés, and a bathhouse. They had Jewish neighbors in the old city; old documents point to the communal property of Arabs and Jews there, even in the same building.[316]

And more on the marketplace and its sounds:

> The cries of the newspaper vendors used to mix with the

calls of chilled 'Sus' and the Tamar Hindi sellers, and the chilled yoghurt with garlic. In the winter, there were the cries of the sellers of the hot Sahlev and the Tamaria in the morning, a symphony that was immortalized by Rimski-Korsakov in *Scheherazade* that will take place as long as the Orient and mankind will exist.[317]

The café of Anton Z'ahar was located at the entrance to the market opposite the square, it also offered its customers hashish smoking. The taxicab office of George Armeni and a restaurant opened in an ally in the square leading to Kingsway.[318] On the southern side, where the restaurant "Abd" was opened later, a Greek managed a dance club which stayed open until the small hours.[319]

Arab cafés that served only coffee with a glass of cold water, a Spinney's gazoz and hookah were on the square and its vicinity serving customers that passed their time playing backgammon. Coffee was also delivered to the shops in the area, although the young man who brought the coffee did not receive payment; instead, the order was registered by chalk on the crossbar of the shop door and later was paid by the owner to the proprietor of the café. Immediate payment was not acceptable indicating a lack of trust.[320]

Arab restaurants were popular among both Arab and Jewish customers; they served typical and delicious oriental food. For breakfast they offered hot beans from a clay jug that stood on the open fire, with olive oil and a boiled egg. During the day they served chickpea (hummus), casseroles dishes of filled vegetables in pots of copper that were presented to the customer to choose the dish he preferred. There were also other plates of Kebab, Shishlik and Senaia, a minced meet fried with tehina or tomato puree. With each meal a glass of cold water was served, and for desert sweet coffee. In restaurants where Muslims, Christians, and Jews dined, alcoholic drinks like Arak were served, together with small dishes of appetizers.

The "Lebanon" restaurant on Jaffa road was the place favored by the Jewish intelligentsia; the "Workers' Kitchen," established for the low income Jewish pioneers, was not considered a restaurant but rather a meeting place; it was both simple and popular; it had tables without tablecloths, benches instead of chairs, and a limited choice of food.[321] The workers' kitchens on Allenby road and Kingsway offered a thick broth and cooked meat. The diners sat on benches next to a long table, eating their food hastily as there were always more people there waiting for their turn. The working class restaurant of "Tnuva," a labor movement collective center for the manufacturing and distribution of milk and eggs products, served self-produce food like eggs, potatoes, and cream that was considered luxurious. White bread was served with a quarter package of Tnuva produced butter. Dessert was a sparse coffee or a cup of tea.

The senior British officials dined in European restaurants on Jaffa street, in the new commercial center down town, in hotel "Hertzelia" and in the German Colony. They were more formal places and the waiters boasted black bow tie and at their waists wore a black brilliant silk scarf.[322]

The population that frequented the many European style cafés was not homogeneous. It was not customary for Muslim women to visit them as a rule, and only few Christian women did. The Jewish women were more open in their social customs; Jalal Irani remembered how he sat with his colleague for work in the British censorship, Ruth Zucker, in a café on the first corner of Hertzel street, the main avenue of the Jewish neighborhood Hadar HaCarmel.[323]

The cafés were diverse; some had a Jewish character, like "Pinati" (my corner) on the corner of Hertzel and Chaim streets, where the guests could dance to the songs of well-known local singers.[324] The German Jewish immigrants typically patronized the European style cafés. "Sternhiem" in Nordau street was similar to cafés in Berlin, Frankfurt, or Vienna, where customers could order large pastries filled with cream and whipped cream and steamy cappuccino. The clients were dressed in style that was more in tune with their European origin and culture, which many still longed for, rather than with the pioneer fashion in Eretz-Israel. Women put on their best robes and men sported elegant suits and ties even in the high summer temperature.

Ernst Jordan opened "Café Jordan" on 5 Nordau street in 1935 with his partner, Carl Rosenthal, this was the first café to be designed by an architect (Lewinski). The café was a popular meeting place of musicians, families, and also many Englishman. Jordan used to conceal in the café weapons of the Haganah and of its right wing rival the Irgun.[325]

Café "Atara" on Balfour street had more relaxed ambiance and many of its young customers wore khaki pants and sandals. The waiters fraternized with the steady clients and one could also leave a note to a friend there. Others wanted to impress their buddies:

> When I received my flight wings I went down Balfour street with my chest forward up to 'Atara' but there was no one who knew me anymore.[326]

British officers and soldiers spent their time not far from there in café "Diana" in the center of Nordau street, drank beer and danced.[327] "Roxi" was a dance club situated in 11 Balfour street in Sira House, its advertisement in the *Palestine guide* showed the Rosenfeled orchestra and couples in elegant evening dress.[328] Café "Kompanetz" was in the center of Bat Galim (daughter of the sea), where British military spent the time following their habit of drinking beer during the day and dancing in the evenings.[329]

"Zaltzman" pension on the Carmel Center also opened a café where piano playing accompanied the serving of afternoon tea, in this refined ambience officers and British officials used to meet with Jewish and Arab friends. With the outbreak of the riots by 1936 the British army confiscated the hotel and the grounds around it, including the bus station that was transferred to the main street Haoren (pine) boulevard.[330]

"Eldorado" was in Carmel Center, "Trokadero" in the corner of Lebanon gate and Panorama street; "Piccadilly" was in Zafririm street on the Carmel and "Arizona" in Ahuza area further high on the Carmel. In the garden next to the former hotel "Prose" on Carmel Center was opened a summer café, "Taverna," where young couples danced to fashionable Hebrew music.[331] Hotel "Prose" was founded in 1893 by the German Frederic Prose, the hotel had great success and was open until 1903. By 1908 it was sold to the English woman Frances Newton, described as "Strong masculine woman that smokes a pipe," she was anti Zionist and actively supported the Arab struggle against Zionism. In 1938 the Mandate authorities declared her a rabble-rouser and she was deported from Palestine by a special decree of the High Commissioner. Miss Newton ordered that her house will not be sold to Jews, but Shabtai Levi succeeded to buy it, using a circumvented way, for a company owned by Baron Rothschild.[332]

There were other entertainments offered to the soldiers-on the entrance to Hativ street there was an "establishment" of Fatma Husseini; Fatma Zahara received her clients in the entrance to the marketplace right next to a hasish smoking place, a number of other establishments were in Jaffa road and Kingsway.[333] Some were of more problematic nature; they disturbed the residents near by that finally decided to present their complaint to the District Commissioner: They wrote that a brothel was opened among the olive trees in 161 Allenby street. The manager was described as "unscrupulous Jew by the name of Abu-Yusef," the writers of the complaint, thirty in number, alleged also that as the place was patronized by senior officials, it was not closed down. The police, on her part, investigated the issue thoroughly and collected testimonies. The writers stressed that the girls working in the brothel were mainly foreigners whom it is possible and even necessary to deport from the country. On the conclusion of the letter, the writers threaten that they will take matters into their hands if the government will fail to solve the problem. Copies were sent to the mayor and the district superintendent of the police.[334]

The casino in Bat-Galim is still regarded as one of the most impressive venues in Haifa and in all of Palestine and became a myth ever since its construction. Designed by Goldberger, an architect who also designed villas in Bat-Galim, and built by 1933-1934. The casino was a social and cultural center, and no gambling took place in it. The casino attracted the residents of Haifa and, in particular, the British army that had camps in the area.[335]

Pnina Vered (Rosenfeld) one of the veterans of Bat-Galim, described the first stages of the building of the casino on the sea:

> They started the construction and it was winter and the sea would demolish everything that was built and in summer they had to start all over again. When my brother, that was a construction engineer, arrived from Switzerland, then he took charge and they built it.
> We used to spend much time there; the owners rented it to a family that decorated the place in an attractive style and we used to dance there every Sabbath. The English also loved the place. I remember that on one Sabbath evening they were in the casino and received a message that there were riots in Jaffa, so they jumped downstairs and hurried back to their camp.[336]

The casino was situated on the tip of Bat-Galim Avenue by the sea, built of innovative construction and in addition supported in the rudiments by crates full of black soil that were used to prevent the infiltration of water. Beside it was a swimming pool; the plan was that the public would enter the changing boots on the entrance floor and leave from there directly to the sea or to the pool.[337]

The main hall was on the ground story, its floor made of prisms of glass; the waves were visible through the transparent glass and the balcony overlooked the sea. The upper floor was built as a gallery overlooking the main floor, the dance floor, and the balcony. There were two bars, one in the corner of the main hall and the other on the roof balcony of 600 square meters. The main hall was decorated in a light green color, silver pillars, and black decorations.[338] The casino, that was famous for dances and entertainment, left its mark on the local people and the British that spent time there:

In the times of the Mandate the casino was real great...It was the most sumptuous club in those days not only in Palestine but in the Middle East as well; the rich Arabs used to come, arriving even from Syria and Lebanon. There was a show of Josephine Baker; there were orchestras, shows, dancers, acrobats...[339]

And another memory:

All the dignitaries, British, and others from all the neighboring countries used to come...Women dressed in gowns and men in smoking jackets. The place was open from evening until morning...Every Sunday evening at five o'clock, according to the best English tradition, the ceremony of five o'clock tea with orchestra for dancing and a bar took place on the casino roof balcony. The place was engulfed with lights and people. [340]

The casino once served as a backdrop for a secret mission of the Haganah in Haifa:

Our secret plan was to invent a birthday party for the sailing club 'Zvulun' that was to take place in the casino of Haifa. On the ground floor of the casino there was an amusement park and among the attractions was a great impressive tent, and I sat there as a fortune teller.[341]

The casino was also to be a stage for a tragic event:

On the 29 November 1947, when the Palestine partition plane was received in the United Nations, we assembled in the square of the casino and on the small balcony in front of us stood the leaders of the borough and gave speeches; among them was the Rabbi, who was so excited that he collapsed and died in front of the members of the community present.[342]

Cinema, theater, and music

The well-known novelist, Arthur Koestler, described the romantic pastime in Haifa of 1926: the inhabitants used to visit the Arab café that also screened movies underneath the open sky; it was called "Paradise café." The silent movies were segments of escapades from the Wild West, the musical accompaniment was carried out by a pianist playing a repertoire combined of two music pieces only, one from *Carmen* for the plays of chase and gunfire and the other from *Tosca* designed for romantic ambience, and so was the gratification of the guests complete:

> A man could sip the sweet hot coffee from small cups, smoke a hookah, watch the stars-studded sky, or follow the events on the fading screen that leaked rain water, and on the nights of a full moon you could not discern a thing on it, and still feel deep satisfaction. [343]

Jalal Irani remembered watching as a child the silent movie showed to the accompaniment of the piano in Jaffa road near Ein Dor street. He went there with his father at the end of the twenties, when he was seven or ten years old.[344]

In 1932, the British High Commissioner Sir Arthur Wauchope came to Haifa for the inauguration of cinema "Ein Dor" where they showed the first talking movie, *The Jazz Singer* with Al Jolson. Ezer Weizmann was an ardent follower of Westerns:

> I went to a concert of Huberman in Ein Dor...It interested me like last year's snow, so I was happy that the roof opened, and he stopped playing because a dog barked...It was an establishment for Westerns, you would get there at two o'clock and leave at six. [345]

"Ora" and "Amphitheater" Cinemas in Hadar HaCarmel were owned by the labor council (Mapha); cinema "Ora"

brought to the public the novelty of three bell rings before
the start of the movie and the gradual dimming of the lights.
"Ora" was burned in December 1940 and reopened in 1947;
"Amphitheater" was built in the twenties as an open cinema that
was also used for hosting public gatherings and performances of
the theaters "H'ohel" and "Matate." By the time of the Second
World War a roof was constructed on it and thus it became a
cinema auditorium active during the whole year.

"Armon" (palace) on Anaporte street, inaugurated in
February 1935, was the larger and most sumptuous cinema
auditorium in the city, containing one thousand two hundred
seats with a gallery and boxes. The roof was opened in summer
by a pressing of an electric button.[346] Cinema "Moria" on the
Carmel was opened in August 1943. By January 1945 an Arab
cinema was opened downtown and in July 1947, a summer Arab
cinema was opened on Jaffa road.

The Jewish theatre in Haifa could not compete with major
theaters like "Habima" or "H'ohel" in Tel Aviv; however, it
witnessed a modest development of its own theatrical life. In
the twenties the Hebrew teacher Ya'akov Friedman established
a theatre that performed every month with the participation of
members of Haifa's elite, like Mrs. Wienshal and Mrs. Dunia-
Weizmann. These activities evoked the resentment of a group
of workers that did not manage to cooperate with the veterans
in the theater and opened its own dramatic stage in Haifa.

The warfare between the two stages included the abduction
of talents and hunting for actors among the new immigrants.
Theatre lovers in Haifa were divided into two camps and the
performances followed each other, until at last the public
decided that the amateurs must all leave the stage and vacate
the place for the professional theatres.[347]

The Dunia-Weizmann conservatory was founded by 1923,
and was run as a teacher's cooperative, enrolling Arab and Jewish
students. Festive concerts were arranged on Saturday nights.[348]

The historically important cultural events of Haifa took
place in the new cinema "Armon" where the Eretz-Israeli
philharmonic orchestra first concerts were played, conducted

by world famous Arturo Toscanini. The opening concert of the orchestra was on a freezing cold evening of 26 December 1936 in a pavilion in Gane Hatarucha (Exhibition Gardens) near Tel Aviv. The concert's program included symphonies of Brahms, Rossini, Schubert, and Mendelssohn.

The first concert in Haifa was planned for a few days later, in "Armon," situated in a tumultuous street; there was apprehension that the noise would spoil the concert, but the bus company and the municipality of Haifa were very eager to help: they published an advertisement in the first page of *Haaretz* daily newspaper announcing that in honor of the concert that would take place the next day, 31 December, by eight o'clock, under the direction of Toscanini, the doors would be opened to the public from seven and 15 minutes, and the traffic of the buses in the area would be suspended until the completion of the concert.[349]

The concert was described by those who attended as "historic" and a "once in a lifetime show," but it did not lack behind-the-scenes drama: the intermission that was planned for half hour was mysteriously prolonged for an hour and a half. Years later, it was acknowledged that the reason was the refusal of Toscanini to continue the concert because of a mistake made by the trumpet player, who played the fourth chapter in the *Second Symphony* of Brahms instead of the third. Toscanini was furious and only after an hour and a half agreed to return to the stand.[350]

In April 1938, during riots in Palestine, Toscanini came back for another series of concerts. This time, opening night was held in Haifa; Huberman, the founder of the orchestra, arrived in Haifa by ship; Mrs. Vera Weizmann, wife of Chaim Weizmann, came from her home in Rehovot accompanied by a large party of titled ladies and gentlemen from England; the commander of the French mandatory forces in Syria drove over from Damascus.

The second concert in Haifa took place on the 26th of April; the sensation of the evening was the interpretation by Toscanini of the preludes to Acts I and III of Wagner's *Lohengrin,* which profoundly touched the heart of the audience in the sensitive interpretation of the orchestra's string section. At the end of the evening, the audience was clapping and cheering, bringing Toscanini back five times. The following day he left Haifa by air, never to return. [351]

The musical events in Palestine were greatly influenced by refugees from Germany and Austria that brought with them the preferences and the standards of Berlin, Vienna, and other cities of central Europe. In a letter home, a British visitor described one of the concerts he listened to in "Armon" played by the Palestine orchestra consisted entirety by Jews: they played the overture to the *Magic Flute* and *Jupiter Symphony* which were, in his opinion, a first rate show.[352]

Transportation and roads

The transportation in Haifa evolved from the carriages to the buses and taxis in the course of the era. The paving of the roads reflects the development of the city and its new neighborhoods, in particular in the Carmel district.

Khamra Square, also called "the carriages square," was the venue of the central station of Haifa. Originally it was mainly used by carriages with collapsible roof, harnessed to two fancy decorated horses. There was a padded seat for three passengers and opposite a collapsible bench for an additional two. In the rainy season, the canopy was covered with a screen of tarpaulin but the coachman remained exposed to the rain.

In the upper part of the square were the stations of the buses to Hadar HaCarmel and to the rest of the country. The passenger in the Jewish bus to Hadar HaCarmel had to pay 7 mils and the cost of the travel downtown was 5 mils. The journey up started on El Hativ street and from there to Stanton street and to the Mountain road, Hertzlia street, Hassan Shukri street, to Hertzel street, buses departed from the square to Bat Galim (no. 7) to Carmel station (no. 5), and to Balad El Suk (Tel Hanan) (no. 1).

In good spirit and great hopes I traveled to the lawyer's

office downtown, which was then a dubious area, populated mainly by Arabs. I went there in a leaping bus...The travelers sat on wooden chairs and the Arab conductor went in the passage.

In spite of the swaying I was able to study the faces of the many passengers. No Englishman would consider traveling in a bus like this. As the bus came from Hadar HaCarmel, most of the passengers were Jews from all over the world.[353]

On the lower side of the square stood the carriages that were called "Hantur" harnessed to one horse or two that traveled along Jaffa road to the German Colony. The coachman was called Arabanji and some time acted as private chauffeur. The Faigine family had an Arabanji that drove them around.[354] The family of Zalman and Dina Nathanzon, the director of Anglo-Palestine (Leumi) bank in the city, enjoyed the services of an Arabanji taking hikes to the remote Mount Carmel. Next to Keller street was a large grove, where they used to have picnics:

> Mother used to prepare a large basket full of delicatessen and we would take a carriage; the Arabanji used to wait for us, and we had a picnic under the pine woods...[355]

At times, they took the Stella Maris road, which climbed on the private property of the Carmelite monastery. At the entrance was a gate, a statue of Maria on its top, where the fees of passage by the sum of 5 mils were collected. The carriage continued from there up to Panorama street, traveling over an unpaved route, but the double springs generally prevented too much hurling from the passengers.[356] The climb of the steep Mountain road was more difficult, as a coachman from those days remembered:

> I asked him (my grandfather) how did you manage with the horses in the road of the Mountain, Sharia El Jabel, which is now Zionisem Avenue? He answered that they had to have interim stops along the way; it was almost impossible to climb this mountain with two horses.[357]

Anton Z'ahar received from the government licenses for taxis that were offered for sale in order to replace the old diligences in the square, and opened a taxi station, "Zahara-Carmel."[358]

The transportation evolved gradually, Hadar HaCarmel was linked with the city by a bus service only in 1925 after the Burj street was paved. Actually it looks like the absence of public transportation services at the beginning of the twenties had a positive contribution to the compactness of Haifa, because it demanded the preservation of a reasonable walking distance between the edges of the city. Lines of regular buses, operated already in the late twenties, but they were divided among at least five companies, which was detrimental to their efficiency.[359]

The Khayat family operated a special bus line to the Khayat beach, a service that left from cinema Armon to the beach and cost one or two mils.[360] Khayat beach was very popular and an important center of entertainment on weekends. There was also a bathing venue in the German Colony next to the railway lines, where a dock of 5 meters by 15 meters was constructed for the visit of the German Kaiser Wilhelm II in the country in 1898. Another place was in the area of the old commercial center somewhat eastward from Khayat street, where the bathers used to undress, traverse the railways, and dip into the sea.[361]

Buses and taxis terminals operated on Mount Carmel by the 30's, opposite hotel "Zaltzman." There were red buses with two benches alongside the windows. Line 4 reached the Carmel but only minibuses that were named line 4a' could travel to the area of Ramat Hadar, as the route was too winding for the big buses. At the beginning of the 40's, several newcomers from Germany established taxi 272727 in the Carmel Center next to Mahanaim street.[362]

Paving new streets

The rapid development of Hadar HaCarmel and Ahuza, created a difficult problem of linking them by roads as result

of the topography of Haifa. The city downtown was linked to
Hadar HaCarmel, the Burj and Stanton streets, and the staircase
of the Prophets for pedestrians. The German Colony was linked
to the center by Vine street and part of the Mountain road and
Khoury street. The requested linkage of downtown and Hadar
HaCarmel with Mount Carmel presented a serious difficulty.
Stella Maris way was private and also lengthy. The Mountain
road was steep and rather long. The third way, Keith-Roach
road, was paved only in the thirties and it climbed to and fro in
order to overcome the heights difference. The forth way, Rupin
road, which was paved by 1946, was winding, and so was also the
way to Neve-Sha'a'nan quarter.[363]

The story of the paving of Keith-Roach road is exceptional.
The development of the Carmel by the Jewish owners of
lands depended on the paving of a road that would enable a
convenient transportation. The plan for its construction was
submitted to the municipality, but was hindered by the District
Commissioner, Keith Roach, asserting that there was no need
for an additional road. David Hacohen, a member of the city
council and one of the principal leaders of the Jewish community
in Haifa, found by chance a special route to the Commissioner's
heart:

> One day a British war ship visited Haifa and the city
> dignitaries including me were invited to a cocktail party on
> her deck.
> I was observing the scenery of the city and the mountain,
> and Keith-Roach approached me and started to praise his
> beautiful city. Right, I said, very beautiful, but it will be
> even prettier if behind the houses above the Technion we,
> you and I, will stretched a road, first right and then left and
> again right up to the heart of Carmel Center.
> My finger sketches aloft the expected road and Keith-Roach
> accompanied her in his eyes, suddenly, mellowed by the
> whisky, he said: 'indeed, important and essential road that
> will be paved and we will name it 'Keith-Roach Boulevard'
> I immediately concurred and we shook hands. [364]

The new road was inaugurated in 1937 by the proud District Commissioner, together with the mayor Hassan Shukri and council member David Hacohen.[365]

But Hacohen was upset by the consent he gave to the District Commissioner, whom he saw as vain and seeking honor and he found a clandestine way to unload his frustration. When one day Watson, the city engineer, complained to him that a mysterious hand bruised the enamel tabulars that carried the name "Keith–Roach Boulevard," he confessed that his was the mysterious hand:

> I dwelled in the city but sometimes when I drove to the Carmel by night, I used to stop next to the tabulars, get out of the car and scratch deep cracks in them, so I vent my compunction.[366]

Hacohen waited for the right moment, as he did not intend to concede: on 26.8.48, about three months after the state of Israel was born, he wrote to the mayor Shabtai Levi a handwritten letter and offered to abolish the street name and to assign instead the name "Wedgwood avenue" and he added:

> I am sure that you will agree that the former Commissioner has no rights that his name will be fixed permanently among us and we assigned it only because he forced us...But to the contrary, by immortalizing the name of Wedgwood we demonstrate the bond between us and the Englishmen that fought for and were loyal to the Zionist interests from inception and in all times.[367]

The long road was divided into several segments and is named nowadays after several prominent men, among them the British Wingate, Kish, and Wedgwood.

The commitment to preserve the character of the city and its landscapes was expressed by the meticulous orders issued by the municipality under the powerful British city engineer

Lionel Watson. He did not accept lightly any infringement of them. In his angry letter to mayor Levi from April 1947, he complained against the British army that barren 23 trees of fig, carob and other trees, some of them on the public way and others on private land in the Mountain road, Ben Yehuda and Tveria (Tiberias) streets. He continued to protest that Haifa was not under martial law and he did not believe that the military had legal authority to cut trees without the accord consent of the owners and contrary to city regulations. He reminded the mayor further that the regulations stipulated that if a resident of Haifa wanted to dig out a tree he must receive a permit from the municipality and the forests department as well.[368]

British ceremonies and events

Haifa and Eretz-Israel, being a part of the British Empire enjoyed many ceremonies, celebrations, and receptions conducted at the time over half the globe. The King's official birthday was a festive event; the lists of the people invited to the reception given by the District Commissioner for King George the Sixth's birthday celebrated on the eighth of June 1939, included names of dignitaries of the city: consuls, industrialists and elected representatives of the municipality.[369] The Christmas party given by the High Commissioner Mac-Michael in 1940 was a prestigious event and officials from Haifa were among the invited guests. Among them were the District Commissioner Polock and his assistant Gibbs, the chief medical officer Bigger, the president of the provincial court Edwards, the police chief Parker, the director of the railway Webb, the city engineer Watson, the director of Barclays Bank Cocks, the director of the harbor Rogers, the director of the refineries Zutter, and the director of the Iraqi petroleum company Stacki.[370]

The most important ceremony during the British Mandate was the festive opening of Haifa's harbor in October 1933, an historic milestone in the annals of the city. The harbor had already been active for a number of months and the first ship to enter it on the second of August, was the *Italy* under the command of the Jewish skipper Shtindler. For the first time, the passengers could descend straight to the dock, without using small boats. [371]

The ceremony was set for Tuesday, 31st October, and planned to take place in the presence of a thousand Jewish and Arab dignitaries; however, the vocal protest of Arab leaders against the Jewish immigration that started some weeks before, reached its pinnacle on Friday before the ceremony. There were many instigation speeches in the mosques, demonstrations without permit, attempts of assassination of Jews, and clashes with British security forces that led to victims on all sides. The Arabs called for a general strike, and in order to avoid violence in the course of the ceremony, all the invitations were revoked at the last moment and only government officials and a number of reporters were invited.

The city still carried a festive spirit. Flags were hoisted from government buildings and the offices of maritime companies, thousands of people crowded on top of the roofs and balconies overlooking the harbor; they watched the ceremony using military binoculars and refined opera glasses and the visibility was perfect. The High Commissioner, Sir Arthur Wauchope, and his entourage boarded the boat of the harbor by 11:20 and sailed to the British ship *Prince Lancastrian*, which had arrived a day earlier and was anchored in the open sea. At 11:35 she lifted anchor and, accompanied by the Royal Air Force planes, sailed majestically into the harbor. When she passed by the harbor entrance, seven cannon shots were fired, followed by 17 gunshots from the navy ship, *Hastings*. The ship docked at 12:15, and the High Commissioner descended from her deck to the sound of the British anthem.

As the ceremony was close to the public, the British guests of honor, estimated by the press as merely eighty officials, took their seats on the platform decorated with flags and flowers, opposite them were many rows of empty chairs. The High Commissioner delivered a speech but in deference to customary procedure, this time it was not translated into Arabic and Hebrew. By 1:30, the best wishes of the Colonial Secretary adressed to the High Commissioner and the people of Palestine were transferred from London by the radiotelegraph. [372]

The District Commissioner at the time, Edward Keith-Roach, wrote in his autobiography that he named the reclaimed strip of land next to the harbor—"Kingsway" as so many kings and their armies marched in along these shores. He named a principal gate to the harbor for Fredrick Palmer, one of its chief constructors.[373]

A fundamental reason for building the harbor was as a terminal for the shipment of oil coming from Iraq in a pipeline constructed by the IPC Company. The opening of the line from Kirkuk to Haifa in 1934 was marked by an excited celebration:

> When IPC completed the oil pipe line to Haifa there was a big celebration and everybody was very thrilled; my father went there dressed properly with a cylinder hat. There is a story that I heard from him, that when the first drops of oil coming from Iraq reached Haifa, they gave each one of the workers a drop in a teaspoon to taste the oil. [374]

The *Times* of 23 January 1935 reported extensively on the opening ceremony:

> The third of the principal ceremonies connected with the opening of the pipe line from Iraq, which began at Kirkuk on January 14, when the King of Iraq started the oil flowing across the desert, took place today when Sir Arthur Wauchope, the High Commissioner, formally opened the Haifa terminal of the line in the presence of a large gathering, with the same ceremonial as that employed by the Comte de Martel, the French High Commissioner for Syria, at Tripoli on Saturday. [375]

Was the project good for Haifa in the long run? Ruth Zuker viewed the oil pipe, even in retrospect, as a curse rather than a blessing:

> The British were interested only in IPC, the pipe line up to the refineries, but the beautiful bay that could have been

like in Nice, Lebanon, Cairo, they took this...They placed
the refineries...The sand was like sugar, had to be for hotels,
holiday and tourism.[376]

The High Commissioner Sir Harold Mac-Michael was a
guest of the municipality of Haifa on the 3rd of August 1944,
a short time before he concluded his tenure. Mayor Levi gave
a tea party and farewell ceremony in his honor. Five hundred
dignitaries sat in the banner-decorated city hall together with
the military commanders of the region, chiefs of government
departments, city councilors, members of the consular corpus,
and religious leaders. Among the invitees were 154 Arabs, 128
English, and 228 Jews.

Sir Harold and Lady Mac-Michael arrived at five o'clock,
escorted by the acting District Commissioner Fowler and his
wife. After refreshments were served, Sir Harold spoke to the
audience; he thanked them for their assistance in the war effort
that proved the strong civilian sentiment in the heart of the
population. He assured them that their future depended on the
collaboration of the Jewish and Arab communities, and added
that they were fortunate that the mayor was level headed and did
not act according to political considerations but for the interests
of the city. He warned them against spoiling in quarrels and
conflicts the great future waiting for Haifa as a central port and
Commerce City on the Mediterranean. After the speech, they
all gathered in the roof garden of the city hall that overlooked
the city and the harbor, then the High Commissioner and his
wife left for the Windsor hotel.

In his letter to Shabtai Levi dated 5 August, Mac-Michael
expressed on behalf of himself and his wife, warm and emotive
gratitude:

We leave the country with a great sorrow and our memoirs
from Haifa in particular will remain a source of great
pleasure. [377]

The Allied victory in Europe was celebrated on the 8th

of May 1945. In a letter to the city engineer Watson, Abraham Halfon, the deputy municipal secretary, detailed the directives on the event: as soon as victory day will be formally announced, the municipality flag, the British flag and other decorative banners will be hoisted on the building; two projectors will be posted on the building. The clerks and workers of the municipality may leave their work immediately. In case the announcement will be after working hours, the following day will be a holiday. He added that parades would not take place, and an official reception would be given in the office of the District Commissioner before noon.[378]

"The biggest reception ever conducted for a dead man," that was the description given by the District Commissioner Keith-Roach to the welcome reception for the corpse of King Faisal of Iraq who died in Switzerland on 8 September 1933 and his coffin was returned to Iraq on the deck of a British cruiser. Keith-Roach spent many days in the preparation of the ceremony bombarded day and night by telegrams from the Admiralty, the Foreign Office, the Colonial Office, Trans-Jordan king Abdullah, Faisal's brother, and almost all the consuls in Jerusalem.

The Commissioner accompanied the former King Ali, brother of Faisal, to the deck where the coffin rested, the guard of honor playing bugles and bagpipes. But as soon as the coffin was taken from the cruiser and reached the enormous crowd of tens thousands of people that arrived in Haifa, the crowed took control of the ceremony and the policemen and the military were carried aside in the flood when everyone tried to touch the coffin.

The ceremony commenced at dawn as the airplane caring the coffin to Baghdad was designed to take off at seven thirty in the morning. The reception committee assembled at the airfield included the members of the Supreme Muslim Council, bishops, military men and government officials. The committee found itself in the center of a large mob that roared and waived his arms; only by miracle did they succeeded in bringing the coffin and King Ali on the aircraft that took off by 7.29. The sweating Keith-Roach returned to his office fighting the crowd, in order to write his report to the office of the Prime Minister.[379]

King George the Sixth's coronation was celebrated on the 12th of May 1937; the formal part included a parade of the Essex regiment that gave a salut to the District Commissioner. All the British children in the area were invited to a celebration of cakes and rolls and later Keith-Roach awarded them with a mug that he designed and was fabricated by a local potter, on one side was the emblem of the city and on the other an inscription to mark the event. Later, he gave a garden party on the lands of a monastery on the Carmel and distributed medals to the people that worked for the Mandate government; among them were physicians, missionaries, social workers, teachers, and also British officials and dignitaries.[380]

The city and its people–Jews, Arabs, and British

A less formal event celebrated by the Jewish community, took place at times when Chaim Weizmann, President of the World Zionist Organization, and later the first President of Israel, came to visit his relatives that lived in Hadar HaCarmel:

> When our uncle would arrive to a Passover 'Seder' feast, it became a celebration in the community; a big turnout used to assemble around the house, Weizmann went out and gave a speech and the evening was culminated by the 'Hora' (Israeli folklore) dances.[381]

Ezer Weizmann's Father, Yehiel Weizmann, worked for the agricultural department of the Mandate's government as forestry inspector until 1928, and then he started to work for the ICI Company for chemical products. Their home in Meltzet street was a stone house of two floors; he remembered it as a classic house of the period of Arab stone cutting, a red tiled roof with attic, garden with three olive trees, loquat tree, and a grapevine hut in the style of those days.[382]

The family had an automobile and telephone, both uncommon in those days; when he lifted the telephone, the operator used to responds in Arabic, English, or Hebrew. The family vacations were spent at times in Cyprus and in the summer in Lebanon:

> I recall trips from Haifa to Beirut in 1928- 1929...We used to travel along the shore, next to the big mills, pass a wood bridge above the Kishon stream, next to 'Shemen' factory we drove on the hard sand along the coast until we reached Acre. Somewhat before Acre we could link to what later became the Acre-Haifa road, from there was a highway to Beirut.[383]

The Weizmann family had contacts with the Arab elite in the city, like the mayor Hassan Shukri and the Catholic Talhemi family from Ussefia, a Druze village; they were invited almost every Christmas to lunch in their house. His father was also on good terms with the Shambur family of Kababeer village on the Carmel that gave their name to the neighborhood of Shambur.[384]

Orde Wingate was a special guest in their house:

> He was a very central figure in my life. He arrived here, in my opinion, according to the recommendation of my uncle Chaim Weizmann and he was welcomed in our house. My mother used to mend his socks; he was not the tidiest man in the world.
> I took trips with him several times...He had a car, in the end he had an azure Chevrolet...I used to open the baggage compartment and would see a rifle with ammunition and hand grenades. Once he told me to take the rifle and clean it. I did not figure out how to dismantle it...
> He was a very interesting gentile; and he probably was under considerable religious influence...He used to sit with my father and talk about the scriptures for hours at night,

and then the British promoted him and sent him away from the country.[385]

The rich Jewish families led a modest life; their children went to the same schools as the children of the blue collar workers:

> Pinhas Rutenberg lived at Rutenberg house of today, on Haoren avenue, I visited him several times with my father; he was a poor worker and Ruthenberg was perhaps the most affluent man in the country. Among the Sepharadic Jews (Oriental Jews) was the family of Shabtai Levi, the mayor; he was an affluent and also generous man; there were also the Hakim family. [386]

The Tiber family owned several big warehouses of lumber and also large businesses, Victor Cohen was an agronome and high-ranking official in the "Picca" Company, and was among the founders of Bat-Galim. He built there a palatial house with a sharpened dome of copper rising above the entrance and the balconies. Cohen arranged parties to the members of the high society, including the High Commissioner.[387]

Grazovski-Gur, father in law of Edwin, the son of the first High Commissioner Herbert Samuel, built his home on Panorama street, not far from Carmel Center. Edwin stayed there at times and participated in the high society parties.[388]

Landowners used to be in the core of Arab society, regarding "noblesse oblige" as the paramount value. The leading families were in competition that was usually manifested in generosity and distribution of favors, lavish reception, and patronage to people under their influence. They were expected to display power and affluence according to their status. There was a concealed contest between the el Halil family, a leading family during the Ottoman period, as well as the Mandate time and the Te family that acquired power during the Mandate time. The competition was manifested in philanthropic activity such as building the mosque of Istiqlal; Ibrahim el Halil and Haj el Halil Te were major players; both were assassinated during the riots (1936-39) and their sons continued the rivalry.[389]

Lavish hospitality contributed to the honor and social status of land owners: 4000 guests came to the wedding of two sons of the landowners el-Maadi family, although just 2000 were invited. Among them were delegations from thirty villages in the district of Haifa. Hospitality was also beneficial in strengthening the connections with prominent government officials and enhanced the standing of the family in the regional political system as well as the national and the Arab in general. Brothers Ibrahim and Tawfiq el Halil gave sumptuous receptions for honorable guests. Among them were the Emir Abdullah of Trans-Jordan, the High Commissioner, the Mufti, and Fahri Nashashibi, nephew of the Jerusalem mayor Ragebe Nashashibi.

A rare Arab hospitality of a Jewish dignitary was reported by Colonel Kish, the Chairman of the Zionist Executive to Eretz-Israel during 1923—1931, in his diary from 12 February 1924:

> I had tea at the home of Hassan Bei Shukri that convened to this party a dozen Arab dignitaries and among them his two brothers in law from the Halil family that were until recently members of the Haifa committee of the Muslim-Christian association and opted to resign from the committee rather than to be dragged to the extremist politics dictated by radicals in Jerusalem.[390]

Muine el Maadi gave a party for the District Commissioner Keith-Roach; others hosted dignitaries like the Prime Minister of Egypt Ismail Zidki. This style of life served as a model for the ascending new social sets of merchants, entrepreneurs, and real estate owners. It crystallized a lifestyle that included summer vacations in Lebanon, holidays in Tiberias or the Hamat Gader hot springs, and trips to Europe.[391]

A fascinating description of a rich man's house, illustrates the magic style of these days:

We stopped next to a palatial stone house built in oriental style; the entrance door was made of Mahogany wood with a key of brass in the shape of 'Hamsa.' A Sudanese servant, dressed in white galabia and a sash of red cloth, received us with smiling white teeth; we passed through a wide corridor to the parlor. The stunning oriental splendor was evident all over the room. The floor was covered by Persians rugs; next to the walls stood divans covered in red velvet, and pillows in various colors. A heavy crystal chandelier was suspended from the ceiling; in spite of the cornucopia and the colorfulness, the room manifested the good taste of the proprietor.[392]

The Haifa's Christian Arabs' internal community structure was reinforced by the establishment of voluntary associations for different purposes, initiated by the Mutran and his assistants: sport clubs, scouts clubs, and women charity organization. The Mutran organized cultural encounters in his residence, the "Mutrania," inviting authors, reporters, and poets.

Christian's clubs had developed cultural activity since the 20's and they invited educated Muslims to present lectures. By 1937 was established a joined culture club for both Muslims and Christians. The Orthodox Arab clubs became the major cultural center of Arab Haifa in the 40's, and the membership included Muslims and members of many different Christian sects. [393]

The colonial hegemony of western countries in the Middle East was generally viewed among the Arabs as a culture-civilization problem, but the Muslims and the Christians had contradictory point of views in that regard. While the Muslims intellectuals accentuated the struggle between the Muslims and western civilizations, the Christians, even those who identified with the anti-imperialism struggle, still felt somewhat like an extension of the western civilization, particularly the Latin and the Anglicans.[394]

Two of the leading contractors were Emil el-Bustani, a son of a well known Lebanese intellectual family, and Camel Abd el Rachman, a son of a builder from a village on the Carmel coast. Together they established the biggest Arab construction company in Haifa, "C.A.T," involved in projects of construction, paving of roads and public works to the extent of five million Palestinian pounds.[395] They received working contracts from the petroleum company under the circumstances that reflected on Haifa's Arab society. Emil el-Bustani benefited from the help of his relative, Wadiea' el-Bustani, who had good connections with the British political and economic elite, and of Taher Kraman, that was a major tobacco industrialist and land owner. Another supporter was Abla Rabiz from Rame village, wife of one of the executives in the company who conducted an open "Salon" for the society of Haifa.

The rapid development led to a contradiction experienced by the Arab elite between economic development in the fields of construction and commerce on one hand and the political domain on the other. It was manifested, for example, in the attitude of Rashid el Haj Ibrahim to the opening of Haifa port. By 1932, he claimed that the ceremonial opening should be used to attract a capital to Haifa, whereas one year later, in 1933 a surge of political demonstrations broke out, and Rashid's party called for banning of the opening ceremony. Radical politicians in Haifa contended that the government wanted to use the ceremony to shift attention from the real basic problems of independence, immigration, and lands to "secondary issues" such as economic development.[396]

The Ottoman culture that was the relevant frame of reference in the beginning of the Mandate period, allotted high social position to government officials and large landowners. Economic pursuits such as commerce and craft skill had a low status and were relegated mainly to the Christians. "El-Doat" was an idiom to achieving the high social status. According to testimonies of Haifa's veterans, these attributes were required from "Doat": connection to the Ottoman senior officials and to their lifestyle, hospitality, benevolence, and giving aegis to the needy.

During the Mandate period a new status rank was created—
"Atzami" men who achieved wealth on their own merits. The
word was derived from the name of a man who used to be the
court minister of one of the kings of Hira in the days before
Islam; he reached a high status only by merit of his personality.
The "Atzami" did not want to form new elite but aspired to
be accepted by the existing elite; one way was to become
connected by marriage to a family of "Doat" and act according
to the norms of generosity, public service, and contribution to
the construction of mosques. In the time of the war prosperity,
the businessmen's position was strengthened alongside the
veteran elite. They did not become competing elite, as they
failed to consolidate a scale of cogent values to be acceptable by
the majority of the Arab society in Haifa.[397]

Mayor Hassan Shukri, the most prominent Arab leader in
Haifa, was regarded as a traitor by the Arab national liberation
movement, charging that he was elected as mayor only as result
of the support of the Jewish community.[398]

Dr. Maged Khamra describes Haifa through the eyes of his
grandfather:

> My grandfather...told me, for example, that the lands of the
> Technion in Hadar HaCarmel used to be the property of
> Khamra; all the land was planted with vineyards, grapes that
> belonged to the Khamra family. When we walked on the
> bridge of Rushmia, over the valley of Rushmia, he told me
> that here in the valley lived people from Gaza and people
> from Um—El Fahem...He told me on his property also in
> the Ard el Zitoun (Allenby road), places that were called
> on the names of prominant families like...Kraman, Suidan,
> Shukha, Rashid el Haj Ibrahim...But it does not exist now.
> My Grandfather told me many stories, on the villa of the
> Khoury family that was a grand villa. He mentioned it
> because beneath the house was the property of the Khamra
> family and opposite was the estate of Touma family who
> were the next of kin of Tawfiq Tubbi family...And like that
> every street that we passed I asked my grandfather how it
> was called because as a carriage driver he took people from

Khamra Square up to the Carmel; he even transported people from Haifa to Jaffa, from Haifa to Acre, he was going places...He was in Nablus...Then everything was open, and he could travel. He wanted to take a trip to Haleb, to Damascus, and he just went. [399]

Women's status in the Arab society was a complex, delicate issue. Social gathering of males and females in a mixed company did not exist in Muslim society, not even in the constraint frame of the family. Only few Muslim couples were, in secret, guests of the High Commissioner. Muslim couples used to dine with their English friends but not with Muslim relatives, friends, or acquaintances.

The tradition of segregation led to a situation that Arab women from the affluent classes rarely traveled abroad at all and to Europe particularly. The few who traveled went mostly to Syria and to Lebanon; a small number also took trips to Mecca as pilgrims. [400] The Muslim leadership in Jerusalem alleged that the veil was required for women as a cultural defense and also as a demonstration that the Arab leaders did not recoil from Zionist pressure. Only twice, in 1929 and 1934, unveiled Muslim women appeared in the presence of the High Commissioner to protest the pro Zionist politics of the British government.

But apparently, national concerns were not paramount among high class Muslim women from Nablus and other places who traveled from time to time to Tel Aviv to visit a fashionable Jewish hairdresser and to cut their hair short in the latest fashion. They shopped in Jewish shops, particularly in the new, updated shops of German Jews. [401]

The first Arab women Organization, the "Christian Public Charity Society for Ladies," was founded in Haifa by 1911. Among its leaders were women of the social elite of Haifa. Madam Fuad Bei Saad was president; Madame Ibrahim effendi Sahioun and Madam Teophil Butaji were among the prominant figures in the organization that was active in particular during the First World War. Another organization was "The Arab Union of Haifa."

Among its members were both Muslims and Christians. The organization linked the women organization in Haifa and in the north of the country and was involved in topics of national significance. Much of its success can be related to its secretary, Madam Sadig' Nassar, granddaughter of El Baha, founder of the Baha'i denomination. She was "a woman of status, culture, and experience." She worked together with her husband, Naguieb Nassar, as the editor of the influential newspaper *El Carmel.*

The first congress of Arab women took place on the 26th of October 1929 with the participation of more than 200 delegates, Christian and Muslim from cities and villages throughout the country. The congress participants adopted resolutions on the required struggle for the abolition of the Balfour declaration, the call for for the establishment of an Arab national government, on economic development, including prohibition of the purchase of anything from the Jews except for land. The resolutions were sent to the British Prime Minister, the British Colonial Secretary, the High Commissioner, diplomatic representatives, and women organizations. The delegates furthermore asked for a meeting with lady Chancellor, wife of the High Commissioner, stating that the Muslim members of the delegation could not appear in presence of the High Commissioner. They were notified that lady Chancellor was not able to receive a delegation that presented proposals of a political nature, but the High Commissioner was ready to receive a delegation of ten representatives.[402]

Muslim religious leaders were mainly interested in the moral conduct of the Muslim woman. The "Association of young Muslims" created by 1928 a code of conduct for Muslim women; it emphasized the objection that a woman would adorn herself in public, including short hair and high heels, requirement for the covering of the head, the face and the neck. They also voiced objection that a woman would leave her house "needlessly," including even for shopping in the market. As late as 1944, conservative groups sent children to the streets to throw dirt and rip the costumes of Muslim women dress in fashionable clothes.

A Kind of cultural war broke out and young educated Muslim men, relatives of the progressive women, organized in order to protect them. A breakthrough was the appearance of an educated Muslim woman, Hiria Mahmad el Khoury, wife of Anis el Khoury, as a lecturer in a mixed society. That led to great antagonism and many efforts were made, unsuccessfully, to pressure her family to prevent her appearance.[403]

Life in the British colony in Palestine was in principal similar to other colonies. At the top of the British close circle stood the high-ranking officials and, as an observer of that society wrote, "The smaller the lake, the bigger the fish." He added that, while being in a distant land, people were dedicated to cultivating the theory of their importance and social leadership, and a man who had a humble ego in England, in small Palestine it expands and any one with a good income becomes a local dignitary. The British officials were not allowed to befriend the "natives," but many disregarded the policy and received invitations to visits in the Jew's or Arab's houses, to an evening of music and social activity.[404]

> The English love to befriend the rich Arabs, well known for their sumptuous hospitality; and they were blinded by the Arab opulence...The rich Arabs host the colonial masters like kings whereas our hospitality is meager...The English invites the Arab effendis to their closed clubs, because they reciprocate with a pampered hospitality in their homes. [405]

Marriages conducted between English men and Christian Arab girls usually suffered from prejudice, unless the bride was a rich heiress...The prejudice was less in case of a marriage between an English man and a Jewish girl from Europe or from Palestine...

Senior Jewish officials of the district government of the Mandate enjoyed a high status in Jewish Haifa. First among them was the district officer Baruch Binna, who also served as a contact between the Jewish establishment and the authorities. Others were the deputies of the British district engineer, among them the Jewish American Perez Etkes. The most senior Jewish official in the railway service was Ya'akov Moshly, director of the railway workshop in Haifa. In the principal railway offices worked Moshe Pikovitch, brother of Yigal Alon, a central figure in the Haganah and Palmach. Yehiel Weizmann, the brother of Chaim Weizmann, was the deputy director of the government agriculture department, in charge of forestry work in the region. Among the Jewish judges were Dr. Aahron Shemesh, Joseph Strumza, district judges in Haifa, and the court secretary Joseph Maman.[406]

Society was organized in small circles: the British officials, the church circle, the Greeks, the Anglo-Jews, the American Jews, the Germans Jews, the Muslims–Arabs, Christians–Arabs and more.[407]

Shabtai Levi wrote about several of the top English officials in the city: Colonel Storrs that served as the first Military Governor of Haifa and was later known as Governor of Jerusalem. He appointed Shabtai Levi and Rafael Hakim to represent the Jewish community of Haifa in the city council for the first time in the community's history.

Another District Commissioner was Colonel Stanton, a pleasant man. The municipality named a street after him. He was followed by Colonel Saims, a socially active man who gave parties with his Italian wife that were attended by the city's dignitaries. The most colorful and famous figure was Keith–Roach whom Levi describes:

> There is no doubt that he was the most flamboyant Englishman among all the District Commissioners of cities in the country, a special character that light and shadow existed in a medley in him. There is no wonder that Keith-

Roach acquired a reputation in the history of this country during the era of the Mandate. [408]

Law was the last District Commissioner of Haifa, strongly attached to the city, a generous and good man who had many contact with both Jews and Arabs. Shabtai Levi remembers emotionally the day in March 1948 when he came to Levi's home to say goodbye to him and his wife and then left their home crying like a little boy. [409]

Sir Arthur and lady Florence Downs' house was at 120 Panorama street, Lady Downs, a sister-in-law of Field Marshal Allenby, was a well known supporter of Zionism; she named the street next to her house in honor of her admired author, George Elliot, the famose author of *Daniel Deronda*.[410] In 1934, lady Downs donated land opposite her house in order to establish a garden in honor of Allenby and as a memorial to his only son, Michael, killed in the First World War in Passchendaele.[411]

Bernard Montgomery, another very illustrious British military commander, arrived in Haifa in October 1938 to command the army units in northern Palestine involved in the suppression of the Arab rebellion. He dwelled in the upper floor at 95 Panorama street in an impressive house built by an Arab family in 1937 in the style of a castle with towers.[412] Montgomery requested to meet Chaim Weizmann who came to Haifa at times to visit his relatives; the meeting took place at the home of the parents of Ezer Weizman who recalled it as "a complete celebration with a motorcycles escort." [413]

The visiting British usually expressed enthusiasm of the city landscape. Mrs. Stuart Erskin praised the splendors of Haifa, Mount Carmel, and the gulf of Acre, but expressed reservation about the way the Jews chose to build the city, stating that they failed to transform it into a new Riviera attracting people to visit during winter. The ugly, crowded streets, the hastily built villas on the Carmel, spoiled for her the loveliness of Haifa. Still she found pleasure in the city:

If you want to see Haifa to advantage you must look down
from a height when the moon is shining on the sea and
thousands of lights make the place look like fairyland. Or
you must go by daylight to the headquarters of the Baha'i
community, from whence you can look down on the wide
sweep of the bay, with cypress and orange trees framing the
picture...[414]

Thomas Hodgkin visited Haifa in July 1935; he was a junior
official of the Mandate government and also served briefly as the
Private Secretary of the High Commissioner Arthur Wauchope.
He stayed at the Carmelite hospice but was asked to leave after
the usual maximum stay of three days; he described the view in
a letter to his mother:

It is beautiful on this promontory, with sea on three sides
and the lighthouse part of the hospice swinging beams of
light around all night-the harbor and the town below, this
afternoon full of sailing vessels with their sails furled and a
few small white sails, and sand and sea on the other side and
falling rocky ground in between. [415]

Towards the end of an epoch

The interaction among the inhabitants of the city was
sometime tense, like for example during the 1921 and 1929 riots,
but even then, during armed conflicts involving Arabs, Jews, and
British, there were also friendships. Abraham Halfon described
in his memoirs how his family was safeguarded during the riots
of 1929 by their Arab neighbors that also supplied them with
food and water when they were barricaded in their house for
three days.[416]

Ruth Zuker described the relations of Arabs and Jews in
quiet periods as compared with times of riots:

The Palestinian people were good, honest, nice people and I
can only commend them. We lived in one of the first houses

in Hertzel street, Negri house on number 85. When there was no one at home we did not shut the door even once, the laundress, the milk man, all of them came in and all of them found their money on the table...We lived together, in the grocery store they did not ask if you are Jewish or Arab, we bought on the account and paid at the end of the month.

We had friends...There was an Egyptian professor who taught law. Another was a lawyer who wore a fez; his name was Camil, he studied at the university in Cairo but was a Palestinian...He recounted that the Arabs in Palestine are indebted to the Jews that brought electricity...Jews and Arabs from the upper classes went together to cafés and also invited each other to their homes. Until the riots, we did not know fear.[417]

Jalal Irani pointed to the distinction that used to exist between the educated people of the two communities, in contrast to the plain people in the marketplace, who, in his view, "did not like each other."

By 1940-1945 he worked for the British censorship office, stationed in a small street in the German Colony; his co-workers were from all the communities. The higher-ranking officials were in general British, although the director of the censorship in Haifa was a Jew named Shvalbe; the principal censor of the country was Edwin Samuel. The relations were cordial; Irani remembered that during the month long Ramadan fast, for example, the Christian Arabs and the Jews refrained from smoking in respect for the Muslims.[418]

The most traumatic event in Haifa in the Second World War was the bombardment of the city by the Italian air force in July 1940. Depiction of an eye witness:

I once descended from the Carmel Mountain with my girl friend and suddenly I saw two groups of five airplanes. We looked at the (oil) installations of 'Shell' next to the power plant and then–Boom.[419]

John Higgins, a British travel agent that arrived on a short-term assignment to Palestine to close Cook's office, wrote home describing the blue skies of Haifa. In his anger he did not refrain from also criticizing the British and wrote that the military and the police were only concerned in looking after themselves and their families. He even complained that the British women were "the worst dressed ever. Bombay lot would look smart in comparison"…It looks like the strikes, bombs, and endless incidents clearly unnerved him.

> This afternoon, for the first time for a week, I got out and went to the Zone at the top of Mount Carmel. It was glorious there. The blue sea 1000 feet below, and we walked through the pinewoods rather like those in Antibes, but it was horrid. You sort of suspected one of the Stern gang might pop out. I am thinking of moving my hotel tomorrow in view of the threat to blow it up.[420]

Richard Crossman, a Member of the British Parliament and of the Anglo-American Committee of Inquiry that visited Eretz-Israel in March 1946, saw the developments in a somewhat more optimistic light:

> …Within ten minutes we were at a party with the usual collection of notables who drink whiskey with commissions in district officers' drawing rooms. Two Archimandrites, several British Council members, British social welfare workers, a city engineer, businessmen, and a few wealty Arabs and Jews. The British there were the best I have met in Palestine.
> After dinner, at ten, a car was sent to take me to visit an Arab trade-union leader. I thought I would be going to a romantic office down in the port district, but we swept higher up to the most expensive residential suburb, and stopped at a magnificent villa, designed last year by a French architect. The trade-union leader was the wealtiest lawyer in town…As always in Palestine, being Labor, he was

more nationalistic than anyone else. I left him at midnight slightly depressed.[421]

The visit in Haifa naturally included also official sessions, he described them in detail:

Back to the gigantic municipal building, completed in 1943, for coffee and chocolate cake with the municipal commission—four Jews, four Muslims, four Christian Arabs. In Haifa, Jew and Arab get on well because money-making bring them together, both on the capital and on the labor side. A Jew, manager of two huge factories run by the Jewish T.U.C. (they were both on strike, comically enough) told us that all worked for the good of the city. [422]
We began to interrogate. Yes, of course, Arab education is a little slow. Were the Jews interested? Well, they have their own schools and education was the responsibility of each community...On the whole, I believe conditions have produced a division, and a real devision, between the working-class representation and business representation, and there are Arab and Jewish wards which elect trade-union representatives. In replying formally, I assured them that I welcomed as a sign of its progressive outlook, **Haifa's development of social conflict in municipal affairs instead of racial conflict.** Ambassador Phillips and Dr. Aydelotte looked a little shocked.[423]

The imminent future grew darker, the days of the Mandate were nearing the end and the national conflict was about to take over, but the municipality and the inhabitants attempted to resume their lives even at the time of growing violence. The public leaders appealed together to the inhabitants to safeguard their beautiful city, "a place that your eyes are aimed at and your hopes are centered in," but history was about to write the next chapter.[424]

The Arabs in Haifa During the British Mandate- Social, Economic, and Cultural Developments

Johnny Mansour

Introduction

The Arab society in Haifa went through a development of far reaching changes, from a traditional society to a modern society that adjusts its economic structure to the proceedings in the surrounds. We will deal here with the social, economic, and cultural issues related to the Palestinian Arabs in Haifa during the British Mandate.

In this essay we will illustrate varied activities of the Arab society in different fields and levels. We specifically mentioned many names, figures, and institutions in an attempt to show the size and order of the activities and their contribution to the advancement and development of the Arab society in Haifa.

Demographic changes and their influence on the social structure

Haifa went through far reaching changes in the social structure during the British Mandate, from a small town in the last days of the Ottoman rule it became the forth city in size in the British Mandate. This change affected very much the balance between the communities that lived in the city, and also the social, economic, educational, and functional structure in the different institutions in Haifa.

The Arab population, which constituted the majority in the city, dwelled in the neighborhoods deployed on rectangular territory that reclined from east to the west, viz from the railway station area in the east to the borders of the German Colony in the west. They were developed from the old city nucleus, inside the walls that were built in 1761 by Sheik Daher al-Omar (1689-1775), the ruler of Haifa and the Galilee.[425] Additional neighborhoods that were built in the period of the Mandate such as Halissa and Abbas were characterized as neighborhoods inhabited by prestigious and wealthy families.

The Jewish community dwelled in the areas that spread on Mount Carmel and parts of its slopes like Hadar HaCarmel, Upper Hadar, Ahuza, Neve Sha'a'nan, and Bat Galim, which is distant from the other Jewish neighborhoods. Some Jewish families dwelled in other parts of the city, like "Ard al-yahud," and "Ard al-ramel." It could be pointed out that the Jewish population inside the city grew in great dimensions and in a consistent way right after the collapse of the Ottoman rule and the beginning of the British Mandate. The growth rate of the Arab population in the city was not proportional to the Jewish population. A considerable part of the Arabs who came to Haifa in order to search for work maintained tight connections with their families that remained in the village.

The Jewish community was blessed with large waves of immigrations, mainly in the 30's. While in 1922, the Jewish residents were about 25% of the population of Haifa, by 1931, the Jewish community accounted for a third of the population of Haifa, and for more than half in the start of the Second World War. The data shows clearly the demographic changes in Haifa during the British Mandate:[426]

> 1922: 18240 Arabs, 6230 Jews, 24470 Total-75% Arabs.
> 1928: 20716 Arabs, 8279 Jews, 28995 Total-71% Arabs.
> 1931: 34148 Arabs, 15923 Jews, 50071 Total-68% Arabs.
> 1935: 37306 Arabs, 18646 Jews, 55952 Total-66% Arabs.
> 1939: 42315 Arabs, 22707 Jews, 65022 Total-65% Arabs.
> 1944: 62800 Arabs, 66000 Jews, 128800 Total-46% Arabs.

The movement of immigration towards Haifa was strong among the two populations during the British Mandate. Each one relied on different and separate sources for its enlargement. The Arabs relied on a movement of inner emigration to Haifa from the adjacent villages of Galilee and Samaria. This was a natural, normal immigration movement that characterized the Palestinian cities and the neighboring states. In addition, the movement of immigration from outside Palestine, in particular from Lebanon, Syria, Trans-Jordan, Iraq, and Egypt accounted for about 10% of all the Arab population of the city.

The factors of the Arabs' immigration to Haifa sum up mainly in the search of workplaces, this after the transformation of the city and the surroundings to a heavy regional industry, especially the refineries and the Haifa harbor. The establishment of wide regional and industrial sites in Haifa pulled workforces to them that the local Arab population could not provide; and started an attraction of workforces from out of the city.

The Jewish immigration is derived from completely different reasons, mainly the Zionist idea and the problematic situation of the Jewish communities in Europe following the rise of the Nazis in Germany, basically national and political factors.[427]

It should be pointed out that the Arabs of Haifa did not cope with the rise of Jewish immigration, both in the numerical aspect and the fact that the Jewish immigrants succeeded to pave their way easily to the central roles and key jobs in the municipality and governmental system. The Jewish population managed its interests in an almost completely independent way by means of arrangement of institutions and organizations, in addition to the takeover of the municipality and its institutions since the early 40's.

The Jewish population enjoyed the strategic location of its neighborhoods and a new and modern construction compatible with its needs. Meanwhile, the Arab population, a majority of which dwelled in the old areas of the city, suffered from a high density of population, particularly in the 40's, and from a lower services level compared to the Jewish neighborhoods. In spite of this, new Arab neighborhoods developed mainly in the western part of the city, such as Abbas, the area of Allenby street, and Wadi al-jimal (Ein Hayam today).

The development of the layout of the Arab neighborhoods came in the aftermath of the formation of a wealthy, resourceful social layer that bought properties in these areas and began to diverge from the tumultuous old areas of the city.[428]

The participation of the Arab community in major managment jobs suffered a set back as result of the processes of transmission of roles and central functions to Jews. What remained were mainly marginal jobs that did not enable promotions to their carriers.

The drastic change for the Arab population in Haifa was in the events of 1948 that brought the immigration of tens of thousands of Arabs from the city of Haifa towards Lebanon, Jordan, Syria and Egypt by sea and land. The "Nakba" (the Arabic nickname for the events of 1948 that preceded the establishment of the state of Israel), caused the collapse of the Palestinian society and the creation of the Palestinian refugees that were deported from their villages and cities by the Haganah forces.

Religious institutions

Haifa's society is characterized by the multiplicity of religious communities. Most of the communites lived in their separate neighborhoods, in spite of the existence of mixed neighborhoods, mainly Christian and Muslim.

The Muslim neighborhoods were in the old city that played an important social and economic role up to the 30's as it was the venue of the central market, but began to lose its centrality after the residence neighborhoods expanded in different areas of Haifa. Ard al-Balan neighborhood, Nazareth road, Wadi al-salib, and Halissa neighborhoods in the eastern part of the city. Muslim families dwelled from the early twenties in the areas of Wadi Nisnas and Abbas.[429]

The Arab Christian communities lived in the neighborhoods of Wadi Nisnas, Al-Zeitoun area (Allenby Road today), and Jaffa road, Wadi al-jimal, Carmel Station, and Vine street (Hagefen today).[430]

All of them built together the mosaic of the population of Haifa and had religious, social, and educational institutions. Each community took care of providing religious services to its members in the neighborhoods of the city.

In the western southern area of the city were few mosques, for instance, the mosque of the Ahmadia community in Kababeer. Kababeer was not considered part of the city of Haifa in spite of the geographic proximity and there was a Mukhtar (mayor) that represented the community in front of the authorities. However, after the establishment of the state of Israel, this neighborhood was annexed to Haifa's municipality. All the Christian churches were in the western part of Haifa, in the different Christian neighborhoods. The Muslim community in Haifa had at that time five mosques:

"**The Little Mosque**" also known as "**Nasr Mosque**" (victory mosque): acknowledged as the oldest mosque in Haifa, was built by Daher al-Omar, the ruler of Galilee, in 1761, at the time of the establishment of new Haifa within the walls. The Muslims call the mosque "The market mosque" as it is located at the heart of the central market of Haifa. A number of stores were built next to the mosque and were proclaimed as Waqf to cover the expenses of the mosque and related services. This mosque is registered on the ground holding that carries the number "10842" sections 55-56 and known at the time by the residents as "al-Hakim" (property of the wise man). The adjacent land that held the number 110 was empty and carried the name of "al-Sibat lane." During the Turkish period and the beginning of the British Mandate, a director of the Waqf was appointed to organize the properties and collect the rents. The first director was Fauzi Timsah. His appointment was authorized by the Supreme Muslim Council, certified by the Mandate government to manage the Waqf in Palestine. At the end of the Turkish period, a Rashidic official school was founded next to the mosque. The author and researcher Abdulla Mukhlis studied in the same school. Near the end of the First World War the building of the school became a small commercial center that dedicated its earnings to the mosque.[431] The Haganah forces bombarded the mosque in the 1948 war in Haifa, which caused great damage to it. The mosque was closed for a long time because residents of the eastern neighborhoods left after the 1948 war.

"**Al-Jerina Mosque**" or "**The Big Mosque**": was built at the end of the 19th century in the northeastern side of old Haifa (the new Haifa of Sheik Daher al-Omar), by the beach that bordered on Jaffa street in proximity to the market. The mosque was spacious and a wide yard surrounded it. Towards the events of Sultan Abd al-Hamid the Second jubilee, the authorities built the clock tower close to the mosque. The passengers of the Hijaz Railway in the Haifa East station could see the clock located on top of the tower. The mosque had a minaret that was ruined by the bombings of the Haganah forces in 1948. Sheik Suleiman was appointed Khatib (the preacher) of the mosque, right after its building, and this role became a legacy in his family which was well known by its nickname "Khatib."[432]

"**Al-Istiqlal Mosque**" (the mosque of independence): was built in 1923-1924 in the eastern side of Haifa. It carried the name "Al-Istiqlal" in anticipation of independence that the Arabs in the Middle East held on to. A basic planning work had been done in the mosque, and quite a few stores were added to it as Waqf that belonged to the mosque. A special public committee was founded to build the mosque, called the "Al-Istiqlal mosque building committee." The head of the board was the Mufti of Haifa Sheik Mohammad Murad and the members were Abdulla Yunes, Khalil Taha, and Abd al-Rahman Haj (former mayor of Haifa). Sheik Izz al-Din al-Qassam became the Sheik of the mosque from its opening in 1924, until his death in 1935. His brother Fakher al-Din was appointed Sheik of the same mosque and he continued to serve the community up to 1948.

This mosque was characterized by different activities that took place there in the religious, social, and political planes. Most of the major demonstrations against the British authorities and the Zionist movement exited from the mosque's yard.

"Haj Abdulla Mosque": the mosque of Halissa neighborhood, located in the east of Haifa. It was built with the contribution of Haj Abdulla abu Yunes. The building had three floors; the ground floor was dedicated to the neighborhood school, the first floor to the social and community services, and the second floor (the last one) to the mosque, which served the citizens of the neighborhood.

The contributor continued to provide money for the activity of the mosque until 1937, when the mosque and the school management were put under the Muslim Waqfs' administration in Haifa following his decision to leave the city and move to Damascus. During the war of 1948, damage was caused to the mosque's structure, particularly from the direction of the attacks coming from the Jewish neighborhood Neve Sha'a'nan.

"Al-Khader Cave": holy to Muslims, Jews, and Christians.[433] The cave is located in the western area of Haifa at the bottom of Stella Maris hill. This is a holy place for Muslims in Palestine, connected to the tradition of the prophet Elias according to the legacy of Islam. The place was guarded and cherished by the al-Haj Ibrahim family (the prominent member of this family was Rashid al-Haj Ibrahim, a businessman and politician who was involved in the political activities in Haifa and other parts of Palestine during the British Mandate). Towards the 40's, the responsibility of this holy site transferred to the Sheik Hassan family. The holy site was in the hands of the Israeli authorities after 1948 and was renamed "Eliahu Hanavi Cave," and some changes have been done to it, which fit the Jewish heritage.

Cemeteries: the Muslim community in Haifa owned several old cemeteries in the eastern part of the city, mainly around Al-Istiqlal mosque. The people of Haifa called another cemetery close to the Hijaz Railway station at the time "The Beis Cemetery," of the Murad's family and some graves of officials and railway laborers.

The Christian religious institutions were distributed between the different communities. Below are Christian institutions, most of which still exist and provide services up to the present day:

A) The Greek Melkite Catholic Community Churches

"**Our Lady Cathedral**": was built in the western neighborhood of Haifa inside the walls of Daher al-Omar. The cathedral was built in the period of Bishop Agapius Doumani by 1862. A small monastery was built in proximity to the church of the reverends, which served the community, and the community also built an elementary school, that was administrated by the church. The church was the center of the community's religious, educational, and social life. It gained an honorable position among the members of the community owing to the fact that the Greek bishop of the Catholic Church's seat was beside the cathedral. The bishop Grigorios Hajjar moved his seat from Old Akka (Acre) to Haifa by the mid 20's. The church began to lose its centrality after the expansion of construction in the western areas of the city, and therefore the leaders of the community decided to build other churches and schools in the different neighborhoods in the city, which had a big concentration of believers. The church was abandoned after the 1948 war and remained closed up to 1982 when it was reopened by the initiative of Camil Shehada and his wife Agnes who established the "House of Grace."

"**Mar Elias**[434] **Church**": located on Ein Dor street. Was founded in replacement of a club that belonged to some members of the community at the end of the twenties. The church was built after the expansion of residence neighborhoods, mostly of Christian Arab inhabitants, towards the west. Bishop Hajjar, a greatly admired bishop of his community, decided to build a church that would serve the community in the new neighborhoods of the city. The church is considered nowadays to be the center of the Bishop's seat, and has undergone a number of renovations and conservation.

"**Angel Gabriel Church**": was built in the beginning of the 30's, in the neighborhood of "Carmel Station" by the contribution of Gabriel Fouad Saad, an esteemed member of the community. In proximity to it the bishop Hajjar built a small school for the inhabitants of the area. The church and the school served the members of the church and the rest of the inhabitants in the neighborhood during the British Mandate. The church was shut down a number of times due to dilution in the number of the members. The activity of the church, contributed greatly to the reinforcement of the economic and socially weak population of the neighborhood.

"**Saint Gregorios Church**": was built in the Wadi Al-Jimal neighborhood in 1935 during the period of bishop Hajjar's priesthood, in order to serve the Greek Catholic community in this quarter.

"**The Savior Church**": Reverend Basilius Khoury's family contributed the building to the Greek Catholic community in the 30's, to serve the religious needs of the inhabitants of Wadi Nisnas area.

B) The Greek Orthodox Community Churches

"**Mar Elias Church**": was built in the western quarter of Haifa inside the city walls at the end of the 19th century. The western neighborhood of the old city of Haifa within its walls is known as "Haret Al-Kanaies" (Churches quarter). This church was the focus of activity for the members of the community during the Turkish period and the British Mandate. The church still serves the community and as result of the residents leaving the area, and the distance from the center of the city, the council of the congregation decided to build a new church on Allenby street in proximity to the accommodation of the spiritual head of the community. The name of the new church will be "Saint John the Baptist."

C)   The Maronite Community Church

"Saint Louis Church": Was built outside of old Haifa's walls at the end of the 19th century by the Khoury's contribution.[435] This church still attracts the Maronite congregation members. Beside the church were an elementary school and a club during the British Mandate.

D)   The Catholic (Latin) Community Church

"The Church of Virgin Mary": located in proximity to "Khamra square" (Paris square of today), was built during the second half of the 18th century. The church served the local members of the community and the foreigners that sustained commerce and business connections in the cities of the Ottoman Empire and most of them came from Europe. This church and other properties are under the supervision of the Carmelite Monastry. The leaders of this community decided in the 50's to build new churches in the areas in which most of the members of the community are settled. A new church of "Saint Joseph" was built on Hamegenim street and serves the community to this day.

E)   The Armenian Community Church

"The Armenian Church": located on Khoury street. This is a small Christian community compared to other communities in Haifa. They arrived from Armenia at the end of the Turkish period and at the beginning of the British Mandate following a series of massacres of Armenians committed by the Turks.

The members of this community are still living among the Arab community, conserving the Armenian legacy and particularly the language. Members of the Armenian community are accepted within the Arab community and take part in most of its social activities.

F)   The Anglican Churches Community

"**Saint John Church**": was built in the 20's on Saint John's street. The church held very intensive activities during the British Mandate because most of the members of this church were English and Australians who worked in the Mandate offices and in the factories placed in Haifa. The council of the church community established an elementary school adjacent to the church, which still serves the members of the community and the rest of the city's inhabitants.

"**Saint Luke Church**": located on Saint Luke street near the Mountain road (Zionisem road today). This is a small church that served the nearby Scottish hospital that was built by "The Edinburgh Medical Mission"[436] beside the priest's house.

A number of monasteries and schools that belong to the different communities exist in Haifa. Listed below are the monasteries that operated during the British Mandate and a large part of them are still serving their communities:

-   "Sisters of Nazareth convent and school" on Abbas street.[437]
-   "Carmelite sisters convent and school" on the Italian street.
-   The convent and the kindergartens named after Saint Anne on Hospital street (Mayer street today).
-   Convent and hospital of Saint Charles in Jaffa road at the corner of the Hospital street.
-   Convent of The Holy Heart of Jesus on Allenby street. Served as a school during the British Mandate

and after the establishment of Israel, it became an institution for the retarded and handicapped.

- "Stella Maris Carmelite monastery."
- "Saint Mary's convent" located in Wadi al-Salib quarter. In the past, the convent was the Khalil family's house. Arab families took shelter in this monastery in 1948 until it was abandoned at the beginning of the 90's. Nowadays this building is registered in the conservation list.
- "Carmelite Sisters convent" (al-Zawra) was located at the "Stone House" that is part of site of the government hospital (Rambam). The monastery served as a school during the British Mandate. The school continued to run until the end of the 50's, when it was sold to the hospital, the sisters moved to Isffia (a small village near Haifa) and the school was shut down.
- "The Carmelite Prisoner Sisters convent." located at the corner of the Mountain road beside the French Carmel quarter. The sisters living in the monastery do not come in contact with the population. They dedicate their lives to Jesus Christ and keep silent almost at all times.
- "Prophet Elias Russian Monastery and Church" Russian church on Hanasie road. Was built by the Russian church at the end of the Russian Czars period as part of a huge project which the Russian church initiated with the support of the czar to build churches, schools, hostels, hospitals,[438] clinics, and monasteries in Palestine and in the nearby states.

Education institutions in the Arab community

The Arab education system in Haifa was composed of two main components: state education and private education. The state education in Haifa at the end of the Ottoman era was below standards. Written evidence on that situation: there are 12 basic schools, three in the city of Haifa, and the condition of the state schools in Haifa itself is extremely dilapidated. The number of students in the state schools in Haifa does not exceed 42, of about ten thousand people living in Haifa. Most unfortunate is the condition of the office furniture and the equipment in the aforesaid schools in comparison to the foreign and the Jewish schools, which were built in Haifa and in the county. There was only one teacher graduate from the teacher's training school, and the others did not have any certificates.[439] The same evidence is related to the girls' education: The parents are willing to educate their daugthers in the schools; the number of the girls that went to school was close to 200 students. [440]

In view of the difficult economic state of the local population, no changes were evident in the state education arrangement by the end of the Ottoman era, even though educational reform took place in the second half of the 19th century, after the declaration of the official law of education by 1869 in which the government determined five levels of education:

Level A: Elementary schools for four years.

Level B: Secondary schools (Rushdia) which were built in the settlements which had a population of over 500 families.

Level C: High schools in the settlements which had a population of over 1,000 families and the studies lasted three years. Schools of this level were in Jerusalem, Akko and Nablus.[441]

Level D: Middle high schools (Sultans schools) only students that successfully passed examinations of the third level were enrolled in them. There was only one school in this level in all of Palestine, located in Jerusalem.

Level E: Schools for training teachers located in major cities such as Istanbul, Beirut, Cairo, and Damascus.

The first state school in Haifa was founded during the Ottoman period, in 1886, in the first level. In another school, established by the government in 1889 in the second level, studied only 20 students.

At the end of the Ottoman period, there were in Haifa three state schools, and eight private schools, four of them French oriented: "Frere," "Sisters of Nazareth," "Sisters of the Sacred Heart," and "Alliance" (a Jewish school). The number of the female students in these schools was only 30. The number of the male students reached 530. The English missionaries established two elementary schools where the number of the female students was 150 and the male students were only 70. The Russians and the Germans established their own schools.[442]

At the beginning of the British Mandate in Palestine, there was an elementary school and a middle school for boys, and an elementary school for girls. The British department of education established a vocational school in 1936.[443]

We should point out that the Arab community did not rely on the services of the state education system, neither during the Ottoman period, nor during the British Mandate. Therefore there began a strong leverage of an establishment of private schools that belonged to the Christian communities and to different monasteries or to the Muslim community, and others that were completely private schools. The Arab community supported the establishment of education institutions throughout Haifa, which reached the highest level of achievements in both local and national comparisons.[444]

The wealthy families in Haifa as in the villages and small towns sent their children to study in these private schools, which quickly earned a name and prestige for themselves.[445]

There are three types of classification of the private schools in Haifa:

A: Private schools.

B: Private schools that belonged to the religious communities.

C: Monastery Schools (connected to the origin countries of the monasteries).

A) Private schools:

One of the famous schools in Haifa was established by Nabih Thabet; he focused on teaching sciences, mathematics, physics,

Arabic and English. The school used a method of teaching that relies on courses taken by small groups of students. The school was located on Allenby street. The parents sent their children to intense professional summer courses. Other schools of this type included "al-Barumi," "al-Wihda," "al-Irshad."[446]

B)   Private schools that belonged to the religious communities:

1) Schools of "Al-Jameia Al-Islamia fi Haifa" (Schools of the Islamic Association in Haifa):

1a) **The Muslim school, "al-Burj"** (the Tower): was located in al-Burj street (Maaleh Hashihrur today), was considered the most prestigious among the Arab Muslim community and accepted also students coming from the suburbs of Haifa. The association administered the school; the educational directors were Sheik Kamel al-Kassab, Naguieb Bleik, Abd al-Latif al-Habbal, and Ahmad Kraiem, who joined the Syrian ministry of education after the war of 1948.[447]

1b) **"Al-Wadad school"**: located on Wadi al-Salib quarter. Sheik Ali Sayed Ja'afar who graduated from Al-Azhar University in Cairo was sent to teach in this school. He frequently preached in the mosques of Haifa and in other cities. [448]

1c) **Schools for Muslim girls.**

1d) **Schools for Muslim boys.**

2) Muslim Private schools:

2a) Elementary school for boys and girls (mixed school) was built in Wadi al-Salib quarter under the supervision of "Madame Khadija" who was known for her strictness with the students and her rules and order within the walls of the school.[449]

2b) **"Al-Madrassa al-Arabia"**: established by Sheik Mohammed al-Sibaei. The school was built next to the Turkish

Hammam (Sauna) in the old city.[450] The school became a hospital known by the name of "Al-Amin," and provided medical services during the 1948 events in Haifa.[451]

3) Schools of the local Christian communities:

3a) **"Al-Madrassa al-Uskufia al-Kathulikia"** ("the Catholic Episcopal School" for boys): this school belongs to the Greek Catholic community. In the early days of this school, it was located next to Our Lady Cathedral Church in "Haret al-Kanaies" (the Churches quarter), inside the old city of Haifa. Bishop Hajjar moved this school from the old city to the area of Allenby street, Ein Dor street, after the regional expansion of the Arab dwellings in Haifa in the 20's of the 20th century. This school was considered one of the most prestigious not only in Haifa, but also all over the area. It was one of the only schools in which the students completed their high school studies.[452]

3b) **"Al-Madrassa al-Uskufia al-Kathulikia fi al-Mahata"** ("the Catholic Episcopal School of Carmel Station"): elementary school, established in the neighborhood of Carmel Station. The teaching was in Arabic, and in addition, the students studied French and English. Priests and teachers from Haifa and Lebanon taught in this school.

3c) **"The Orthodox Elementary School"**: under the supervision of "the Orthodox Community Council of Haifa." Operated many years in Allenby street, was closed following the events of 1948. However, the same council reopened a secondary school in Haifa at the end of the 50's of the last century. This school is known for its achievements among the Arab society all over the country.

3d) **"The Maronite Elementary School"**: established beside the Maronite Church. The teaching was done in Arabic, and in addition French and English were studied. The staff of teachers included the local people and teachers from Lebanon.

C)   Monastery Schools:

1. **"Frere School"**: (The brothers): belonged to the French Jesuit Order. It was founded in 1884 on Jaffa Road. Arabs, Jews, and foreign students studied in this boys only school. The official language of teaching was French and in addition Arabic and English. The school was also a boarding school since a great number of students came from different places in Palestine and from the south of Lebanon. [453]

2. **"Sisters of Nazareth School"**: was founded in 1856 by "The Sisters of Nazareth Order" from France. The school was a girls only school. Its first location was near the Latin Church in the old city in the direction of Kingsway. After the openning of the Haifa port the school was transferred to its new buildings on 7 Abbas street.

3. **"The Selesian School"**: was located on King George road (Hameginim road today). Was a boys only vocational school. The official teaching language was Italian and in addition Arabic and English. The school was shut down during the Second World War after manifestations of support of Mussolini, the fascist ruler of Italy and his regime, an enemy of Britain who ruled Palestine at the time.[454]

4. **"Carmelite School for Girls"**: under the supervision of the Carmelite Sisters Order. Established at the beginning of the 20th century on the Italians street. The official teaching language was Italian and in addition Arabic and English. The school became a mixed one after the closing of "Frere School" at the beginning of the 60's.

5. **"Carmel Saint Joseph School"**: mixed school for boys and girls. The school was under the supervision of the Carmelite Sisters. Was located at the stone house at the entrance of the governmental hospital, and was closed down after the building

was sold to the hospital. The students were distributed between the rests of the schools in the city.

6. **"Saint Luke School"**: this school belonged to the Evangelist community. A vocational high school for boys, located near the priest's residence. As the number of students increased there was a need to move it to the Tirat al-Carmel area. The school continued to operate until 1948, when the IDF forces overtook it, today the building serves as a military convalescence house. Many students from Tirat al-Carmel village and from the small triangle villages (Ijzim, Jaba' and Ein Ghazal) used to go to that particular school because of its proximity to their villages.[455]

7. **"The English High School for Girls"**: was established on Shabatai Levi street (nowadays "The Haifa Museum"). Wealthy families sent their daughters to study in this school. The school was administered under the British education department's instructions, and according to British methods.

8. **"The Monastery and School of The Holy Heart"**: located on Allenby street. In the beginning it was an elementary school. Two secondary classes were added to it near the end of the British Mandate.[456]

The private schools were characterized by practically full autonomous educational management. The syllabus included a combination of the official programs of the mandatory educational system together with the syllabus of the monastery's origin country or order, which the school belonged to. There was very rough competition between the schools and particularly for the obtaining of the highest British matriculation certificates, which award a studies grant in England. The private schools were very positive towards the instruction of the Arab language. The schools and their managements were careful to appoint the best Arabic language and literature teachers. A great part of the Arabic language and other language teachers were from Lebanon, Egypt, France, and England.

The table summarizes the number of students in the different schools in Haifa in the school year 1942\ 1943:[457]

1. Male students in schools—4194
2. Female students in schools—2937
3. Boys in the education age 5-15 years in Haifa—7000
4. Girls in the education age 5-15 years in Haifa—6550
5. Percentage of boys in school of the boys population—60%
6. Percentage of girls in school of the girls population—40%

From the table we learn that a high percentage of the Arab children in Haifa attended school, the high percentage of girls should be especially mentioned.

The development of the different education systems in Haifa aided the advancement of many of the intellectual Arabs that were integrated in the government's administration local offices and institutions, in spite of the limitations due to a preference for Jews in the different levels of clerical work in the local and national administrative offices. The contribution of the schools made a stamp on the social and cultural fields and was reflected in the westernization of certain aspects of the Arab communities' lives that were influenced by different education trends.

Haifa: the Arab Palestinian press center

Haifa was a focus of activity to a great number of newspapers and journalists beginning from the end of the Ottoman era until the end of the British Mandate. A large part of the newspapers that were published in Haifa were sent to other cities of Palestine and to the Arab states.

During the Ottoman period, the Palestinian press presented national political approaches in a very restrained and careful way; however, following the First World War and consolidation of the British Mandate, the newspapers in Palestine obtained the freedom of expression and action among the Arabs.

The main roles the editors of the newspapers in Haifa took on themselves were presenting events, news, information, articles, and comments on the subjects of society and literature. But the development of interest in Zionism and the related occurrences in the struggle between the Zionist movement and the national Arab movement forced the majority of the newspapers to refer to it so intensely. The Arab Palestinian press was also aware of the wave of Zionist immigration, as a large part of the Jewish immigrants was directed to Haifa.

Without any professional training and early related knowledge of journalistic methods, the Palestinian press in Haifa made a very hard argument against Zionism and the Jews' takeover of the institutions in Haifa and the rest of the cities and the centers during the British Mandate. Some of the editors caused the leaders of the Palestinians to deal with Zionism and the British authorities by a long series of editorial and informative articles about the Zionist movement and its intentions.

The Palestinian press in Haifa did not limit its interest to the Arab matters only related to the question of Palestine, but they also dealt with the questions that concerned the Arab leaders in general, and particularly in the neighboring states.

The growth of the Arab population in Haifa and the increased number of the literate and free professionals on the one hand, and the growth of the Jewish population and the deepening of the gap between Arabs and Jews in Haifa on the other hand, presented difficult challenges for the newspapers and their editors. They were imposed to find a supply of accredited information on the events in the city and guiding the public to forms of reaction to the current news and subjects, such as the immigration of the Jews, the sale of land and the autonomy aspired by the Jewish settlements.

Below is a list of the newspapers and the magazines published in Haifa at the end of the Ottoman period and until the end of the British Mandate:

-     *Al-Nafae'es*: literature magazine, the editor in chief

Khalil Baydas. Was founded in 1908 as a weekly magazine and then issued twice a week from 1909. Baydas moved his offices to Jerusalem in 1911.

- *Jirab Al-Kurdi*: political satirical newspaper, founded in 1908. The editor: Mitri Halajj. Published once a week.
- *Al-Carmel*: a political, economic and social newspaper, founded in 1908. The editor and publisher was Naguieb Nassar. Published once a week, and twice a week from 1910. Was known as one of the most influential among the Palestinian newspapers. Nassar adopted a policy of unforgiving criticism of the Palestinian leadership when it dissociated itself from the national positions in which he believed. Nassar was nicknamed the "Sheik" of the Palestinian press. He was arrested several times by the authorities and his newspaper was closed for a few days when he crossed the lines according to British censorship. It continued to appear until April 1948, that is, up to Haifa's takeover by the Haganah forces. Subsequently Nassar transferred his office to Nazareth but he died before the Haganah took Nazareth.
- *Al-Nafeer*: general newspaper edited by Ilia Zakka, it was started in Jerusalem in 1908 and was transferred to Haifa by 1913. Published once a week. Zakka had good relations with Zionist activists, and there are claims that he received financial support from the Zionist movement to improve its image and to circulate Zionist ideas among the Arab population in Haifa and the other cities of Palestine.
- *Al-Hammara Al-Qahira*: political and satirical newspaper. The editors were Khalil Zaqout and Naguieb Janna. Was founded in 1911 and closed down after a short period.
- *Al-A'ssa Liman A'ssa*: political, literature and satirical newspaper. Was founded in 1912 and appeared once a week. The owners decided to stop its publishing

due to the high cost during the First World War. The newspaper was published again by 1920 until 1922 and edited by Ibrahim Adham.

- *Al Mahabba*: a weekly newspaper founded in Beirut as a magazine for the Orthodox Christian studies in 1899 and by 1912 moved to Haifa. The editor was Fadellallah Fares Abu Hallaqa. The newspaper was known for its policy to defend the rights of the Zionist settlement in Palestine.[458]

- *Al-Sa'eiqa*: politics and literature newspaper, the editor was Jamil Ramadan. Founded in 1912 and published once a week. Closed down after few months.[459]

- *Haifa*: laborers newspaper, founded in 1921 and published once a week. The editor was Ilia Zakka. Was dedicated to defend the rights of the Palestinian peasants. Printed in "Al-Nafeer" printing house in Haifa.

- *Al-Sallam*: Arab Jewish newspaper, the chief editor was Niseem Maloul. Founded in 1919 and published once a week. Dealt with social affairs, and introduced a pro-Zionist approach. The publishing of the newspaper ceased after the editor received a job in the Mandate government in Jerusalem.[460]

- *Zahrat Al-Jamil*: literature magazine, the editors were Jamil al-Bahri and his brother Hanna. Founded in 1921. The editor changed the name of the magazine to *Al-Zahra*.

- *Al-Zahra*: magazine of contemporary literature, drama, ethics, history, published twice a month. The chief was Jamil al-Bahri until he was murdered in September of 1930, and then his brother took over the editing of the magazine.

- *Al-Tabel*: political, social and satirical newspaper, the editor was Ibrahim Kraiem, was founded in 1921 and published once a week.

- *Al-Urdon*: official newspaper. Was founded in 1923 by

Khalil Nassar and Bassila Jadaa'; continued to operate until 1927. Nassar continued to publish the newspaper from Amman by himself.

- *Al-Yarmuk*: political newspaper, was founded in 1923 and published five times a week. The owner was Rashid al-Haj Ibrahim, and the chief editor was Kemal Fares. Later the ownership passed on to Ali Bashir and Subhi Fouad al-Raies and after a while to Aza Qassem.[461]

- *Al-Iqdam*: political newspaper was founded in 1926 and published once a week. Moved to Jaffa two years later. The editors were Yusef Salloum and Salim Hilu, the latter, from Lebanese origin, lived in Haifa. Closed at the end of 1937.[462]

- *Al-Zuhour*: literary magazine, the founder and chief editor was Jamil al-Bahri. Published twice a week. Different writers and authors supplied the magazine with diverse articles; among them was bishop Hajjar that made use of the magazine to propagate his opinions, and the Muslim researcher Abdulla Mukhlis who used to publish articles concerning the cooperation between Muslim and Christian intellectuals during the Middle Ages, in the main cities of Islam states. The magazine editor also attached booklets every now and than on different subjects, as a present to the readers. The editing passed on to Hanna al-Bahri, brother of Jamil, after the assassination of Jamil in 1930. The magazine continued to be published up to May 1931.[463]

- *Al-Nahda*: political newspaper, the editors Jad Suidan and Kaisar Abyad. The general editor was Wadia' Sanbar. Founded in May 1929 and published until April 1930.[464]

- *Al-Majala Al-Tijarrya*: the official newspaper of the commercial bureau in Haifa; was founded in 1925 and published once a month.

- *Nashrat Al-Ghourfa Al-Tijaria*: the editor was Fouad

Tabaa'; dealt with business and commercial issues and activities. Published once a month and later on once a week in two languages: Arabic and English. The first issue was published in March 1945.

- *Kashaf Al-Sahraa*: scouts newspaper, the editors were Atef Nurrallah and Mutlaq Abd al-Khaleq. Founded in 1931 and published once a month.

- *Al-Carmel Al-Jadeed*: a similar version of the *Al-Carmel* newspaper edited by Nagueib Nassar that he published after closing his famous newspaper.

- *Al-Bushra*: official newspaper of the Ahmadya community in Kababeer village near Haifa. The founders and editors were Attallah Al-Jalandahri and others from the community.[465]

- *Akher Sa'a*: daily newspaper that dealt with political and literature issues. The editors were Yusef A'zar Salloum and Anas Khamra. Was printed by the Haddad printing house at the entrance of Wadi Nisnas neighborhood. The issue date of the license is September 30th 1938.

- *Al-Samir*: political, economic, social newspaper, the editor was Muneer Haddad. Licensed in 1940 and was published only for several months. .

- *Al-Rabita*: The Greek Catholic official community magazine. Founded in Haifa by the bishop George Hakim the leader of this community. The date of the license is 17th January 1944. The magazine published the views of the bishop. Continued to operate up to the start of the 90's. The last editor was Father Nathaniel Shihada.

- *Al-Itihad*: the official Communist newspaper, the chief editor was Emil Gabriel Touma, founded in 1944. The newspaper was published once a week and after a long time became a daily newspaper. This is the only political newspaper that remained active after 1948.

- *Al-A'mel Al-Arabi*: this newspaper dealt with labor, social, economic, and political issues, was the official newspaper of the Arab Palestinians Labor association.

The editor was Dr. Omar Khalil and the first issue was published in December 1945.

- *Al-Mihmaz*: a social, economic, and political newspaper, published once a week. The editor was Muneer Haddad. The first issue was published in February 1946.

- *Al-Hares*: Muslim newspaper, published once a month. The chief editor was Sami Yusuf Abu Hammad. The first issue was published in June 1946.

- *Kaukab Al-Carmel*: a spiritual Christian, literature and culture newspaper. The editor was Father John Tonb, head of the Latin parish in Haifa. Published once a month in Arabic and French. The first issue was published in September 1946.

- *Akhbar Filasteen*: daily political, social, economic, and culture newspaper. The editor was Anas Khamra. It was printed by "Al-Nafeer" printing house. The first issue was published on April 6th, 1948 and continued until the fall of Haifa on the 22nd of April 1948.

- *The Palestine Daily Mail*: daily political and commercial newspaper. The editor was Muneer Haddad; the first issue was published on September 8th 1934.

- *Times of Palestine*: daily political newspaper, the editor was Muneer Haddad; the first issue was published in 1933. [466]

Sports and scouts activities

Most of the athletic activity and the scout's movement were connected to the schools or to religious associations that operated in the city during the British Mandate. There was a strong impact made by the British that created an athletic ambience among the Arabs in Haifa. The British—soldiers, administrators, and their families, held many sport activities and established sports club associations throughout the city. Several wealthy Arabs families integrated in the arrangement of the English sport activities that were going on in the city.

The athletic activity of the Jews was also noticed by the

Arabs, particularly the sportsmanship activities held by different sports organizations like Maccabi and Happoel.

Many of Haifa's Arabs visited the neighboring Arab states and observed different sports competitions, particularly football, which attracted thousands of people, and later on encouraged the establishment of various sports clubs. An additional source that contributed to the sports enthusiasm was the Haifa newspapers that took care of publishing sports news as part of the media rating.

As early as the 40's the sports clubs succeeded to move ahead to national competitions with other clubs from Jaffa and Jerusalem, and to win championships. The clubs and their teams attracted a great audience of activists and fans and became a part of the leisure culture of the local Arabs. It should be pointed out that many spectators in the competitions came especially from the Galilee villages and joined the fans.

The well-known clubs in Haifa that attracted players and fans were "Shabab al-Arab," "al-Tirsana," "al-Nadi Al-Riyadi al-Islami," "Huechemen," "Humentmen" (The last two belonged to the Armenian community in Haifa and they were members in the main clubs of the Armenians in Lebanon, and had members from the Arab community in Haifa). Also well known were the football teams of social clubs or Christian community clubs such as "The Catholic Club" and "The Orthodox Club." Almost all the football fields were concentrated in the "al-Mawares" area (neighborhood of Kiryat Eliezer today).

The football fields belonging to the clubs were arranged so that the first was east west of the Islamic club, after it was "Shabab al-Arab" and the last was "al-Tirsana." The clubs collected entrance fees from the spectators and the fans, to cover different expenses of the clubs' activities and the advancement of other sports branches. Almost all the competitions and the games took place on Sundays, as it was the official resting day in the city.

During the 40's, Haifa clubs played against Lebanese and

Syrian sports clubs. The last game was held in September 1947 between the "Shabab al-Arab" club and the Allepo (Syria) club group, which ended in a tie. The spectators come from Akko, Shefaram, Kefar Yasif, and other villages of the Galilee. The Allepo club team was known for its good players and the tie was enough for Haifa's fans to be proud of their football team. Several players of Haifa's sports clubs were included in the Palestinian National Team and participated in the matchs held in other Arab countries.

The clubs organized games against British clubs and teams during the Second World War, one well known game took place between the Haifa football team and the British coastguard team in the presence of the High Commissioner Alan Cunningham, and the outcome was the defeat of Haifa's football team, which could not win while playing against the experienced and skilled English team.[467]

Another kind of sport which attracted attention among the Arabs was wrestling. Adib Kamal, a wrestler and a referee established a wrestling club in the 30's in Haifa. One of the most well known competitions that took place during the British Mandate was between Sanharib Saliba from Haifa and Mardo, a champion of the Jerusalem clubs. The competition took place in the summer of 1945 in the "al-Tirsana" club yard. Thousands flocked to encourage the champion of Haifa. The newspapers published in Haifa promoted the marketing of the competition and contributed to the attraction of a large audience. Sanharib succeeded to rout his opponent and then began the celebrations in the streets of Haifa. Sanharib was later routed by Palestinian wrestling champion Adib Dasouki from Jaffa. Dasouki arrived for the competition in Haifa escorted by hundreds of his fans. However, in the second competition held between the two of them later, the result was a tie.

In basketball, the Selesian school club stood out the location of this club was in King George road. The coaches of the school sport club took care of introducing this branch of sport to the students and the school team. The managment established a club and called it "The Selesian Club." Italian coaches were invited by to train the members. The club reached high sports standard compared to other clubs and sports teams in the same branch.

Scouts movements activity among the Arabs in Haifa began immediately after the entry of the British forces to Palestine. The Catholic scout movement was the first one to be established among the Arabs in Haifa in 1923 and later among the Orthodox, Armenian, Maronite, and Muslim communities. At the same time, private scouts movements were also established in Haifa. The typical activities of the scouts focused on the organization of camps for the members, and different processions on Christian and Muslim holidays or on receptions for dignitaries like the great reception of Abdulla the Emir of Trans-Jordan in Haifa in 1946. The scouts participated in the big funerals in Haifa, such as King Faisal's funeral in September 1933 when his coffin was brought to Haifa from Switzerland. He received an official and public ceremony and from Haifa the coffin was flown to Baghdad; and the funeral of bishop Hajjar in October of 1940. These two funerals were attended by thousands from Haifa and the area.

The Arab scouts movements contributed to the deepening values of motherland love, national identification, and helping the needy people without prejudice of religion, nation, or race. Youth and scouts movements that were set up in Haifa and other cities in the country under the name "al-Najjada," held a variety of activities that combined scouts elements and politics. The movement also carried out military activities against the Zionists organizations during the 1948 events. It's headquarter in Halissa neighborhood (at the corner of Hagiborim street), was attacked by the Haganah forces between 21 and 22 April 1948, the battle was one of the hardest battles between the Arabs and the Jews in Haifa in 1948.

We should mention here that scouts began attracting girls only from the mid 40's because scouts were perceived as being for men only, and the activities required being outside the house for long periods of time. But this perception changed gradually due to impacts of the British and Jewish societies in the city.

Transformation in employment patterns: professionals and intellectuals.

The change of the Ottoman rule at the end of the First World War caused drastic changes in the occupation structure among the Arabs in Haifa. Groups of professionals that have acquired modern skills began to form, as did the intellectuals and people involved with social matters whose contribution was wide and branched inside their society in Haifa and in the national and Arab level as well. Three main factors contributed to these changes:

A) The new government caused changes in the perception of the Palestinian Arabs and their leaders. The British administrative proceedings were utterly different from that of the Ottomans, which the Palestinians were used to for four hundred years.

B) The Palestinian Arab society started a slow and gradual integration into the British Mandate system of jobs, such as the central government and the local government, all in very limited dimensions though.

C) The Jewish immigration from Europe to Palestine, increasing particularly after the rise of the Nazis in Germany, contributed to the reduction of the options for Arabs for integration in key jobs in British Mandate institutions in Haifa and the area. The British preferred for many reasons to employ Jews for key positions in the different government bureaus, as part of an implementation policy of the Mandate that was given by the League of Nations.

Facing the new situation created in Palestine following the new British Mandate government and the increase of the Jewish immigration waves, the Arabs in Haifa and the suburbs faced difficult political, economic, social, and cultural challenges. They managed their lives almost without any connection to the British authorities, which were authorized to qualify the country for independence for the sake of the welfare and the advancement of the citizens in Palestine.

The Palestinian Arab leaders and intellectuals quickly realized that the challenge of building an advanced society rested on their shoulders and consequently they began a process of establishing Arab institutions that provided essential services to the citizens of different fields of life. It should be noted that the Arab Palestinian community in Haifa was not prosperous and did not have a strong economic, administrative, and social background. This was a community that had just been released from a corrupted and crumbled Ottoman rule that provided only the lowest, most minimal services and facilities to finance its expenses. The Palestinian society in general and in Haifa in particular, suffered from poverty and difficulties at the end of Ottoman rule and during the First World War. As result of the previous situation, this society lacked supportive tools that would help building of social and economic arrangements. Facing such challenges, the Palestinian society in Haifa, some individuals, and small groups began to establish social, educational, and economic movements or committees that gradually integrated into the social life of Haifa's Palestinians.

During the Mandate period the Palestinian society was an independent society that built itself unaided, and tried to survive the opposing challenges it faced. The increase of the Arab population in Haifa caused a rise in demands for services in the various branches vital for the existence of the society.

There were many lawyers in Haifa; some of them became famous after winning complicated and critical cases. Some of them played an intensive role in the national Palestinian movement, such as Wadiea' al-Boustani, Mahmoud al-Madi, Yusef Sahioun, Anas Khamra, Ameen Jarjoura, Hanna Asfour, Abd al-Kareem al-Karmi, Hanna Nakarra, Sheik Mahmoud

Khatib, Sheik Abd al-Aziz Sibaai, Sheik Saeed (the last three were religious judges in The Muslim Courts).

Some of the Haifa's intellectuals contributed to the Palestinian cultural and literary movement and the Arab one in particular. Haifa played an important role in the developent of the press, as we mentioned before, as well as the literary, theatrical, and political activities. Many Intellectuals lived and took part in cultural, educational, social and political activities in Haifa.

Writers from Haifa published their work in Palestinian, Egyptian, and Lebanese newspapers and magazines. In the 20's and the 30's this was a miracle for a society in the making. Specified below are several names of these writers who published their works in Haifa during the British Mandate or after they left Haifa for the neighboring Arab states of Lebanon, Syria and Jordan.

Jamil al-Bahri (1895-1930) distinguished in varied cultural activities, such as editing newspapers and magazines, translating works from French and English to Arabic. The main translations were plays staged in schools at the beginning of the 20's, and after that, in Ein Dor and other theatres in Haifa.[468]

Hassan al-Buheiri (1921-1998) was born to a poor family in Haifa. He published poetry books (four books in the 40's) and continued his literary activity from Damascus after 1948. He took part in operations against British and Jewish targets during the events of 1948.

Khaled al-Hassan (1928-1995) born and educated in Haifa. He was one of the founders and leaders of Fateh and PLO.

Khayriea Kasmia (1936-) born in Haifa, a senior lecturer and researcher at Damascus University, she specializes in Arab and Islam studies.

Raji Habeeb Sahioun (1920-2004) the Sahioun family had properties in Haifa and the area. Several family members took part in the social and political life. Raji worked as a teacher in Haifa and Safad. He joined the Palestinian broadcast service and later the Jordanian. He took part in establishing the PLO when working together with Ahmed al-Shuqairy. He published many books; the last one was *Not to Forget*.

Abdulla Mukhlis (1878-1949) was born in Syria, moved to Haifa and in the last years of his life he lived in Jerusalem. He took a central part in the cultural and political activities in Haifa and the area. He wrote many articles and books about the history of Arabs and Islam. He was a member of the Arabic linguistic council in Damascus.[469]

Nabil Badran (1937-) researcher in education, his famous research: *Education and modernism in Arabic Palestinian society* was published by the Palestinian studies center in Beirut, 1968.

Najlaa' Nassour (1947-) born in Haifa, historian. Her most famous research was about "the disruption of Arab education due to the occupation in Palestine" (published in Beirut, 1971).

Nouh Ibrahim (1913-1938) poet and a folk story teller. He wrote and recorded national songs and was known for his battle against the British and the Jews. He associated with Sheik Izz al-din al-Qassam.

Wadiea' al-Bustani (1888-1954) a lawyer of Lebanese origins. Arrived in Haifa after the British occupation, he took part in different activities in Haifa and in the National Palestinian Movement; he participated in various conferences and committees and wrote articles and books in different historical and Arabic literature.

In the late stage of the Mandate, young writers began to publish political articles in the local newspapers, especially the official newspaper of the Communists *Al-Itihad*; the most distinguished were Emile Habibi, Emile Touma, and Boulos Farah, who had Communist views.[470]

In the health area, a few distinguished doctors contributed to the advancement of the health and medical practice in Haifa. The Arab doctors in Haifa established a medical association "al-Jameia al-Tibiya al-Arabia." Dr. Rashid al-Tamimi was elected head of this association. He was the chief doctor of the Islamic hospital in Haifa. Dr. Gabriel Abbyad was his deputy manager. A group of doctors from several medical expertises were also members:

Dr. Saad Musalam (internal medicine),

Dr. Emile Sabela (family doctor),

Dr. Clemanse Hindi (obstetrician),

Dr. Ibrahim Zourob (the municipality doctor),

Dr. Maurise Sahioun (cardiologist),

Dr. Nadim Khoury (the refineries doctor),

Dr. Outhman Khamra (internal medicine),

Dr. Naief Hamza (surgeon and the director of the government hospital in Haifa),

Dr. Johanes Tourban (forensic medicine director in the health department).

There were pharmacies in the different neighborhoods of the city, mainly in the downtown area near the doctor clinics, among them the pharmacies of Rashid Nassar, Salim Sahioun, Ibrahim Damian, Tanas Attalah, and Omar Abu Ghazala.

Some of the midwives in the city studied their occupation by heritage from their mothers, and only few of them studied formally, such as, Afifa Abu Ghazala (in the Christian quarter), Ifat Adham (al-Abassiya neighborhood), Majdiya Irani (Nazareth road), Waddad Habibi (Abbas street), Maryam Zureiq (the government hospital), Saniya and Muzayan Zifri (the eastern quarter), Fatima Makari (wadi al-Salib neighborhood).

The medical services were given privately to the people. There was no medical organization in the Arab sector as established by the Jewish sector in Haifa and in other parts of Palestine. The citizens received medical services privately by the doctors and the pharmacies. The midwives helped pregnant women give birth at home and in the 20's were established in the hospitals of the city, mainly the government hospital in Bat Galim, the Italian hospital, the German hospital and other small maternity hospitals. Some of Haifa's monasteries served medical aid and free emergency treatments for the needy people, like the Sisters of Nazareth Convent and the Holy Heart Monastery.

A few professional and qualified Arab architects found plenty of work in the developing construction and expansion of the neighborhoods in wide parts of the city. The municipality and the government initiated great projects in Haifa, but only few had been designed by Arabs. The Arab engineers designed houses and sumptuous buildings part of which still exist in the different areas of the city. The Arab Engineers of Haifa established their association named "Nikabat al-Muhandisin al-Arab fi Haifa" (Arab Engineering Association in Haifa), in 1934. The offices were at Miss Newton building in Stanton street. The Board members were Yusef Hazboun (chairman), Emile al-Boustani (secretary),[471] Tawfiq Menassa (treasurer), and Ahmad Fares, George Menassa, Francis Angel, Mansour Azzam, Adib Asaad (members).[472]

Personalities who held nationalist viewpoints stood out in the political field. While they were Haifa citizens they took part in forming Palestinian politics and shaping ideologies, since a great number of political events took place in Haifa. There were also influential people among the decision makers in different planes of the Zionist-Palestinian conflict. Among the prominent people were:

Rashid al-Haj Ibrahim (1888-1955): he was a businessman and statesman. One of the founders of the "Al-Istiqlal" party, the Islamic Association chairman in Haifa and member of the city council of Haifa and head of the "National Arab Committee" in Haifa during the events of 1948. Strongly opposed the British policy in Palestine. The British Mandate authorities arrested him, along with other nationalist opponents in 1937 and exiled them to Seychelles islands.

Sami Taha (1911-1947): one of the Arab Palestinian labor movement founders. Elected head of "Jameiat al-Umal al-Arabiya al-Filastinia" (The Arab Palestinian Labor Association). Taha represented the Arab laborers' interests, and succeeded in improving conditions for them. He did not hesitate to proclaim labor disputes and strikes in governmental factories such as the refineries in Haifa. He was a member of the Haifa city council. Taha was assassinated in the entrance to his home in September 1947, apparently by the orders of al-Mufti Haj Amin al-Husseini (The Mufti of Palestine). The assassination occurred due to a conflict of interests between Taha's and the Mufti's followers.[473]

Abd al-Rahman al-Haj (1870-1946): the mayor of Haifa (1923-1927). Prominent in the developing of a number of construction projects in the city.

The Sheik Izz al-Din al-Qassam was the preacher of Al-Istiqlal mosque in Haifa. He was born in Syria. He succeeded to change the policy of the Palestinian resistance movement against the Mandate authorities in the first half of the 30's, from a political battle to a military one. He proclaimed a battle without compromises against the British, and gathered Muslim activists from Haifa and Galilee and even from Jenin. The authorities declared him an outlaw and fought him and his men persistently until he was murdered by the British soldiers in Ya'bad forests near Jenin in 1935. Qassam quickly became a symbol for the Palestinian struggle against the British Mandate authorities, and beginning in the 90's, a symbol of the armed struggle by the Hammas movement against the IDF and the Israeli settlers in the Gaza strip and The West Bank.

Bishop Grigorios Hajjar (1875-1940): head of the Greek Melkite Catholic Church in Haifa and the Galilee. He supported a national political line and declared in several opportunities that he and his church oppose the partition of Palestine into two states. He was known for his spiritual and political speeches that emphasized the historical affiliation between the two components of the Arab nation "The Muslims and the Christians." His most famous speech in front of the "Peel Commission" in 1937 was very concrete and portrayed the dangers the Palestinians faced daily.[474]

Many personalties took part in the social and political activities in Haifa and in the national arena. They contributed to the establishment of an urban Palestinian society in Haifa, which was well on its way to develop a political ideology that was expected to lead to the founding of an independent Palestinian state or at least achieve Palestinian autonomy. There is no doubt that the national-political conflict between the Zionist movement and the national Palestinian movement left its mark on the lives of the Palestinian society in general and on the Arab Palestinians in Haifa, since Haifa became a significant attraction for the Zionist immigration since the 30's.

The events of 1948 happened so suddenly for the citizens of Haifa that it was not possible for them to continue the political effort together with other Palestinian forces. On the other hand, the heavy offence of the Haganah forces destroyed all the socio-economic leadership arrangements of the Arabs of Haifa. Groups of Haifa citizens were deported from the city or left their city to protect their lives and their children's life. In addition to that they were affected by rumors that were spread about the mass killing committed by the Haganah forces and the Irgun in Palestinian cities and villages in the Jerusalem's area (The massacre in Deir Yasin) and other places.

Changes in the construction of the social-cultural activity

The Palestinian Arab society in Haifa sharply shifted from the Ottoman period to the British Mandate on different planes, and when referring to the social-cultural activity we claim that the move placed it in the center of the activity, both on the local and national level. The community created a varied and vibrant action and set the stage for an increase in the organizations and unions dedicated to the improvement of the society culturally, educationally, and socially.

The Arab society in Haifa during the British Mandate period was characterized by a large number of unions, associations, clubs, theatres, cafés and movie theatres, which attracted a large and varied audience from Haifa and other places, especially cities and villages from the Galilee.[475]

Initially, the associations and unions had a social oriented character, but in the beginning of the 20's and especially after the declaration of the Mandate, some of the associations and unions started to deal with the major political issues.

The British Mandate government did not interfere in the life of the Palestinian Arab society at all. It established a small number of state schools and left the education in the hands of the church and private institutions that operated schools and education and culture institutions of their own simultaneously. The groups that had a part in providing education services for the Palestinian Arab society in Haifa and many other villages in Palestine were mostly schools and institutions that belonged to the churches and private unions.[476]

The lack of a massive presence, and even the indifference of the Mandate government in the matter of education, created a void, which the Christian, Muslim, and private organizations and institutes took care to occupy, maintaining multiple fields of activity (educational, financial, medical, political, sports...)

On the other hand, the Palestinian Arab society in Haifa faced the intensive activities of Jewish associations and organizations in Haifa, challenges that were not easy. The immigrant Jewish society had in general a progressive organizational background, while the Arab society of Haifa had to take care first of its subsistence needs, and only later move on to establish the different institutes, organizations, associations, and unions.

The associations and unions had to create a Palestinian Arab society in Haifa, with a strong sense of belonging to the place, to Palestine, and the Arab nation, in order to face the strengthening of the Zionist movement and its institutions in Palestine between two World Wars.

The welfare associations and organizations had to consolidate an established social-political perspective, but the path to fulfill it was interrupted in the midst due to the difficult events of 1948, which befell the Palestinian Arab society and divided it into many parts.

Below is a detailed list of organizations, associations, unions and clubs that operated in the Arab society mostly in Haifa, although communities outside of Haifa benefited from their services as well:

"Al-Jameia Al-Islamia" (The Muslim Union): established in 1919. Considered one of the oldest associations officially listed in the mandatory government offices in Haifa.[477] Founder of the union and director was the Sheik Muhammad Murad the Mufti of Haifa. The union offered help and assistance for those in need from the Muslim community in Haifa. It operated a school and a health clinic.[478]

"Al-Jameia Al-Masihiya" (The Christian Union): established by the end of the First World War. Its president was Fouad Sa'ad, one of the respected Christians in Palestine.[479]

"Jameiat Al-Shabiba al-Masihiya" (The Young Christians Union): began operating at the end of the Ottoman period under the name of "Jameiat Nahadat Fitian Al-Rom Al-Catholic" (The Greek Catholic Youth Revival Union). Its president was Adib Jedaa'. The main part of its activity was cultural matters[480] and it produced a number of plays performed in Haifa in front of large audiences.

"Jameiat Al-Saidat Al-Masihiya" (The Christian Women Union): established right after the First World War, dealt with issues of the Christian Arab Women's advancement through a variety of cultural and social activities.

"Jameiat Tahathib Al-Fatat Al-Islamia" (Educating the Muslim Girl Union): established in the 20's. Organized social parties for the Muslim holidays, and collected donations from the Muslims in Haifa and outside it, to help the needy.[481]

"Jameiat Al-Nahada Al-Iktisadiya" (The Economic Revival Union): its objective was to help promote the different economic fields. Among its members were lawyers, journalists, and authors. Naguieb Nassar, the editor of *Al-Carmel* newspaper, initiated the establishment of the union that received a license from the government. The opening party was held on March 16th, 1922, and the board of directors members were Naguieb Nassar, Wadiea' al-Bustani, Rev. Salah Saba, Muhammed Ali Bei al-Tamimi, Abdulla Mukhlis, Rushdie al-Shawa and Theopil

Boutagy. This union did the groundwork for the establishment of a professional union of the free-professionals, not only in Haifa but also outside it.[482]

"Jameiat Al-Nahda Al-Orthodoxia" (The Orthodox Revival Union): the union's members called for the independence of the Orthodox group from the burden of the Greek priesthood centered in Jerusalem. Its founders were influenced by the spirit of the Orthodox Arab movement that operated in Jerusalem for the same cause of abolishing the Greek priesthood. Among its members were Fouad Attallah, Elias Bahu and attorney Hanna Nakarra.

"Nadi Mowathafi Sikat Al-Hadid fi Haifa" (The Railway Clerks in Haifa Club): taking care of the social and cultural needs of the railway clerks.

"Jameiat Ta'awoun Al-Kura" (Village Assistance Union): established in 1924, in Haifa, its main objective was to improve the Palestinian farmers' state. The villages of the Haifa district benefited from its services. The union organized lectures on different subjects, especially on agriculture.

"Al-Nadi Al-Kathouliki" (The Catholic Club): established in July 1922 by the initiative of young Greek Catholics in Haifa.[483]

"Nadi Al-Shabab Al-Arabi" (The Young Arabs Club): was established at the end of 1936. Its founders were attorney Hanna Nakarra, Subhi Abd al-Khaleq, poet Mutlak Abd Al-Khaleq, author Borhan al-Din al-A'boushi, Khalil Eid and attorney Anas Al-Khamra. The club organized many educational, cultural, and political activities, also lectures and different symposiums. This activity concerned the authorities, which got a court order to close down the club during the Second World War as it was suspected of hostile activity.

"Jameiat Al-Shuban Al-Muslimin" (The Young Muslims Union): was established in Haifa in 1928 by Rashid al-Haj Ibrahim, was influenced by the unions of the "Youth Muslim movement" in Cairo after the establishment of the Muslim Brothers movement over there, also aimed against the increasing number of Christian unions in Haifa and other places, especially the fear of the missionaries of several Christian unions that operated in the city and were not Arab. This union established three branches in the Carmel triangle villages of Jabaa', Ijzim, and Ein Ghazal. It founded three committees: education for the illiterate, sports, and first aid committee.[484]

"Jameiat Al-Itihad Al-Nisa'ee" (The Feminine Unity Union): established in the 30's, "to teach illiterate girls and educate them in a way fit for modern life in society." This union established branches in different parts of the country.[485]

"Al-Jameia Al-Adabia Al-Ilmiya" (The Literature-Science Union): established in 1932. The objective was "to encourage science and literature activities and projects in Haifa."[486]

"Jameiat Tathkiff Al-Fata Al-Arabia" (Educating the Young Arab Girl Union): established in the 40's, the objective was to "raise the young Arab woman's position in society."[487]

"Jameiat Al-Takadum Lelsyrian" (Promoting the Syrian Ethnic Group Union) established in 1934. Its objective was to raise money for building a school and a church for the community, through a variety of activities.[488]

"Jameiat Al-Tulab Al-Arab" (The Arab Students' Union): established in 1945. Its objective was to assist students and promote studying among them.

"Nadi Al-IKha'a Al-Arabi" (The Arabic Brotherhood Club): established in 1945.

"Nadi Ansar Al-Fadila" (The Talisman Supporters Club): established in 1944. The club activities included lectures and publishing pamphlets in health and hygiene issues.[489]

"Nadi Al-Tamthil wal-Tahathib" (The Actors and Education Club): established in 1930 by Iskandar Ayoub Badran. His objective was to educate the young generation through theatre plays. His activity ceased for a certain period and continued by the initiative of Fouad Oweis in 1938.[490]

"Nadi Shabab Al-Arab" (The Young Arabs' Club): established in the 30's. One of the most famous sports clubs in Haifa and the North.

"Al Rabita Al-Adabiya fi Haifa" (The Literary Union in Haifa): established in 1928 and its occupation was organizing lectures and meetings related to literary issues.

There were many village and family unions in Haifa: "Jameiat Shabibat Kfar Bar'am" (Kfar Bar'am's Young People in Haifa association) established in 1939. "Nadi Shabibat Kfar Kana" (Kfar Kana's Young People Club) established in 1945. "Rabitat Al-Shabab al-Bourini" (Bourin's Young People movement) established in 1945. "Al-Jameia Al-Khairiya Al-Gaziya" (The Gaza People's Assistance in Haifa Association) established in 1934. "Jameiat Al-Nahada Al-Misriah" (The Egyptian Revival Association) established in 1946, offered assistance and services to the Egyptian community in Haifa, especially railway and the refinery clerks and workers in Haifa. "Jameiat Al-Maddy" (The Maddy Family of Ijzim Village Union) established in 1947. "Al-Nadi Al-Ayuni Al Khairy" (The Voluntry Ayuni Club) established in 1947 by the citizens of Haifa who were originally from Jish (Gush Halav- village in Upper Galilee). "Jameiat Al-Hashul" (Hashul Family Union) established in 1945 by the family members who were originally from Jish village. "Rabitat Al-Haddad" (Haddad Family Union) established in 1945 by the author and journalist Muneer Ibrahim Haddad who owned the "Haddad" printing house (located in Wadi Nisnas). The objective of this union was to bring together all Arab families by the name of Haddad regardless of any family relations.

The social-cultural activity among the Arab citizens of Haifa was characterized by a variety of fields brought to the public by the different clubs and unions in Haifa. There is no doubt that it set the grounds for a growth of theatrical activity which provided different plays for the city's people and other groups outside the city.

The theatrical activity during the Ottoman period was held only on school grounds, especially in the private schools. Outside the schools this activity was done by the storyteller. The storyteller phenomenon ("Hakawati" in Arabic) continued to exist in Haifa until the 20's, when a few movie theatres, which included a stage for plays, were built, such as "Ein Dor" theatre.

The Hakawati knew dozens of stories by heart. He walked around the cafés about the city, and when the place was full he would begin with a song. Later he would tell the stories, and they warmed at times the atmosphere among those present. The stories he read to the public were old folk tales, part of them taken from Arab literature from the Jahalic period (before the Islam). Several of the Hakawati storytellers would walk around the neighborhoods and gather an audience, tell stories, and receive mere mils for it. Sometimes they received payment in different forms such as food or clothing.[491] The Marionette Theatre was common in Haifa and the other cities of Palestine. The theatre actors came from "Bilad al-Sham" (Syrian cities) and preformed all over the city for several mils or bottles of oil and wheat.

A different theatrical phenomenon that was common during the Ottoman period and which lasted until the 30's was the "Miracle Box" (Sanduk al-A'jab). The person carrying it would hang around the city's neighborhoods and called the kids and adults to come and, for very little money, see pictures through a small hole on the back of the box after covering their heads with the cloth attached to the box.

The theatre, as it operated in the West, began to produce plays in Haifa in the 20's. Jamil el-Bahri was among the first pioneers of this field. Being a journalist and an author he supplied his readers a great deal of material performed in the city. His first story *Qatel Akhihi* (His Brother's Murderer) that was published in 1919 was played in the 20's dozens of times in Haifa and in other cities of Palestine, Syria, and Lebanon. With the beginning of the British Mandate, theatrical activity came to life mostly in Haifa. Writers like Al-Bahri and others provided literature-theatre material in a way that suited the Arab society. A big part of the plays were translations of plays and stories written in different languages, especially English and French.

The contribution of the private schools was important for the promotion and development of the theatre movement in Haifa; the first plays were performed by school students in front of their parents.

Haifa's theatre quickly broke loose from the world of schools and the restraints it naturally had, after the move to the large cafés in the city that allowed performances of the different plays in the nearby gardens, such as Al-Balad café and Al-Enshirah garden.

The end of the 20's and beginning of the 30's witnessed the building of movie theatres and theatres like the ones in Ein Dor, Armon and "The Arab Theatre." As soon as the building was done, groups of actors and choirs began to flow towards Haifa and present their plays to a very large audience from Haifa and the area. Al-Ajwaq Al-Thalatha (The Three Choirs) band, lead by the greatest Arab actor in Egypt, George Abyad, came to Haifa to perform plays. The Egyptian Ramsis band, led by Yusef Wahbi, came and preformed plays like *The Confession Throne, Rasputin*, and *The Slavery* before a large audience. *Al-Nafeer* newspaper constantly emphasized Haifa Theatre Union's activity to promote and deepen the theatre culture among the Arab inhabitants in Haifa and the area.

After the series of success that was achieved by the Haifa Theatre Union, other groups belonging to social-cultural clubs in Haifa began to put on plays of their own or to bring over groups from neighboring countries. The Islamic Union in Haifa put on a play called *Fahed Trabulsi* on "Zahrat al-Shark" (Rose of the East) theatre stage. The Selesian Club put on two plays: *Kisra Wal-A'rab* (Persia Ruler and the Arabs) and *Intikam Kahen* (Reverend Revenge). Other clubs joined this activity, such as the Islam Sports Club in Haifa performed its play *Matamea' al-Nissaa* (Lust of Women) and *al-Assud wal-Na'aman* (The Lions and the Na'aman) by actors from Haifa's scouts.[492]

The biggest and most professional actors group was "Al-Carmel Group" led by the greatest actor in Haifa's theatre and in Palestine, Iskandar Ayoub Badran. They successfully performed Shakespeare's *Hamlet* in front of a huge audience. Women and girls from his group share some of the parts, like Assmaa Khoury and Thouraya Ayoub Badran (Iskandar's daughter).

Iskandar Badran opened a professional theatre according to the convention of those days. He had firm connections with the greatest actors in Egypt and Syria, invited most of the groups from Egypt to perform to Haifa's audience. He joined Yusef Wahbi's plays with a few chosen actors from his group; small part actors or they were brought for adjusting the play to the location in which it was put on. That means that the Egyptian groups did not arrive with a full cast, and there was a need for a certain amount of actors so Badran provided a few replacements. A number of violinists and other musicians participated in the plays.

Great and famous singers arrived in Haifa from Egypt and Lebanon, such as Farid Al-Atrash and his sister Asmahan and their bands. Umm Kulthum came from Egypt and her songs were played in al-Inshirah and Karakin garden.[493] Dabkeh and dancing groups participated in folk dancing festivals organized in Haifa. The theatrical activity brought to the growth of different groups and bands among the Arab public in Haifa, which perceived this field as a layer of building the culture and entertainment life it lacked, and were not given by the Mandate rule whose main activities were administrative.

Alongside the branched theatrical activity, a number of movie theatres were established all over the city by Jewish and Arab entrepreneurs, together and also separatly. At first they screened silent films and later on dubbed movies in different languages, mostly English and Arab.

A number of private schools screened movies to their students, in the language spoken at the school, such as the Selesian School in which the language spoken was Italian. Movies in Italian were shown, most of them propaganda movies made by the fascist party led by Mussolini (as was mentioned above, this school closed down at the beginning of the Second World War by the British in suspicion of hostile activity).

Almost all the movies produced in Egypt were presented immediately in Haifa on the large movie screens in the city's theatres. Movies of the greatest actors such as Yusef Wahbi, who transferred from the theatre to the movies; other movies were starred by Farid Al-Atrash which included a large collection of his and his sister Assmahan's songs and other large bands were shown. Other Arab actors who starred in the movies were Anwar Wajdi, Ismail Yassin, Abd Al-Salam al-Nabulssi, Nagueib al-Reihani, Madiha Kamel, and Bishara Wakim. Lila Murad, an Egyptian singer and actress from a Jewish family was loved by the audience in Haifa. She played alongside Anwar Wajdi and sang beautiful songs that are still sung in family events.[494] The audience included Arab and Jewish inhabitants of Haifa and a considerable number of Arabs who came to the movie theatres in Haifa very early in the day of the play to secure a seat.

The complex cultural, educational and commercial activity in Haifa created a large consumption of paper, and so a number of printing houses providing services in the book, newspaper, and commercial fields were established. Below is a list of Arab printing houses in Haifa:[495]

"Akher Sa'a" (The Last Hour), owned by Yusef Azar Salum. Located on Allenby Street.

"The Ahmedian Group" printing house in Kababeer. Provided printing services mainly to the ethnic group's members.

"Al-Matba'a Al-Tijariya Al-Ahliya" (Private Commercial Printing House), owned by Sheik Taher Farhan and the folk poet Nouh Ibrahim. Located near Al-Istiklal mosque.

"Matba'at Al-Taqadum" (The Development Printing House) owned by Fouad Salam, on Iraq street (Kibbutz Galuiot today).

"Matba'at Haddad" (Haddad Printing House), owned by the writer and journalist Muneer Haddad. The printing house was first built on Allenby street and moved to The Wadi street.

"Matba'at Dar Al-Tiba'a walnasher al-Filistinia" (Palestinian Printing House and Publishing), established by Mahmud Yusef Issa, located on Nazareth street.[496]

"Matba'at Al-Zaituni" (Al-Zaituni Printing House), operated in the 30's.

"Matba'at Kashaf Al-Sahra" (The Desert Discoverer Printing House), established by Yunis Mahmud Al-nafa, located on the Railway street.

"Matba'at Al-Najah" (The Success Printing House), was established by Adib Al-Hijawi, next to Haifa's Saraya.

"Matba'at Al-Nafeer" (Al-Nafeer Printing House), established by Suheil and Zaki Zaka, received a license in 1933.

"Al Matba'a Al-Watania" (The National Printing House), established by the author and journalist Adib Jeda'a. This is the oldest printing house in Haifa, built in 1908. Its contribution is apparent mainly in the start of the newspaper publication in Haifa and of books which were translated to Arabic mostly by Al-Bahri. This printing house provided wide services to all-Arab population in Haifa and the North.

"Al-Maktaba walmatba'a Al-Arabia" (The Arab Library and Printing House) was owned by Sheik Muhammad Nimer Khatib, located on Stanton street, was licensed in 1947.

"Matba'at Ahmad Menimni" (The Ahmed Menimni Printing House) was on the Mahata (station) street.[497]

We can sum up by stating the fact that the Palestinian Arab society in Haifa was dynamic and highly mobile. This society succeeded in adopting forms and components of the modern western society. Undoubtedly, the Arab society faced different and difficult challenges in the culture and entertainment fields also. On the one hand, it was a growing society, demographically speaking, and it needed cultural services, and on the other hand, it had to deal with the social and economic Jewish development which deepened its roots of activity in Haifa. The Arab society quickly realized the responsibility it had to bridge the social gaps between themselves and the Jewish population, which was mostly composed of immigrants. So the focus was put on developing different culture and education directions that would lift the Arab society a level up and help it progress and not be left behind.

That is why the various culture activities held in the society and were connected to the centers of the Arab cultural activity, places like Cairo, Damascus and Beirut pointed to the strong connection among the Arabs in Haifa and the rest of Eretz-Israel to the general Arab culture.

The development of the Arab laborers' movement

The change of rule in Palestine in 1918 brought extreme economic changes for the Palestinian population. The construction under the Turkish rule was classic, crumbling, and based mainly on manual labor, without any industrial network in the full sense. The British began to initiate industrial projects in different areas of the country, especially in Haifa's area, which seemed like a future center of all industry and economic activity.

In light of the growing demand for workforce in industry and the services related to it, hundreds of Arab laborers from the Galilee area and the rest of Palestine began flowing to Haifa as early as the late 20's; later, there were thousands who constituted a workforce in the big and important projects of the heavy industry initiated by the Mandate government and private entrepreneurs.

The British foresaw Haifa's future from the beginning as a major center for the British army's forces in the Mediterranean and it was required to establish the management and the industry that would partly assist these forces.

During the 20's, factors of the Zionist movement and the Hebrew laborers in Palestine union, which established a power center for its activity in Haifa, played an active role. The Jews participated in most of the economic and industrial projects in Haifa; the concession for manufacturing electricity and providing it as a monopolistic corporation was given to Pinhas Rutenberg. The key roles in the government economic offices were given to Jews. The jobs that were basically related services, not involved with decision-making, were given to Arabs from Haifa or from other places in the country.

The reluctance to appoint Arabs for key roles or central jobs caused a lower income rate than that of the Jews. This affected the standard of living and contributed with time to widening the economic gap between the two populations living in the same city. The income gaps would exist for years and all attempts to bridge them would not bear fruits. The Arab laborers in Haifa worked in almost all types of jobs open to them, in order to provide living for their families, whether in Haifa or in the villages they came from.

One of the railway clerks named Abd al-Hamid Haimor, of Syrian origin, wanted to establish a union that would take care of the railway laborers and clerks in the beginning of the 20's, but without proper legislation he could not realize his plans. He and a few others decided to establish a club for the railway workers and listed it in 1923 under the name of "Nadi Umal Sikat Al-Hadid Al-Arab" (The Arab Railway Laborers' Club). Many of the laborers in the railway and different occupations joined the club. The Jewish union's management perceived this act as a threat to its existence and announced its willingness to fire Arab laborers employed in the construction and paving branches with the aim of influencing the club mentioned above and remaining the dominant force controlling the occupation resources.

As a response to the union's steps, the club's board members decided to establish the "Al-Lajna Al-Akhawia la-Umal Sikat Al-Hadid" (The Railway Laborers Brothers Committee), in order to support anyone who was dismissed. The heads of the club met with Sheik Izz al-Din al-Qassam in Al-Istiqlal Mosque in Haifa and told him about all the problems the laborers faced and the circumstances of their employment and approved his advice to establish a trade union that would be on the same level as that of the Jewish union and represent the interests of the laborers belonging to all branches of employment. Haimor applied for a license for establishing and operating a workers' union and received it at the end of 1923, under the name of "Jameiat Al-Umal Al-Arabia Al-Filastinia bi-Haifa" (The Palestinian Arab Laborers Union in Haifa). Haimor received officially the license from the authorities on March 21st 1925. He declared this date as Laborers' Day. The union established branches in almost all of the big cities and some of the Palestinian Arab villages.

The Palestinian Laborers' Movement went through three main stages that formed its identity, image, and influence on the workforce and the political issues of the time. The first stage was between the years 1925-1935 (the year that Sheik Izz al-Din al-Qassam was murdered by the British). This time period was characterized by the building and establishing the laborers' movement. The concern was to improve the worker's status by raising his salary and minimizing the working hours and ensuring some of the social conditions he deserved. At this stage, small unions were established for some of the occupation branches such as cigarette company workers' union in Haifa (Kraman, Dick and Salti and company—Dubek today). Bakery Workers union, Truck Drivers union, Municipality workers' union, etc...

One of the prominent figures in the laborers movement was Sami Taha who was appointed coordinator by the Palestinian Arab Laborers' union, between the trade unions and the different employers. He also took care of the widening circle of the union members. The union succeeded in announcing a series of big strikes in 1931 and 1932 demanding a raise in the workers' salary and avoiding firing Arab workers. The strikes were also against the Arab employers who fired Arab workers. The most important strike during that period was organized in the Iraqi Petrol Company (I.P.C.) and broke out in February 1935. This strike lasted ten days and caused great damages for the petrol company and for other companies and sectors dependant on it. This stage ended in the murder of Sheik Qassam and the announcement of the Arab mutiny in response.

The second stage was between 1936 and 1939 and was characterized by the big strike and a series of actions against the British government in response to its lenient policy towards the immigration and the Jewish settlement, according to the Arabs' claim. Almost all work factors among the Palestinians took part in the strike and declared a mutiny against the British authorities as response for supporting the Jewish settlement and neglecting the Arab population throughout the years.[498]

The third stage was between 1940 and 1948. That was the golden period of the union, and a very strong recovering period for different industry and occupation branches in Palestine and particularly in Haifa. The British government decided that Haifa would be one of the main logistic and supply centers of its forces. This decision caused an increase in the workforce and attracted ten thousands workers to the British military facilities and the related services providing vital products to the British and Allied armies participating in military activities in North Africa and the East basin of the Mediterranean.

In spite of the increasing job opportunities in Haifa and the area, after the Second World War, the Zionist union and Zionist groups began establishing factories that provided the British army's needs with the aim of making profits and taking over the job-market, that attracted mostly Arab workforce. As a response the Arab laborers union decided to concentrate its powers in widening the professional unions' circle by letting other sectors in. The focus was on adding workers who were employed in factories and companies that provided different services for the British military forces and the Allies armies. "The British Military Camp Workers' Union" was established, approximately 28,000 of its workers registered as members in the union.[499]

Later on, unions such as "Public Works Department," "The Telegraph, Post and Telephone Workers' Union," "Haifa Harbor Workers' Union," "Haifa's Refinery Workers' Union," "British Spinney's Company Workers' Union" (the British company that provided different merchandise to the British army in Palestine and in Trans-Jordan) were established. The union's leadership saw a need in deepening the awareness of the laborers by turning them into an influence and pressure group on the Mandatory government in order to actualize vital achievements that would improve the status and life of the Arab worker in Eretz-Israel. The leaders of the union believed the most efficient way was announcing a series of strikes in many branches vital to the everyday activity of the government, especially those related to the British army.

The famous strikes: Haifa's municipality workers' strike after the mayor Shabtai Levi decided to reduce 30% of their salaries and fire hundreds. The British military camp workers' strike, British Spinney's workers' strike, Haifa's harbor workers' strike, refineries workers' strike, and other strikes of different sectors which sometimes helped raise the salaries and also improve the conditions of employment offered by the government or private companies.

The unions' leaders quickly realized there was an immediate need to provide guidance and direction to its members who were operating within the rights anchored in the different labor laws in Palestine. In addition, the leaders began to establish different associations and groups that would assist the laborers in improving their financial situation and offer financial support for building independent industrial projects of Arab laborer groups or entrepreneurs. The union opened a special employment office in 1944 as the public and military-related jobs began to narrow down and thousands of workers were unemployed. That is when the union came into action, by making lists of the unemployed and their qualifications, passing them on to factory owners and Arab contractors in order that they would hire them. The union promised minimal wages for the workers who became members, after the wave of dismissals when the Second World War ended.

The international organization of laborers decided to recognize the union as an official group representing the Arab laborers in Palestine. Sami Taha, the secretary general of the union, was invited to participate in the world convention of the organization in London in 1945. Hanna Asfour, the union's legal consultant, accompanied him.

At the same time, a group of young Communists went against the union and began attracting the attention of a large part of the working public, aiming to elect a new leadership for the workers based on the doctrines of Marx and Lenin. This group called itself "Usbat Al-Tahrur Al-Watni" (The National Liberation Group). The battle between them and the Palestinian Arab Laborers' Union proliferated; central branches from Jerusalem, Nazareth, Gaza, and Jaffa left the union and joined the Communists. These branches were called "Mou'tamar Al-Umal Al-Arab" (The Arab Laborers' Congress).[500] Three delegations participated in the international laborers' convention: the Hebrew Laborers' Union, the Palestinian Arab Laborers' Union and the Arab Workers' Congress.

In spite of the division in the Palestinian Laborers' movement, the Palestinian Arab Laborers' Union maintained its position and continued leading the work force in the social and economic systems in Haifa and other areas of Palestine where it did not have representation.

In light of the union's success in protecting the workers and standing up to the pressures of the Communist opposition, the latter saw that their efforts to create a rift did not go well, and so they blamed the members of "The Arab Workers' Congress." In addition to that, deep cracks were created in the Communists' structure due to the support of big layers of Arab members, as did Jewish members, in the United Nations partition resolution in 1947.[501]

The secretary-general Sami Taha and his associates in the union continued in their roles despite the division and cracks that occured in the General Palestinian Laborers' Movement, until Taha was murdered in September 1947, as mentioned above, by the Mufti Haj Amin al Husseini's messengers, as the Mufti objected to some of Taha's political moves, including a series of meetings he held with the Hebrew Laborers Union's leaders.

Immediately after the murder of Taha and following the resolution of Palestine's partition, the country faced turmoil and violent events erupted between different Jewish military organizations (Haganah, Irgun and the Stern group) and the Palestinian forces. After the Palestinian forces lost and the declaration of the state of Israel was made, the Arab states' armies joined the battle and so began a difficult war between Israel and the Arabs. In this war also, the Arab states' armies suffered defeat. The Palestinian population had to deal with great damage to their infrastructure, and worst of all, thousands were driven out of their homes by the Jewish military organization forces and later on by IDF.

The Palestinian Laborers' Movement suffered a complete devastation by these difficult events. Especially after its leaders were banished and relocated in different neighboring countries. Several of the union's leaders who moved to Jordan decided to continue the union's activities from the West Bank areas.

We should mention that in addition to the laborers' union and the professional unions, commerce bureaus were established in the main cities of the country and were recognized by the Mandate authorities. These bureaus represented their members in front of the mandatory government in matters of economy and for receiving assistance from the government offices in establishing certain projects. Haifa's commerce bureau was established in 1920. Towards the end of the 30's, Mikhail Touma was president, Rashid al-Haj Ibrahim was vice-president, Shafiq Sarakbi was treasurer, and the members were: Tawfiq Majdalani, Aziz Mikati, Kaisar Abyad, Taher Kraman, Shukri Saba, Salim al-Fityani, George Tawill, Anis al-Khoury, Elias Haddad and Tawfiq Zeibaq (secretary). The last president of the office was Kamal Abd al-Rahman.

The Palestinian Laborers' Movement succeeded in raising the issues of the laborers' rights in the country and outside it. It was also an influential force on the economic life in Haifa and the country. This was evident mostly in the series of strikes that it announced and in the hidden battles between its leadership and the Mufti al-Husseini and his followers. The Mufti viewed the movement and its secretary-general Sami Taha as a competition in organizing the laborers and influence in the country. There is no doubt that Taha's status as leader of the workers in Palestine strengthened due to the union's success in the battle against the Mandate authority and its activities for the workers. The leaders of the union managed to stand against the power of the Hebrew Laborers' Union (Histadrut) and even to have advantages over it.

Arab neighborhood development

The life of the Arab society in New Haifa (Haifa al-Jadida) that Dahar al-Omar built in 1761 surrounded by walls (built in order to protect the city, as was customary in Levantine cities), defined and shaped different forms of social-economic and cultural patterns. The Arab society lived in defined quarters within the walls of Haifa: the Muslim quarter in the eastern part of the city where the mosques and the education and social institutions were concentrated, and the Christian quarter in the western part of the city, where the churches and education and social institutions were concentrated. These were two separate and independent service systems; but the geographical division did not prevent cooperation between the two populations in the economy, social and politics fields. The ethnic key is the one that determined Haifa's social life basically until the end of the 19th century.

During the second half of the 19th century many families began to exit the walls in two directions: the first was east (Ard al-Yahud, Ard al-Blan, and Halissa neighborhoods), the second was west (Wadi Nisnas, Abbas, Zaitoun-Allenby, Wadi al-Jimal-Ein Hayam.) The main reasons for stepping out of the wall limits were the growing crowdedness; the lack of solutions, especially by the Ottoman rule, the inhabitants began building their houses in the areas near the walls so as not to distance themselves from the economic, social, and ethnic centers.

The expansion of the building in the areas mentioned caused a transfer of a considerable part of the living needs and so the city within the walls began crumbling. Stepping outside the walls contributed to expanding Haifa's urban space already at the end of the Ottoman Empire. It also inspired the inhabitants and the immigrants to help build a city different from the old one.

The city inside the walls provided most of the social and economic needs of the inhabitants until 1948. The location of the central market (between Zim building and al-Jerina Mosque) remained a force of attraction for new and old inhabitants who visited it to buy food and imported products from Lebanon, Syria, Iraq, Egypt, and different European countries. This is a completely typical Levantine market. In the areas between the western part of the city right after Jaffa gate (by Khamra square-Paris square of today) and the fringes of Al-Istiqlal Mosque in the east, markets were extended in the curved alleys of the city within the walls, where different products were stacked as well as local and imported merchandise that can supply all kinds of demands. The alley markets (Suq al-Shewam-the Syrian Market, Suq al-Abyad-the White Market) were lively and crowded all days of the week.

In spite of the city's expansion and the establishment of the commerce houses in the new parts outside the boundaries of the walls, most of the Arab inhabitants remained loyal to the classic areas inside the city, surrounded by the walls. The walls began to disappear from the city's scenery in the 20's, until nothing was left of it, after the 1948 events.

Building new neighborhoods outside the walls changed the city structure in the economic, social, and functional features, some of which maintained a unique ethnic character such as the Muslim neighborhood of Halissa; Wadi Nisnas that was a Christian neighborhood until the beginning of the 30's when Muslim families began buying or renting houses there, or certain areas in neighborhoods that became mixed Christian-Muslim.[502] This new trend of creating mixed Christian-Muslim neighborhoods got stronger during the Mandate period in light of the circumstances of the Jewish-Arab conflict on Palestine, and the basic necessity of close cooperation between all layers of the Arab population in Haifa, in its two components— Muslim and Christian. In addition to that, winds of the national Arab movement in general and Palestinian especially, were blowing strong and cast their shadows over the character of cooperation.

The building momentum in the neighborhoods outside the walls or the areas near them accelerated mainly in the 30's, with the establishment of big factories and new investments that were set off by the Mandate government and private entrepreneurs, a considerable part of which were Jewish. The British were an important factor in the economic development of the city in that period. The economic enterprises accelerated in a non-direct way the processes of building big and wide buildings in the Arab neighborhoods in Haifa. Their aim was to provide dwelling to hundreds of families who transferred from the nearby villages or the Galilee villages and even from south of Lebanon villages to work in those factories and provide livelihood for their family. The house owners were either among the city's richest people or came from Lebanon and Syria to invest in projects that would advance their business further, especially those related to housing and commerce in the different parts of the city.

The Jewish immigration to Haifa in the 30's was one of the driving factors in developing the building of the flat areas of Haifa and some of the western and eastern slopes of the Carmel range.[503] However, the form in which the Arab neighborhoods expanded along the coastline with a climb on some of Carmel's slopes was very natural, seeing that the society did not distance itself sharply from the city's center. The distancing was gradual and slow.[504]

In conclusion, there is no doubt that Haifa's Arab society was aware of the functional changes that affected the urban and the demographic structure. A deeper examination shows that this society was present in all the political, economic, social, and cultural events. However, making the decisions without an Arab authority or at least a concerned Arab leadership brought the rise of private interests that supported the development progress that matched their economic and status needs.[505]

The Jews' influence in the city was intensive and came to clear expression in their takeover of the municipality and the economic and neighborhoods power centers, beginning in the 40's. This process caused a weakening in the Arabs' ability to make crucial and future decisions having to do with Haifa. That is why the Arab society decreased its participation in the events in Haifa and was engrossed in its own matters only.

Epilogue

Coexistence-History, Myth, and Hope for the Future?

Life in Mandatory Haifa was multi-faceted and fascinating; there were daily contacts between populations mostly in the economic field, as the political order, especially in the municipality, was forced from above by the British rule. There was a conflict on different levels between political institutions that represented two populations that did not have shared values in many issues and was separate, even if not totally, in society and in education.

In the Arab context, the political system in Haifa was an integral part of the national system but also had special elements. Haifa was included in the political struggle but was not part of the national loyalty networks built as political coalitions between families; being a young city it was not under the influence of major old families. There was a constant need for practical considerations that did not necessarily go hand in hand with the temperamental politics of the 30's and 40's. The Arab leadership in Haifa was accused of being too restrained, as the national leadership, for instance, forced the strike in the harbor on them by murder threats.[506]

In the civil society there were dual elements in the economic and urban fields and among the government employees; in social life a division prevailed, but many personal friendships existed as well. Voluntary organizations were separate, except for international institutions such as the Rotary and the Free

Masons. In the Free Mason's Carmel chamber, for instance, the activity went on until the end of the Mandate. The members were mostly Protestants and with them a few Greek Orthodox and Muslims, Rashid el Haj' Ibrahim and Haifa's District Commissioner Simms were among them.[507]

Companies and firms belonged mostly to one nationality but there were also dozens of partnerships in different branches. The social relations were narrowed very much down to contacts made at work.[508] The British managed mostly flexible and complex policy of balance in Haifa. At times the shared Jewish and Arab institutions like the municipality run the city by mediating between separate national institutions.

Haifa was different from any other area in the country in all aspects of civil society, but not in terms of political relations. Its economic structure and the government sector centrality did not allow a separate existence of the two civil societies. The British viewed basic strategic, transport and economic interests in the center of the mandatory policy in Haifa and not the relations of Jews and Arabs. A permanent severity of the contradictions, as opposed to a sporadic tilt this way or the other would have hurt the British interests.[509]

The relations between Arabs and Jews in the civil society of Haifa were multi-faceted; in commerce relations there was much importance to personal trust. Vashitz also notes that Haifa's Jewish and Arab veterans emphasized that the quality of the relationship with a business partner determined usually more than his nationality.[510] Haifa attracted people because of its lovely scenery and its progress opportunities, while they came to terms with the mixed reality of the city. Representatives of the Jewish public usually aspired to avoid political polemics and focus on the everyday problems.

The Jews who settled in Haifa were mostly secular, and did not feel the need to build a separate national Jewish city, as did those who chose to settle in Tel Aviv. Haifa's labor council, lead by Aba Hushi, perceived the mixed city as an important tool for development and opposed the idea of a separate Jewish bay city.

Moshe Smilansky analyzed the essence of this difference, speaking in the meeting of the investigation board held by the Jewish Agency in 1940 to examine Jewish-Arab relations:

.... (In the riots) Haifa suffered relatively less than Tel Aviv, since the riot disaster was caused by Tel Aviv, by the Tel Aviv psychology, the psychology to isolate itself, the psychology not to see the Arabs, not to see the reality in the country. If the system of a mixed settlement prevailed in all parts of the country we would have been better off financially, politically, in terms of the relation with the Arabs.[511]

To sum up, the objective factors that encouraged the relations and the cooperation were:

1. Shared economic interests.
2. Population structure—considering that the majority of the inhabitants were flexible, with cosmopolitan attitude. The special contribution of the Sepharadic Jews who knew the language and habits of the Arabs, and the cosmopolitan character of the city.
3. City structure—the harbor and the commerce center were all situated downtown in one center, many neighborhoods were mixed and shared workplaces also created ongoing contact.
4. Haifa was a new city and most of its inhabitants, Jews and Arabs, were absorbed into it due to the development of the harbor and the city.
5. The city was distant from the center of national politics in Jerusalem.
6. The development of the balance of power: at first the Jewish sector was weak and had to be considerate of the Arab sector. Later on there was sense of equality in the municipality.[512]

In terms of the Zionist effort of "nation building," Haifa was not a province: about 20% of the Jewish investments in the 30's were made in Haifa. The harbor, oil refineries, and concentration of industry—all contributed to its unusual importance for the Jewish settlement leaders.[513]

The Jewish development brought prosperity to the landowners, house owners, and merchants. The Arabs had land and the Jews had capital and knowledge. This also had affect on the quality of the Arabs' lives; the percentage of Arabs paying city taxes and thus entitled to vote in the municipal elections was the highest in the country, compared to the Arab population. The high standard of living was not the Arab laborer's share as well; his own salary was not usually higher than his colleague's in Jerusalem or Jaffa. In the 20's and 30's the Arab public was dependant on the services of Jewish doctors and engineers. Even later on, those in need applied for the assistance of Jewish lawyers thanks to their expertise and experience, regardless of national matters.[514]

The image of the Jews in the Arabs' eyes was composed of different layers, the traditional religious layers and the modern anti-Semitism were naturally not positive, but Arab journalism could not ignore the actual image of the Haifa Jewish resident as an enterprising person building a developed society, yet carrying the threat of a western takeover. The European lifestyle and the free relationships between men and women in the new Jewish society and the modern women's fashion caused an angry response from conservatives such as the Mufti of Haifa and the Catholic Mutran but fascinated the young Arabs.[515] One of the oddest and most intriguing phenomena in the Arab-Jewish relations in Haifa was the split personality of the Arab that cooperated with the Jews because of shared economic interests but also belonged to a political system that was battling against Zionism, Jewish immigration, and settlement.

That is why in relatively quiet periods the economic interest had a higher priority than the political one. In the 30's, the city's horizons broadened with the construction of the harbor, and the Arab newspaper *Al-Carmel* prophesized a big future:

> ...Haifa began to progress in rapid steps towards prosperity and civilization...The harbor will connect East and West, simplify the trade of agriculture from the East and industrial products from the West.[516]

The Arab sector developed, but the Jewish sector grew at a more rapid pace and as result caused a feeling of relative deprivation: between the years 1922-1944 the two populations grew, the Arab population at 241% and the Jewish in 959%. From a majority of 75% in 1922 the Arabs deteriorated to a state of numerical equality. The existence of the dual economy, which was the basis of the Arab-Jewish relations, was dependant on the British Imperialist presence; clearly without the British arbitrator it could not exist.[517]

Indeed, towards the end of the British Mandate, when security and stability began to deteriorate and the confrontations between the two ethnic groups increased, the municipality published, in December 1947, "A declaration to all the citizens of Haifa":

> Haifa, your city, which is prospering thanks to its unique position in land, air, and sea, has become a place that your eyes are aimed at and your hopes are centered in, especially since it reached a high level of progress in all aspects — economics, industrial, commerce and also social aspect... You should maintain the calm and the order and stay away from general or private collisions, and avoid robbery, looting and igniting; these actions do not add dignity to our city...[518]

The mayor Shabtai Levi and his two Arab deputies Haj' Taher Bei Kraman and Shehada Shelah, signed the declaration.

Several months later, the Mandate period ended and with it the special arrangement it held. The city went through deep war vicissitudes and many of its Arab inhabitants left. However, the record of the council members and the senior officials in the municipality of January 1949, compared to the one published in September 1946, shows that there was no major change at least in the membership of the city council. The mayor was Shabtai Levi and his deputies were Shehada Shelah and Haj' Taher Bei Kraman. The municipality secretary, Jiris Khoury, left his post and was replaced by Abraham Halfon, his deputy.[519]

Goren notes that in 1948-1950, and in later years, a special contribution to the post war recovery process was made by local leaders, including the Arab representatives, who wished for involvement in the city life. It is a manifestation of the continuity of Haifa's particular nature as a mixed city.[520]

They all must have been aware of the great difficulties but still thought of their city as one which would continue to flourish in the future, and the municipality as one that, as they wrote in the declaration, "had all the citizens' welfare in mind, and was free of political, ethnic or sectarian tendencies."[521] And maybe their greatness was that they managed to pass on this vision to the succeeding generations, to transform it into a myth that fulfills itself in the lives of the Jewish and Arab citizens of Haifa, who are proud even today of their city's uniqueness and the important message it sends to the country and the world.

Notes

Prologue

[1]Gilbert Herbert and Silvina Sosnovsky, *Bauhaus on the Carmel*, Yad Ben Zvi, Jerusalem, 1993, p.10.

[2]Deborah Bernstein, *Jews and Arabs' relations in Haifa's Job market 1920-1948* (Hebrew), (printout) no date, p.1.

[3]Lawrence Oliphant, *Haifa* (Hebrew), Yad Ben Zvi, Jerusalem, 1976.

[4]Bernstein, op.cit.

[5]Ian Garrick Mason, *"Cosmopolitanism There and Now,"* St' Lawrence Institute for Advancement of Learning, 9/12/2004.

[6] Ibid.

[7]*Encyclopedia Britannica,* www. Britannica.com/eb/article 26905, 12/9/2004.

[8]*Wikipedia,* 12/9/2004.

[9]Daniel Pipes, "The Muslims against the Arabs," *Ma'ariv,* 20.8.2004.

[10]"Last Night in Alexandria," *Tarbut,* 12/9/2004 (Hebrew).

[11]Nathan Shaham and Shemuel Katz, *Journey in Eretz-Israel* (Hebrew), Levin Epstein, Tel Aviv, 1966, p.117.

[12]A.J. Sherman, *Mandate Days*, Johns Hopkins University Press, Baltimore and London, 2001, p.139.

[13]Ibid., p.166.

[14]Street advertisment from the 40's, inviting the British soldiers to a five o'clock tea in Panorama Garden, to the music of the "Joe Nadel's Swingers."

[15]Benny Nachshon, "People and Families in the History of the Jewish Settlement in Haifa," Sarah and Meir Aharoni (Editors), *People and Actions in Haifa* (Hebrew), Maxim Publishing, Kfar Saba, 1993, p.127.

[16]Shlomo Erel, *The "Yeks" - 50 Years of German Speaking Immigrants* (Hebrew), Reuben Mass, Jerusalem 1989.

[17]Yoav Gleber, *New Homeland - Immigration and Absorption of Central European Jews 1933-1948* (Hebrew), Yad Ben Zvi and Leo-Beck Institute, Jerusalem, 1990.

[18]Ibid., pp.228-229.

[19]Yoram Melzer, *Haifa's Hideaways,* 28.8.04 (Hebrew).

[20]Ibid.

[21]Ya'akobah Cohen, *The Secrets Died With Him* Ynet, Article/ 1,2506,L-25.8.2004. The Palmach was the elite combat unit of the Haganah.

[22]Ruth Zucker, *I Spy?* (Hebrew), the Ministry of Defense, Tel Aviv, 1997.

[23]Haviv Cna'an, *The Fifth Column–Germans in Eretz-Israel in 1933-1948* (Hebrew), Hakibbutz Hameuhad, Tel Aviv, 1968.

[24]Tamir Goren, *Shared Municipality in a Mixed City* (Hebrew), Ph.D. dissertation, University of Haifa, April 2000,   first Volume, p. 10-11.

[25]Ibid., pp.13-15.

[26]Yossi Ben-Artzi, *Turn A Desert to the Carmel* (Hebrew), Magnes, The Hebrew University, 2004, pp. 328-329.

[27]Ibid., p.335.

[28]Scott A. Bollens, *On Narrow Ground*, State University of New York press 2000, pp. 341-343. The book presents a comparative research on the policy in Jerusalem and in Belfast in the shadow of the Ethnic-National conflict.

Arabs and Jews in a Dynamic Job Market - Eli Nachmias

[29]Eva Feld, *Life in Mandate Palestine* http: Jewishmag.com/55mag/commencement.htm, 17/9/2004.

[30]*My name is Munira,* http: womenforPalestine.com/020403V2/pp testimonies.htm, 17/9/2004.

[31]Samira Abdennour, *I Cannot Visit My Father's Grave* (17/11/2000), Palestineremembered.com/Haifa/Story 1990.html, 24/9/2004.

[32]Interview with Moshe (Musa) Botton, 9.8.2004.

[33]Mordehai Shreiber, *Land of Dreams-Memories of the Establishment of the State* (Hebrew), Shinegold, 1997, p. 59.

[34]Mordehai Ron, *Haifa of my Childhood Days* (Hebrew), Ariel, Jerusalem, 1993.

[35]Sharon Rotbard, *White City-Black City; an Anatomy of a murder of a city* (Hebrew), 16.6.2004, w.bimkom.org/dynContent/articles.

[36]Yair Ron (editor), *Souvenir Edition for the Inauguration of the Baha'i Gardens on Mount Carmel* (Hebrew), published by the world Baha'i Center, May 2001.

[37]Leopald Trepper, *My Red Orchestra* (Hebrew), Idanim, Jerusalem, 1975.

[38]*From the memoirs of Major-General William Hargreaves of his service in Palestine*, Kcl.ac.uk/Ihgma/Top.htm, August 2003.

[39]*Written report by Adolph Aichman, 4.10.1937, of his visit in Palestine and Egypt.* (Document given by office 06 in Israel's Police Department head office, for Aichman's trial). Tuvia Friedman's personal archive, Haifa.

[40]David De Prise, *Workers Movement in Haifa, 1919-1929* (Hebrew), Ph.D. dissertation, the Senate of Tel Aviv University, October 1991; Peter Y. Medding, *Mapai in Israel*, Cambridge University Press, 1972; Baruch Zaltz and Eli Nachmias, *Mapah in Red Haifa* (Hebrew), Ahva, Haifa, 2003; Zadok Eshel, *Aba Hushi Man of Haifa* (Hebrew), the Ministry of Defense, Tel Aviv, 2002.

[41]David Hacohen, *Time to Tell* (Hebrew), Am Oved, Tel Aviv, 1974; Habib Can'an, *In the Eyes of a Palestinian Policeman* (Hebrew), Massada, Givata'im, 1980; Eliyahu Orbach, *From the Father Land to the Fathers' Land-the First Jewish Doctor in Haifa* (Hebrew), Yad Ben Zvi, Jerusalem, 1997; Arieh Meholal, *Haifa-Past, Future and Present* (Hebrew), department of trade and industry, Haifa, 1995; Carl Singer, *From the Memoirs of an Israeli Detective* (Hebrew), Haifa, 1991; Nesher factory, *Cement and his Creators* (Hebrew), Yavneh, 2002; Mordehai Naor, *Oil Refineries: 60 Years of Energy* (Hebrew), the oil refineries, Haifa, 2000; Amos Carmel, *Like The Eye of Electricity* (Hebrew), Ministry of Defense, 1998.

[42]Leumi Bank of Israel, *Leumi-100 Years* (Hebrew), 2003.

[43]Alex Carmel, "Haifa in the 19th Century," Eli Shiller and

Yossi Ben-Artzi (editors), *Haifa and its Sites* (Hebrew), Haifa Municipality and Ariel publishing, 1985, p. 68.

[44]Nahum Willbush, "The Beginning of the Settlement in Haifa," S. Shalom and S. Kramer (editors), *Carmelit* (Hebrew), Dvir Publishing, Tel Aviv, 1953, pp. 196-197.

[45]Alex Carmel, *History of Haifa During the Turkish Days* (Hebrew), Yad Ben Zvi, Jerusalem, 1977, p. 161.

[46]Alex Carmel, "Haifa in the End of the Ottoman Period," Arnon Sofer and Baruch Kipnis (editors), *Atlas of Haifa and the Carmel* (Hebrew), Society of applied science studies in the University of Haifa, 1980, p.50.

[47]Carmel, *History of Haifa*, op.cit., pp. 196-197.

[48]Nahum Gross, *The Spirit Does Not Stand Alone* (Hebrew), (studies on Israel's economic history in the new era), Magnes Publishing, Yad Ben Zvi, Jerusalem, 1999, pp.50-51.

[49]Alex Carmel, "Haifa in the End of the Ottoman Period," Mordehai Naor and Yossi Ben-Artzi (editors), *Haifa During its' Development 1918-1948* (Hebrew), Yad Ben Zvi, Jerusalem, 1989, pp. 17-18.

[50]Gad Gilber, *The Tendencies in the Palestinians' Demographic Development, 1870-1987* (Hebrew), The Moshe Dayan Center for Middle East and Africa Studies, Shiloah Institute, Tel Aviv University, 1989, p. 12.

[51]Hadara Lazar, *Hamandatorim* (Hebrew), Keter, Jerusalem, 1990, p.189.

[52]Yosef Klausner, "Magic and Alienage" Yosef Nedava (editor), *Haifa, Oliphant and the Zionist Vision* (Hebrew), Haifa University, The Zionist Cathedra named after Reuven Hecht, Haifa, no mention of publishing year.

[53]David Hacohen, "Segments of Memoirs," Ibid., pp. 70-71.

[54] Ibid.

[55]Shabtai Levi, "My Memoirs," Nedava, op.cit., p. 116.

[56]Yossi Ben-Artzi, "Haifa's Uniqueness and Development During the Mandate Period," Naor and Ben-Artzi, op.cit., p.27.

[57]Ibid., p.30.

[58]Ibid., pp.34-35.

[59] Yoram Melzer, "*Bat Galim-Revealed Layers*" (Hebrew), Notes. co.il/ioram/3578.asp,20/5/2004.

[60] Patrick White, *Palestine*, abc.au /white /life, 2/5/2004. Patrick White, who stayed in Palestine as an Australian soldier, won the Nobel Prize for literature in 1973.

[61] Shimon Stern, *Development of Haifa's Urban Alignment in the Years 1918-1947* (Hebrew), Ph.D. dissertation, the Hebrew University of Jerusalem 1974, p.152.

[62] Tom Segev, *Palestine under the British* (Hebrew), Keter, Jerusalem, 1999, p.289.

[63] Ibid.

[64] Yonathan Fine, "Developing Haifa's Harbor in the British Policy 1906-1924, Strategic Considerations," *Cathedra* (Hebrew), Yad Ben Zvi no. 89, p. 127.

[65] Ibid., p.128.

[66] Mordehai Naor and Dan Giladi, *Israel in the 20th Century, From Settlement to State 1900-1950* (Hebrew), Ministry of Defense, Tel Aviv, 1990, p.12.

[67] Hebrew Commerce and Industry Bureau of Haifa and the district, *Haifa-City of the Future* (Hebrew), Haifa, 1932, p.5.

[68] Wilbush, op.cit., pp.196-199.

[69] Ladislas Farago, *Palestine on the Eve*, Putnam, London, 1936, pp. 233-237.

[70] Naftali Arbel (chief editor) and Moshe Lisak (editor), *The Great Periods in Israel's History, Recovering in the Shadow of the British 1918-1929* (Hebrew), vol 5, Revivim Publishing, Tel Aviv, 1980, p.71.

[71] Herbert Sidebotham, *Great Britain and Palestine*, Macmillan and Co., London, 1937, pp.119-120.

[72] Herbert Sidebotham, *British Interest in Palestine*, Macmillan and Co., London, 1931, p.3, pp.20-23.

[73] Stern, op.cit., p.135.

[74] Zionist Information Bureau for Tourists in Palestine, *Guide to New Palestine*, Ninth Edition 1936-1937, Ariel Press, Jerusalem, pp.71-72.

[75] Zohar Alufi, *Haifa Committee of the Jewish Agency* (Hebrew), M.A. dissertation, the Hebrew University of Jerusalem, 1993, p. 7.

[76] Ibid., p.8. (Alufi notes that Ben Gurion said in relevance to this

matter that without determining a final date for its expiration, the temporary Mandate could last forever).

[77]David Ben Gurion, *Memories* (Hebrew), vol 5, Am Oved, Tel Aviv, 1973-1975, p. 120. It is important to note that Ben Gurion, who was disappointed by the offer that was made by the "Peel Commission" to keep Haifa under mandatory rule, analyzed Haifa's status in his memoirs:

"The existing condition in Haifa is ideal for England: fifty-fifty, when the Jews and the Arab are equal-Haifa is English. If we could turn Haifa into a Jewish city we would gain a key position that would make England need the Jews... There are 150,000 Jews in Tel Aviv, Haifa has only 50,000. It is necessary that Tel Aviv will be bigger and stronger than Jaffa, but 100,000 or 200,000 and even 300,000 does not alter the political nature of Tel Aviv. At the same time adding 50,000 Jews to Haifa would change the whole character of the city. If the Jews were three quarters instead of half of the citizens of the city (an addition of 100,000) or even 2/3 (addition of 50,000) ...Haifa would become a Jewish fort..." Ibid., pp.404-405.

[78]Naor and Giladi, op.cit., p.244.

[79]Ya'akov Shorer, *Touring Haifa* (Hebrew), Ministry of Defense, Tel Aviv, 2003, pp.21-28.

[80]Charles D. Smith, *Palestine and the Arab Israeli Conflict*, St. Martin's Press, NY, 1988, p.119.

[81]Binyamin Yaffa, A *Portrait of Eretz-Israel 1840-1914* (Hebrew), Dvir/Carta, Tel Aviv, 1983, pp. 194-195.

[82]Yosef Barslavski, *Have You Known the Country (a) The Galilee and the northern valleys* (Hebrew), Hakibbutz Hameuhad, 1947, p.312. Barslavski adds that as more steam ships came to Eretz-Israel's coasts, their captains realized that the anchorage in Haifa is more convenient than in Acre. Haifa's apparent upsides and the diminishing importance of Acre harbor's, caused the consulates and ship agents of England, France, Austria, Russia etc., to move to Haifa, even though the city had a very small population (Barslavski is referring to the middle and end of the 19th century).

[83] Yeshaihu Freidman, *The Question of Eretz-Israel in the years 1914-1918* (Hebrew), Magnes, Jerusalem and Tel Aviv, 1987, p. 121.

[84] Deborah Bernstein, "Jews and Arabs in Nesher Factory," *Cathedra* (Hebrew), Yad Ben Zvi, no. 78, 1995, p.83.

[85] Sherman, op.cit., p.178.

[86] Nahum Gross, "The Economic Policy of the Mandatory British Government in Eretz-Israel," *Cathedra* (Hebrew), Yad Ben Zvi, no. 24 July 1982, pp.155-156.

[87] Gideon Bigger, "The Strategic Perception of Haifa in the Eyes of the British Government," Naor and Ben-Artzi (editors), op.cit., p.60.

[88] Moti Golani, "Haifa's change-Britain and the Civil War in Eretz-Israel: December 1947-May 1948," Anita Shapira (editor), *State on the Way-The Israeli Society in the First Decades* (Hebrew), Zalman Shazar Center of Israel's History, Jerusalem, 2001, p.44.

[89] Amir Ben Porat, *Where are those Bourgeois-History of the Israeli Bourgeois* (Hebrew), Magnes, The Hebrew University, Jerusalem, 1999, pp.7-9.

[90] I. Bradley, *The English Middle Classes Are Alive and Kicking*, Collins, London, 1982.

[91] Ben Porat, op.cit., p.26.

[92] Ben Halperin and Yehuda Reinhertz, *Zionism: the Creation of a New Society* (Hebrew), Zalman Shazar Center of Israel's History, Jerusalem, 2000, p.159.

[93] Yigal Drori, "Roots in the Exile and in Ottoman Eretz-Israel - The Path of Six Members of 'the Civil Circles' to Zionism and Eretz-Israel," *The Zionism* (Hebrew), 1995, p.117.

- Note- on the "Civil Circles" and the like, see: Yigal Drori, *Between Left and Right, the "Civil Circles" in the Twenties* (Hebrew), University Enterprises, Tel Aviv, 1990.

- Yigal Drori, "The Organization of the Middle Class in Israel-Political Settlement Attempts in the Twenties," *Cathedra* (Hebrew), Yad Ben Zvi, Jerusalem, no. 44, pp.116-125.

- On the beginning of the General Zionism in the country, see ibid., and Yigal Drori, "The General Zionists in Israel in the Twenties," *The Zionism, 10* (Hebrew), 1985.

[94]Moshe Lisak, *The Elites of the Hebrew Settlement in Eretz-Israel During the Mandate* (Hebrew), The University Library/Am Oved, Tel Aviv, 1981, p.22.

[95]Elyakim Rubinstein, "From a Settlement to State-Institutions and Political Parties," Binyamin Eliyav (editor), *The Settlement in the Days of the National Home* (Hebrew), Keter, Jerusalem, 1976, p.260.

[96]Moshe Lisak, "Immigration, Absorption and the Building of a Jewish Society in Eretz-Israel During the Twenties," Moshe Lisak (editor), *History of the Jewish Settlement in Israel Since the First Immigration* (Hebrew), Bialik Institute, Jerusalem, 2001, pp.181-182.

Also see: Yair Aharoni, *The Political Economy in Israel* (Hebrew), the Hebrew University, Am Oved, 1991, pp.66-67.

[97]Dan Giladi, *The Settlement in the Fourth Immigration Period* (Hebrew), University Library, Am Oved, Tel Aviv, 1973, p.118.

[98]Shlomo Kodesh (editor), *The Bat Galim Anniversary* (Hebrew), the Bat Galim Committee, 1949, p.18.

[99]Yehuda Hayut, "The Influence of the Settlement's Ideology on the Development of the Krayot in Haifa's Bay," Yoram Bar-Gal and Aharon Kellerman (editors), *Horizons in Geography* (Hebrew), The Geography department, Haifa University, Haifa, 1979, p.22.

[100]Yosef Katz, *Private Initiative in the Construction of Eretz-Israel in the Second Immigration Period* (Hebrew), Bar Ilan University, Ramat Gan, 1989, pp.164-167. See also Ben-Artzi's book, *Turning a Desert to the Carmel,* op.cit., pp.13-19.

[101]Protocol: *the first gathering of the Jewish merchants in Haifa, 16.8.1919,* from the files of the Merchants Bureau in Haifa.

*On Wadiea' Bustani see Yair Safran's article, "A.D Pichoto" *Haifa* (Hebrew), Haifa History Society Journal, 1, 2004, p.9.

[102]Letter from 7.12.1919 to the Merchants Union in Jaffa, by the

chairman Nathan Kaiserman; secretary Ya'akov Zilberman (Caspi), from the files of the Commerce Bureau in Haifa.

[103]Details from the convention of the Jewish Merchants in Haifa in Apek-13.11.1919. From the files of the Commerce Bureau in Haifa.

[104]"Yediot Aharonot: Announced by Telephone from Haifa," *Doar Hayom*, 15.6. 1921.

[105]Yigal Drori, "The Beginning of the Economic Organizations in Israel in the Twenties," *Cathedra* (Hebrew), Yad Ben Zvi, no. 25, p.99.

[106]Journalists' Union in Israel, Haifa and the North http://www. haifapress.org.il/ 26/8/2004 (Hebrew).

[107]Industrialists' Union in Israel-Haifa and the North Branch site, 20/12/2003: Information on the routine professional activity of the Industrialists' Union provided in the book by Emmanuel Fortuna (editor), *The Industry in Haifa and the North* (Hebrew), published by the Union of the Industrialists of Haifa and the North, Haifa, 1993.

[108]Yair Aharoni, *Structure and Behavior in Israel's Economy* (Hebrew), Goma/Cherikover, Tel Aviv, 1976, p. 323.

[109]Ibid., p.329.

[110]Ibid., pp.326,327.

[111]Yael Yishai, *Interest Groups In Israel* (Hebrew), The Hebrew University, Am Oved, 1987, p. 38.

[112]Avi Bettleheim, *The Merchants* (the story of the commerce in Eretz-Israel - 70 Years of the Commerce Department of Tel Aviv-Jaffa) (Hebrew), Commerce Department of Tel Aviv-Jaffa, Tel Aviv, 1990, p.78.

[113]Yosef Gorney, *The Labor Union 1919-1930* (Hebrew), Tel Aviv University, Hakibbutz Hameuhad, Ramat Gan, 1973, p.59.

[114]Yossi Beilin, *The Hebrew Industry-Roots* (Hebrew), Keter, Jerusalem, 1987, p.89.

[115]Ben Porat, op.cit., p.66.

[116]Tamir Goren, "Why Did the Arab Inhabitants Leave Haifa? A Study of a Divided Question," *Cathedra* (Hebrew), Yad Ben Zvi, no' 80, 1996, p.176.

[117]Gideon Bigger, "The Industrial Structure of Eretz-Israel's

Cities in the Beginning of the Mandate Period," *Cathedra* (Hebrew), Yad Ben Zvi, no' 29, September 1983, pp.82-83.

[118]Deborah S. Bernstein, *Constructing Boundaries, Jewish and Arab Workers in Mandatory Palestine,* State University of New York, Albany, 2000, pp.49-55.

[119]Ibid.

[120]Baruch Kimmerling and Joel S. Migdal, *Palestinians-The Making of a People,* The Free Press, New York, 1993, p.25.

[121]Dan Giladi, "Industrial Initiatives in Eretz-Israel in the Twenties," Nahum Gross (editor), *Jews in the Economy* (Hebrew), Zalman Shazar Center Publishing, Jerusalem, 1995, p.349.

[122]Ibid.

[123]Department of Custom, Excise and Trade, *First Census of Industries,* Jerusalem, 1929, p.17.

[124]Z. Avramovitz and Y. Gleft, *The Arab Economy in Eretz-Israel and the Middle East countries* (Hebrew), Hakibbutz Hameuhad Press, 1944, p.64.

[125]Ibid., p.86. Avramovitz and Gleft note that even though the number of shops in mixed cities increased, the Arabs opened them for Jewish customers.

[126]Ibid., p.93.

[127]Ibid., p.94. See also: C. Empson, *Economic Conditions in Palestine,* July 1935, Report by the British Commercial Agent in Haifa to the Department of Overseas Trade.

[128]Mahmud Yazbak, "The Arabs in Haifa: From Majority to Minority, Processes of Change (1848-1870)," Ephraim Karsh (editor), *Israel Affairs,* A Frank Cass Journal, vol. 6, no. 3&4 Spring/ Summer 2000, p.132.

[129]Ibid., p.134.

[130]May Seikaly, *Haifa-Transformation of a Palestinian Arab Society 1918-1939,* I.B Tauris Publishers, London, 1995, p.26.

[131]Ibid., pp.81-90.

[132]Ibid., pp.91-92.

[133]Yizhak Klein, *The Arab Community in Haifa in the Mandate Period: Political, Economic and Social Survey* (Hebrew), Haifa University, Middle-East Studies Center, Haifa, 1983, p.26.

[134]Ibid., p.27.

[135]Ibid., p.28.

[136]Ibid., p.29. Yizhak Klein relies on Yosef Vashitz's book, *The Arabs in Eretz-Israel* (Hebrew), Hapoalim Library, Merhavia, 1947, pp.81-133.

[137]Ya'akov Shimoni, *Eretz-Israel's Arabs* (Hebrew), Am Oved, Tel Aviv, 1947, pp. 235-236.

[138]Ya'akov Shavit, Ya'akov Goldstein, and Chaim Be'er (editors), *The Lexicon of Eretz-Israel's Personages 1799-1948* (Hebrew), Am Oved, Tel Aviv, 1983. Also see: Arab dignitaries in Haifa, in Seikaly, op.cit., pp.233-236.

[139]Haifa's Labor Council, *As Told by the Pioneers-Twenty Years of the Union in Haifa* (Hebrew), Beit Hapoalim, Haifa, 30/12/1940, p.8.

[140]Ibid., p.10.

[141]Ibid., p.51.

[142]Ibid., p.56.

[143]Eliyahu Biltzky, *In Creation and in Struggle, Haifa's Labor Council 1921-1981* (Hebrew), Am Oved, 1981, p.120. Biltzky is relying on articles written by Z. Lilach, "New Factories in Eretz-Israel in 1925," *Trade and Industry* (Hebrew), edition 24, 31/12/1925. also: Y. Gleft, "The Hebrew Industry in Eretz-Israel," *Trade and Industry* (Hebrew), no.17, 30/10/1925.

[144]Biltzky, op.cit., pp.381-404.

[145]Haifa Municipality, *Miller House-The Story of Miriam and Yosef Miller* (Hebrew), 1970.

[146]Wilbush, op.cit., pp.198-199.

[147]Yehoshua Ziman, *The Eretz-Israeli Economy in Numbers* (Hebrew), Davar Press, 1929, pp.22, 24.

[148]Fortuna, op.cit., pp.107-201, present a detailed list of industries. For more on Haifa's industry history: Mordehai Naor, *Industry-The Stories of the Industrialists and Industry in Israel* (Hebrew), The Industrialists' Union in Israel, 2001

[149]Ze'ev Vilnai and Eliezer Boneh, *Eretz-Israel Guide* (Hebrew), Stimatzky Publishing, Jerusalem, 1935, pp.321-335. Also: Benjamin Lewensohn, *Guide to New Palestine 1936-1937*, Jerusalem, 1937.

[150]Ibid., p.323.

[151]Ibid.

[152]Hebrew Trade and Industry Bureau in Haifa and the District, *Haifa-City of the Future* (Hebrew), 1932, p.40.

[153]Vilnai and Boneh, op.cit., p.327.

[154]Ibid., p.336.

[155]His Majesty's Government, *The industry exhibition organized by the Palestine's (Eretz-Israel) government, Cairo 1941* (Hebrew).

The exhibition was held in nine halls, 42 Haifa factories and companies exhibited their products (14.89%); 155 companies from the Tel Aviv area (54.9%); and 26 from Jerusalem area (9.21%).

[156]Sir John Hope Simpson, a lecture on immigration, settlement and developing the country, 1930, chapter 9, p. 70 and up (a memo reported to the parliament by the Colonial Secretary on request of His Majesty, October 1930).

[157]Ibid., p.80.

[158]Ibid., p.84.

[159]Bernstein, op.cit., p.80.

[160]Zvi Even Shoshan, *History of the Laborers' Movement in Israel* (Hebrew), (second book), Am Oved, Tel Aviv, 1966, p.120.

[161]Dan Horowitz and Moshe Lisak, *From a Settlement to a State-Eretz-Israel's Jews in the British Mandate Period as a Political Community* (Hebrew), Am Oved, Tel Aviv, 1977, pp.36-38.

[162]Smith, op.cit., p.23.

[163]David Horowitz, *The Economy of Eretz-Israel*, (Hebrew) Massada, Tel Aviv, 1954, page 84.

[164]Yehoshua Ziman, *Building the Country (1882-1945)* (Hebrew), the Small Zionist Library, Jerusalem, 1946, p.44.

[165]Dan Horowitz and Moshe Lisak, *Distresses in Utopia* (Hebrew), Am Oved, Tel Aviv, 1990, p.42.

[166]Gross, op.cit., p.174.

[167]N. Polak, *The Hebrew Settlement on the Eve of the War* (Hebrew), Poalim Library, Merhavia, 1945, pp.59-60.

[168]Ben-Artzi, "The Uniqueness of Haifa and its' Development During the Mandate Period," op.cit., p.36.

[169]Ibid.

[170]Eliezer Boneh, *Eretz-Israel - the Country and the Economy* (Hebrew), Dvir Publishing, Tel Aviv, 1938, pp.273-274.

[171]Ziman, op.cit., p.112. Ziman's data refers to 1946.

[172]J.H. Kann (Late consul of the Netherlands in Jerusalem), *Some Observations on the Policy of the Mandatory Government of Palestine*, Martinus Nijhoff, The Hague, 1930, p.11.

[173]David Horowitz, op.cit., p.112.

[174]Horowitz and Lisak, op.cit., p.33; Seikaly, op.cit., pp. 92-93, also notices the segregation processes.

[175]Bernstein, *Constructing Boundaries* op.cit., p.80.

[176]E. Schmorak, *Palestine's Industrial Future*, Reuven Mass, Jerusalem, 1946, p.201.

[177]Yazbak, op.cit., pp. 143, 145. See also Mahmud Yazbak, *The Arab Immigration to Haifa in the Years 1933-1948*, M.A. dissertation, Haifa University, History of the Middle East Department, October 1986.

[178]Ibid.

[179]For instance: Yehoshua Froidenheim, *The Government in Israel* (Hebrew), Reuven Mass, Jerusalem, 1973; Moshe Gurion (Wager), *Introduction to the History of the Local Government in Israel* (Hebrew), Tel Aviv University Publishing; Economics and Law School, Jerusalem, 1957; Daniel Y. Elazar and Chaim Klechaim (editors), *The Local Government in Israel* (Hebrew), Jerusalem Center for Public and State Affairs, Jerusalem, 2001; A. Kazrin, *The Local Government in Israel* (Hebrew), Yahalom Press, Tel Aviv, 1949, and: Anglo-American Committee of Inquiry, *a Survey of Palestine*, vol. 1, 1946.

[180]For instance: Seikaly op.cit., Tamir Goren, *Co-operation Under the Shadow of Confrontation: The Formation and Function of the Municipality of Haifa as a Mixed Representative Institution During the British Mandate*, University of Haifa, The Jewish-Arab Center, 2001.

Elyakim Rubinstein, "Jews and Arabs in Eretz-Israeli Municipalities (1926-1933) Jerusalem and Other Municipalities," *Cathedra* (Hebrew), Yad Ben Zvi, no. 51, April 1989, pp.122-147.

[181]Rubinstein, ibid., p.122.

[182]Elazar and Kelchaim, op.cit., pp.6-7.

[183]Z. Zilbigger, *The Government and Law Arrangements in Israel*

(Hebrew), the Government Publishing Press, Jerusalem, 1954, pp. 186-187.

[184] Eliyav, op.cit., p.238.

[185] Hacohen, op.cit., p.96.

[186] Abraham Halfon, "Haifa, My City," Nedava, op.cit., p.69.

[187] Levi, op.cit., p.112.

[188] Rubinstein, op.cit., pp.123-124.

[189] Mahmud Yazbak, "Immigrants, Elite Groups and Common Organizations in the Arab Society in Haifa," op.cit., p.380.

[190] Seikaly, op.cit., pp.57-58.

[191] Yossi Ben-Artzi and Tamir Goren, "In the Hands of the Creators: Designing the Urban Space of Haifa's Arabs in 1948," Eran Rezin and Rihav (Boni) Rubin (editors), *Geographical Researches of Israel* (Hebrew), The Hebrew University of Jerusalem, Jerusalem, 1988, p.7.

[192] Esco Foundation for Palestine, Inc. *Palestine-a Study of Jewish, Arab and British Policies*, Yale University Press, New Haven, 1947, vol. 1, p.527.

[193] Goren, op.cit., pp.36-37.

[194] Seikaly, op.cit., pp.56-57.

[195] Ibid., p.551.

[196] Haifa municipality's director general's office, *History of Haifa Municipality's Data*, (Hebrew), November 1998.

[197] Ibid.

[198] For a description of the jobs and assignments see: The Hebrew Community in Haifa, *Haifa's Community in the Years 1932-1941* (Hebrew), Haifa, 1942, and also: Israel's Knesset in the country of Eretz-Israel, *the Hebrew Community in Haifa Committee, Actions (April 1944-March 1945)*, July 1946.

[199] See Hadar HaCarmel Committee's duties in: The Journalists' Union in Tel Aviv, *The Journalists' Year Book of 1947* (Hebrew), (chapter on Haifa, pp.108-112), and also: *The Anglo-Palestine Year Book 1947-1949* (F.J. Jacoby editor), Anglo-Palestine Publications, Ltd. London, pp.316-317.

[200] Ann Mosley Lesch, *Arab Politics in Palestine, 1917-1939*, Columbia University, 1979, p.71.

[201]Lieutenant Colonel F.H Kish, *Eretz-Israeli Journal* (Hebrew), Ahiasaf Publishing, Jerusalem, 1939, p.88.

[202]Esco Foundation for Palestine, op.cit., pp.736-737.

[203]Ya'akov Reuveni, "The Jewish component in the Mandate Government Mechanism—Economic and Political Aspects," *State, Government and International Relations* (Hebrew), The Hebrew University of Jerusalem, Leonard Davis Institute for International Relations, Jerusalem, 1990, no. 31, p.44.

[204]Ibid., pp.50-51.

[205]Nadav Halevi, "The Jewish Economy in the Settlement Period," Shmuel Stempler (editor), *The Settlement During the New Time-Milestones Before the State* (Hebrew), Ministry of Defense, Tel Aviv, 1983, p.211.

[206]The National Committee, *The Settlement Economy Book of 1947* (Hebrew), Tel Aviv, 1947, p.504.

[207]Yosef Vashitz, "Social Changes in the Arab Settlement of Haifa During the British Mandate: Merchants and Other Entrepreneurs," Avi Bareli and Nahum Carlinski (editors), *Economy and Society in the Mandate Days 1918-1948* (Hebrew), Ben Gurion Heritage Center, Ben Gurion University in the Negev Publishing, Beersheba, 2003, p.424.

[208]Ibid., pp.424-425.

[209]Peretz Cornfield (editor), *Palestine Personalia 1947*, Tel Aviv, 1947.

[210]Shahar Huneidi, *A Broken Trust, Herbert Samuel Zionism and the Palestinians, 1920-1925*, I.B Tauris London, 2001, p.228.

[211]Anita Shapira, "Political History of the Settlement 1918-1939," Moshe Lisak (chief editor), *History of the Jewish Settlement in Israel Since the First Immigration* (Hebrew), The National Israeli Academy for Sciences, Bialik Institute, Jerusalem, 2001, pp.110-111.

[212]Anita Shapira, "The Struggle for 'Hebrew Labor' in the Thirties," Yosef Gorney, Avi Bareli and Yizhak Greenberg (editors), *Work Notebook for the Organization of Workers* (Hebrew), Ben Gurion Heritage Center, Kiryat Sdeh Boker, 2000, pp.213-214.

[213]Ibid.

[214]Nathanel Katzburg, "The Second Decade for the Mandate Rule in Eretz-Israel 1931-1939," Moshe Lisak (chief editor), *History of the Jewish Settlement in Israel Since the First Immigration* (Hebrew), part 1, op.cit., p.363.

[215]Horowitz and Lisak, *From a Settlement to a State*, op.cit., pp.44-46. In their book, *Distresses in Utopia*, op.cit., Horowitz and Lisak note that the dominant ideology in the Jewish settlement supported getting comprehensive autonomy, ibid., p.43. Dan Giladi also express consent to this claim, by saying that earlier in the settlement history, we detect a condition in which, "all the public, for all its different orientations were for Hebrew labor," op.cit., p.174.

[216]Eshel, op.cit., p.77.

[217]Haifa's Labor Council, *As told by the Pioneers*, op.cit., pp.57-57.

[218]Ibid., p.59.

[219]Amnon Lin, *Before the Storm* (Hebrew), Karni, Tel Aviv, 1999, pp.70-71.

[220]Ibid., pp.71-72.

[221]Deborah Bernstein, "Jews and Arabs in Nesher Factory," op.cit., p.105.

[222]Yossi Schwartz, *"Arab-Jewish working joints struggles prior to partition in Palestine,"* http:narxist.com/MiddleEast/Arab_Jewish_struggles1.html 18/10/2004.

[223]David de Prise, "Work and Authority Battles Among Industry Workers in Israel: 'Nesher' Factory Workers in the Twenties," Gorney, Bareli, Greenberg, op.cit., p.245.

[224] Eshel, op.cit., pp.77-78.

[225]Aba Hushi, *Israel Laborers' Alliance* (Hebrew), Hava'ad Hapoel, Tel Aviv, April 1943, p.36.

[226]Ibid., p.32.

[227]Ibid., pp.21-22.

[228]Gorney, op.cit., pp.152-153.

[229]Interview with Amnon Lin (Linkovski), 31.10.2004. Amonon Lin, born in kibbutz Mishmar Haemek, married Aba Hushi's daughter, Ruth. He operated among the area's Arabs; became the manager of "Eretz-Israel Laborers' Alliance." In the Independence War he served as an officer in "Carmeli" division.

Later on he was elected to the Knesset and served as a member of central Knesset committees.

[230]Letter from the National Labor committee to Mapah, 6.6.1934, on the subject of: "Recruiting laborers for the railway work." The Work and Pioneer Archive-Lavon Institute (no file number).

[231]Data from December 1943, by Mapah management: The Arab laborers in Haifa in December 1943, the professional arrangement." According to that the number of Arab laborers in Haifa reached 15,672; the Work and Pioneer Archive-Lavon Institute (no.file number).

[232]ISSEI, International Society for the Study of European Ideas, Ninth International Conference, *The Narrative of Modernity: Coexistence of Differences* 19/10/2004, http:// issei2004.haifa. ac.il

[233]Muhamed Amara, "Relationship Between the Arab Minority and the Jewish Majority in Israel," Chaim Opaz (editor), *When Peace Comes-Influences and Social Aspects* (Hebrew), Education, Culture and Sports Ministry, Jerusalem, 1995, p.48.

[234]Adi Ofir,"Jewish—Arab Coexistence: the Politics of Rationality," Avi Sagi and Yedidiah Z. Stern (editors), *Democratic Culture* (Hebrew), Bar Ilan University and the Israeli Institute for Democracy, vol.6, 2002, p.12.

[235]Arthur Herzberg, "The Roots of the Arab Resistance towards Jews in Eretz-Israel," Eli Eyal (editor), *New Directions, Zionism and Judaism Journal* (Hebrew), no. 8, October 2003, pp.14-17.

[236]Bernstein, op.cit., p.215.

[237]Abraham Sela, "Society and Institutions Among Palestine's Arabs in the Mandate Period: Changes, Lack of Mobility and Demise," Bareli and Carlinski, op.cit., p.307.

[238]Hacohen, op.cit., pp.99-101

[239]Yazbak, op.cit., p.142.

[240]Vashitz, op.cit., pp.422-423. Yazbak wrote that when the terror and the damage to the Arab economic sector in Haifa increased, traditional politicians and merchants called to stop the strike and the violence. The rebels, who had nationalistic

viewpoints, declared that those calling to stop the strike are traitors and operated a terror campaign against them.

²⁴¹Ephraim Krisher, "The Joint Organization in the Implementation Test," Yosef Vilfend (editor), *Ma'asaf* (Hebrew), Givat Haviva, c-d, August 1972, p.171; also see Lin, op.cit., and: Zvi Even Shoshan, *History of the Laborers' Movement in Israel* (Hebrew), Am Oved, third book, Tel Aviv, 1966, p.164; and: Gideon Karsel, *The Union-40 Years* (Hebrew), Culture and Education, Tel Aviv, 1960, pp.47-49.

²⁴²Protocol of the Haifa City Council meeting 1.6.1925, Haifa city's Archives.

²⁴³Ibid., 8.7.1925.

²⁴⁴Ibid., 16.7.1929.

²⁴⁵Ibid., 12.12.1929.

²⁴⁶Ibid., 1.5.1930.

²⁴⁷Ibid., 2.6.1931.

²⁴⁸Ibid., 25.4.1932.

²⁴⁹ Ibid.,4.10.1934.

²⁵⁰Ibid.,24.1.1935.

²⁵¹The "cohabitation" concept was adopted by the French politics system where President Francois Mitterand, from the left wing, created in 1986 a weakened "coalition" with the right wing, with Jaque Chirac as Prime Minister at the head of it; according to this perception, French "cohabitation" was a temporary cooperation, while distributing loose authorities; see definition of cohabitation in: Ian McLean, *Oxford Concise Dictionary of Politics*, Oxford University Press, Oxford, 1996, pp.78-89.

²⁵²Fred J. Khouri, *The Arab-Israeli Dilemma*, Syracuse University Press, New York, 1983, p.22.

People, Places and Events in Haifa's History - Daphna Sharfman

²⁵³Alex Carmel, *The History of Haifa During the Turkish Days,*

op.cit., p.197 and Zeev Vilnai, *Haifa in the Past and Present* (Hebrew), Tel-Aviv, 1936, pp.93-94.

[254]Carmel, ibid., pp.164-169.

[255]Ibid., pp.180-184.

[256]Ibid., pp.184-185.

[257]David S. Ruhe, *Door of Hope* (The Baha'i Faith in the Holy Land), George Ronald, Oxford 1983, second revised edition 2001, pp.130-131.

[258]Emile Havivi, *Ahtiye* (Hebrew), Am Oved, Tel Aviv, 1988, pp.93-94.

[259]*The letters of Gertrude Bell*, Penguin Travel Library, Great Britain, 1987, pp.115-117.

[260]Carmel, op.cit., pp.185-186.

[261]Northern Palestine was considered than part of Syria.

[262]Shabtai Levi, "My Memories," Nedava ,op.cit., p.83.

[263]Ibid., p.85.

[264]Ibid., pp.186-197.

[265]Y.K Silman, *Haifa, its History and Settlement* (Hebrew), Amanut, Tel Aviv, 1931, pp.50-51.

[266]Gideon Bigger, *A Crown Colony or National Home* (Hebrew), Yad Ben Zvi, Jerusalem, 1983, pp.83-84.

[267]Ibid., p.85.

[268]Amiram Harlaf, *Between the Carmel and the Sea* (Hebrew), Haifa, 1998, pp.50-51.

[269]Interview of the author with Jalal Irani, born 1920, and his sister, Nazuk Bahaj, decendants of Ali Riza, brother of Baha u'lla'h, founder of the Baha'i faith, 12.3.2004.

[270] Ron, op.cit., p.87. Spinney's was a British company that was the major supplier of the British forces in Palestine, Trans-Jordan and Iraq, and also managed food stores. Spinney's imported merchandises from the British Empire and the people of Palestine were able to buy delicatessen such as Canadian butter, Cadbury chocolate from Britain and apples from Australia that made the long way in wood boxes, adorned with a painting of an Australian native wearing a head kerchief and a peacock feather.

Spinney's even had a special train that carried merchandise to its stores.

[271]Ibid., pp.87-88.

[272]Vilnai, op.cit., p.108.

[273] "Information for the Travelers: The bus stands again in the last station before Jordan," *Haaretz*, 9 Mars, 2004.

[274]Vilnai, op.cit., p.109.

[275]Douglas Duff, *Knight the Galilee* (Hebrew), Ariel, Jerusalem and Absalom Institute, Tel Aviv, 2002, pp. 192-194.

[276] Irani, interview, op.cit.

[277] *Home Port-The Story of Haifa Port* (Hebrew), Haifa City Museum, Curator Yehudit Matzkel, October 2002, p.109.

[278]Ibid., p.175.

[279]Peltours, 1st November 1947, Haifa City Achieves (HCA) 364/36. The municipality of Haifa received a letter from the owner of a travel agency in Beirut with branches in the region who wished to offer the municipality to buy 50 copies of a tourism guidebook for the sum of five Palestinian pounds, Ibid.

[280]The annual meeting of the Association for Development of Tourisms in Palestine, King David Hotel, Jerusalem, the speech of the association's President, 16 January 1936, Ibid.

[281]The annual meeting, 25 January 1937, Ibid.

[282]The annual meeting, 28 February 1938, Ibid.

[283]In April 1936 the Arab leadership in Palestine, led by Haj Amin-al–Husseini declared a general strike to protest against, and put an end to Jewish immigration to Palestine. The strike was called off in October, while the Peel Commission deliberated and eventually recommended the partition of Palestine. With the rejection of this proposal, the revolt resumed during the autumn of 1937, marked by the assassination of the District Commissioner Andrews in Nazareth. The violence than continued throughout 1938 and eventually petered out by 1939. (*Wikipedia*)

[284]Gleber, op.cit., pp.228-229.

Dr. Bodenhaimer-Biram writes in her letter in autumn 1933 to Landawer, one of the association's leaders, that it is urgent to cultivate mutual understanding and good will among the Jews even before dealing with the Jewish-Arab relations in Palestine.

[285]Ibid., pp.245-246.

[286]Ruth Sharfman immigrated to Palestine from Poland in May 1935, in an interview with the author (her daughter), 9 January 2007, she described the memorable first time that she saw the approaching coast of Haifa: "Into the all enveloping blueness of shimmering sea and sky, a darker streak appeared on the horizon. As the ship made her way towards the shore it grew bigger and bigger into the elongated shape of the Carmel Mount. Slowly the white town emerged out of the bluish haze and like a developing photo print grew clearer with every few moments. The blue changed into green clad slopes of the mountain towering above the harbor."

[287]Vilnai, op.cit., p.109.

[288]Herbert and Sosnovsky, op.cit., pp.51-52.

[289]Publication of "Lot," the archives of the Haifa History Society (HHS).

[290]A flight schedule published by Khal.E and Ch, of Kingsway 42 and 126, HCA, tourist portfolio, Ibid.

[291]A letter of 9 July 1939, HCA.

[292]Ibid.

[293]A letter of 15 Av (August) 1939, Ibid.

[294]Ron, op.cit., p.95.

[295]Hacohen, op.cit., p.75.

[296]An advertisement published in a guide to Palestine, issued for British and Australian military. Gail Hoffman, *Pocket Guide to Palestine*, Peltours, Jerusalem, 1940, p.90.

[297]Harlaf, op.cit., p.16.

[298]Hacohen, op.cit.

[299]Zeev Vilnay, *Steimatzky Palestine Guide*, Steimatzky, Jerusalem, 1942, p.317.

[300]Zadoc Eshel, *Those women, Haganah women members in Haifa* (Hebrew), Ministry of Defense, Tel Aviv, 1997, pp. 112-114.

[301] Interview with Hilda Lev, HHS, 24.3.1999. Her family opened a sanatorium in Pinski street which was also a high class hotel.

[302] Silvina Sosnovski, *The Development of Modern Architecture in Haifa 1920-1940, Planning of Commercial Centers* (Hebrew), Hatechnion, October, 1983 p. 30.

[303] Herbert and Sosnovski, op.cit., pp.259-261.

[304] Vilnay, op.cit., p.323.

[305] Letter from the president of the association to the Chief Secretary, 14 November 1942, HCA, 379/34.

[306] Letter, December 1942, Ibid.

[307] Letter to the mayor, 16 July 1944, Ibid.

[308] Ibid.

[309] Sherman, op.cit., pp.48-49, see also f.n. 61.

[310] Ya'akov Davidon, *That was Haifa* (Hebrew), Mai, Haifa, 1925, pp.57-63.

[311] Ron, op.cit., p.82. Interview with Rachel Bell-Turkasma, 10.5.99, interview with Abraham Monson, 18.2.2002, HHS.

[312] Ibid., pp.90-91.

[313] Zuker, op.cit., p.24.

[314] Interview with Ruth Sharfman, op.cit., she remembered that the vendors, knowing that most of the Jewish residents were immigrants, proclaimed the fish in Yiddish calling "lebedi-ge-fish, lebedi-ge-fish" (live fish).

[315] Interview with Zafrira Belgur, Zvi Faigine's daugther, op.cit. Her family lived in Khamra Square, they had good relations with their Arab neighbors until the riots of 1929, when they were forced to move to the all Jewish neighborhood of Hadar HaCarmel. They built their house on the Carmel.

[316] Interview with Dr. Maged Khamra, HHS, 29.11.2000.

[317] Havivi, op.cit., p.84.

[318] Interview conducted by the author and adv. Eli Roman with Yusef Musa (Abu Victor), in Khamra Square, 24.3.2004. His father was a policeman and he also joined the police, worked with a Jewish Sergeant, Alfred Bart, about him he said: "I was like a son to him."

[319]Ibid.

[320]Ron, op.cit., p.79.

[321]Hacohen, op.cit., p.71.

[322]Ron, op.cit., pp.92-93.

[323]Irani, interview, op.cit., he noted the prices of the simple food at that time, humus with foul and bread cost one, or one and a half mil, the same amount was charged for a pita bread with peppers and tomatoes, the daily wages of a worker was about five mils.

[324]Harlaf, op.cit., p.11.

[325]Interview conducted by adv. Eli Roman with Gideon Jordan, July 2005.

[326]Interview with Ezer Weizmann, the Seventh President of Israel, HHS, 24.6.2003.

[327]Harlaf, op.cit., p.24.

[328]Hoffman, op.cit., p.90, see also interview with Yitzhak Rimon, 26.3.2003.

[329]Harlaf, op.cit., p.55.

[330]Interview with Moshe Kline, HHS, 10.6.98.

[331]Harlaf, op.cit., pp.65-66.

[332]Shorer, op.cit., pp.78-79 and see also: Norman & Helen Bentwich, *Mandate Memories*, The Hogart Press, London, 1965, p.65.

[333] Musa, interview, op.cit.

[334]A letter from 18.7.45, HCA, 7915,381/49.

[335]Herbert and Sosnovski, op.cit., pp.150-151. They also mention the architect Erich Mendelson's plan to build in Bat Galim houses and hotel near the sea. He was in touch with the owners of the Shepeard's hotels company in Cairo, but could not raise the required 50,000 pounds.

[336]Interview with Pnina Vered, HHS, 24.2.2000.

[337]Shorer, op.cit., p.186.

[338]"Casino Bat-Galim, Haifa," *Building in the Near East* (Hebrew), Tel Aviv, May 1938, pp.67-69.

[339]Interview with Asher Vered, HHS, 24.2.97.

[340]Shorer, op.cit., p.187. Quoted from Avi Kfiri, "The Legend of Bat Galim," special issue on Haifa, *Rehov Rashi*, 28.10.83.

[341]Zuker, op.cit., p.92, the special operation was conducted in order to obtain the signature of a high ranking British official. It was copied on forged documents that helped the Haganah to bring safely to Palestine the 800 holocaust survivors known as "Teheran Children."

[342]Vered, interview, op.cit.

[343]Arthur Koestler, "Haifa in the Twenties," chapter from his autobiography: *Arrow to the Blue Sky* (Hebrew), Naor and Ben-Arzi (editors), *Haifa Development 1918-1948, Idan* 12 (Hebrew), Yad Ben Zvi, Jerusalem, 1989, p.246.

[344]Irani, interview, op.cit.

[345]Weizmann, interview, op.cit.

[346]Harlaf, op.cit., pp.9,17-18,33-34.

[347]Davidon, op.cit., pp.137-139.

[348]Interview with Michal Brenner, daughter of Gita Dunia-Weizmann, HHS, no date.

[349]Ruth Jordan, *Daugther of the Waves*, Taplinger Publishing Company, New York, 1982, pp.177-178.

[350]Ibid.

[351]Ibid., pp.181-182.

[352]Sherman, op.cit., pp.166-167, see also f.n. 223.

[353]Zuker, op.cit., p.24.

[354]Belgur, interview, op.cit.

[355]Interview with Carmela Bernsthein and Ehuda Zeliouk, the quotation from the latter, HHS, 27.6.2001.

[356]Ron, op.cit., pp.77-79.

[357]Khamra, Interview, op.cit.

[358]Musa, interview, op.cit.

[359]Stern, op.cit., p.130.

[360]Weizmann, interview, op.cit.

[361]Irani, interview, op.cit.

[362]Kline, interview, op.cit.

[363]Stern, op.cit., pp.118-119.

[364]David Hacohen, "Jews and Arabs in Haifa Municipality," I*dan* 12 (Hebrew), op.cit., pp.237-239.

[365]Ibid., photo in page 238.

[366] Ibid., p.239.

[367] A letter from David Hacohen to the mayor, HCA, file 8597, 401/9.

[368] A letter of Watson to the mayor, 8 April 1947, HCA, file 8607, 401/18. The regulations are still valid.

[369] HCA, file 5568, 280/16.

[370] HCA, file 7694, 376/7.

[371] Vilnai, op.cit., p.104.

[372] Jordan, op.cit., pp.142-144.

[373] Edward Keith-Roach, *Pasha of Jerusalem*, the Radcliff Press, London, New York, 1994, p.137.

[374] Weizmann, interview, op.cit.

[375] Herbert and Sosnovsky, op.cit., p. 47.

[376] Interview with the author, 24.2.2004.

[377] Haifa City Archives, file 8747, 407/1.

[378] Haifa City Archives, file 8567, 400/3.

[379] Keith-Roach, op.cit., p.165.

[380] Ibid.,p.189.

[381] Brenner, interview, op.cit.

[382] Weizmann, interview, op.cit.

[383] Ibid.

[384] Ibid.

[385] Ibid. In 1936 Wingate was assigned to Palestine to a staff office position and became an intelligence officer. He saw the creation of a Jewish State in Palestine as being a religious duty toward the literal fulfillment of Christian prophecy and he immediately put himself into absolute alliance with Jewish political leaders. (*Wikipedia*).

[386] Interview with Yitzhak Rimon, op.cit.

[388] Shorer, op.cit., p.189. Picca was a company founded by the Baron Rothschild for the settlement of Jews in Palestine.

[388] Benni Nachshon, historical tour of Haifa, 5.12.2003. Edwin Samuel wife was Hadassah.

[389] Yosef Vashitz, *Social Changes in Haifa's Arab Settlement During the British Mandate* (Hebrew), Ph.D. Dissertation, the Hebrew University, June 1993, p.311.

[390]Fredrick Kish, *Eretz-Israel Diary* (Hebrew), Ahiasaf publication Jerusalem, 1939, p.112. The brothers in law were Ibrahim Bei and Tufic Bei Halil, the first murdered by Arab terrorists in 1937.

[391]Vashitz, op.cit., p.311.

[392]Zuker, op.cit., p.73.

[393]Vashitz, op.cit., pp.135-136,151.

[394]Ibid., pp.152-153.

[395]Ibid., p 179.

[396]Ibid., pp.198-199.

[397]Ibid., pp.189-192.

[398]Khamra, interview, op.cit.

[399]Ibid. Toubi was elected in 1949 to the first Israeli Knesset as representative of the Communist party, he served until 1990.

[400]Ruth Woodsmall, *Muslim Women Enter a New World*, London, 1936, pp.73, 355.

[401]Michael Assaf, *The Relationships between Arabs And Jews in Eretz-Israel 1860-1948* (Hebrew), Tarbut Vehinuch, Tel-Aviv 1970, and see also in Matiel E.T. Mogannam, *The Arab Woman*, Herbert Joseph, London, 1937, pp.61-62.

[402]Mogannam, Ibid., pp.70-74.

[403]Vashitz, op.cit., p.126, see also f.n. 83, page 277.

[404]Horace B. Samuel, *Unholy Memories of the Holy Land*, the Hogart Press, London, 1930, pp. 189-191.

[405]Zuker, op.cit., p.18.

[406]Hacohen, in Nedava, op.cit., pp.71-72.

[407]Samuel, op.cit.

[408]Levi, op.cit., pp.168-169.

[409]Ibid., p.170.

[410] Nachshon, op.cit.

[411] Shorer, op.cit., p.114.

[412] Ibid., p.89.

[413]Weizmann, intrview, op.cit.

[414]Mrs. Stuart Erskine, *Palestine of the Arabs*, George G. Harrap & co. London, Bombay, Sydney, 1935, pp.234-236.

[415]Thomas Hodgkin, *Letters from Palestine, 1932-36*, Quartet Books London, New York, 1986, p.136.

[416]Abraham Halfon, "Haifa, my city," Nedava, op.cit., p.62.

[417]Zuker, interview, op.cit.

[418]Irani, interview, op.cit.

[419]Weizmann, interview, op.cit.

[420]Sherman, op.cit., pp.217-218, see also f.n. 288. The Zone is the secured British area on the French Carmel.

[421]Richard Crossman, *Palestine Mission,* Harper and Brothers Publishers, New York and London, 1947, p.141.

[422]Ibid., p. 142-143.

[423]Ibid., my emphasis. The Anglo-American Committee of Inquiry was a joint British and American attempt made in 1946 to find a policy to resolve the growing conflict between Jews and Arabs in Palestine. The Committee approved the American condition of the immediate acceptance of 100,000 displaced persons into Palestine. A binational state was to be established in Palestine, in which the interests of both communities were as carefully balanced and protected under the British Mandate until a UN. Trusteeship will be implemented. (*Wikipedia).*

[424]HCA, file 8615, 401/25, declaration from 11.12.1947.

The Arabs in Haifa During the British Mandate- Johnny Mansour

[425]Sheik Daher al-Omar destroyed Old Haifa neighborhoods in 1761, in the area of Al-Carmel station near the current port, and established the New Haifa within the walls. Years later it was known as the Old City by its inhabitants, especially after the building of the new neighborhoods outside the walls in the second half of the 19th century.

[426]See May Ibrahim Seikaly's book, *Hayfa Al-Arabiyah 1918-1939,* Mua'sasat Al-Dirasat Al-Filastinia, Beirut, 1997. (Arab Haifa, 1918-1939 published by the Institute for Palestine Studies, Beirut, 1997), p.68. the book is originally a Ph.D. dissertation, published in English, Seikaly May, op.cit.

[427]For further detail see Yossi Ben-Artzi, *Formation of a Dwelling Model and the Moving Characteristics of Haifa's Arabs* (Hebrew), Studies in the Middle-East, Haifa University and The Jewish-

Arab Center, Haifa, 1980. Mahmud Yazbak, "The Arab immigration to Haifa, 1933-1948: Quantity Analysis according to Arab Sources," *Catedra* (Hebrew), Yad Ben-Zvi, 65 (1987), p.131-146.

[428]Klein, op.cit., p.114. Attached a map of the Arab neighborhood dispersing according to testimony.

[429] Klein, ibid., p.115.

[430]Ibid., p.116. Additional details about each neighborhood and its social-economic status.

[431]Hussein Ighbaria, *Haifa, Altarikh Waldhakira* (Haifa, the History and the Memory), Social Development Committee (SDC), Haifa, 2001, p.275-276.

[432']There is still a street near Khamra square (Paris today) by the name of Khatib family.

[433]Zuhayr Ghanayim, *Liwa''Akka fi'ahed al-tanzimat al-'uthmaniyah, 1864-1918* (The District of Acre during the Ottoman Tanzimat Period), Mua'sasat Al-Dirasat Al-Filastinia, first edition, Beirut 1999, p.244. Quoted from the Sijil Al-mahkama Al-shareia in Haifa from 1905.

[434]All Christian churches in the East use "Mar" before the name of the church. Mar is "holy" in Aramaic.

[435]Maronite family from Lebanon that immigrated to Haifa during the second half of the 19th century. Bought lands in Haifa and Yagur (the lands in Yagur were sold to the Jewish lands foundation K.K.L). Salim Khoury, one of the city's wealthiest people, built his castle at the end of Anaporte street, where Migdal Hanevi'im stands today.

[436]The Scottish medical delegation established hospitals in Nazareth and Tiberias. Three English doctors worked in the hospital in Haifa, see Zuhayr Ghanayim, op.cit., p.263.

[437]The first convent was near Jaffa-Kingsway (Haatzmaout street today). Was transferred to its current location in the beginning of the 30's with the start of the reclaiming of the sea in order to built Haifa's harbor.

[438]The Russian Orthodox Empire built a small hospital in Haifa

in the beginning of the 20th century. See Ghanayim, op.cit., p. 264.

[439]Muhammad Rafik and Muhammad Bahajat. *Wilayat Beirut, Al-Qism Al-janoubi* (District of Beirut, the Southern area). Lahed Khater publishing, third print, Beirut, 1987. (The first edition came out in Turkish in 1335 to the Hijra-1916), p. 237.

[440]Op.cit., p.237. It should be noted that both writers of the aforementioned book took a wide tour in Wilayat Beirut, and wrote their notes.

[441]*The Palestinian Encyclopedia* (studies volume), The Education and Teaching, first volume, p.529, Abd elhadi Hashem (chief editor), the Palestinian Encyclopedia Society publishing, Damascus, 1984.

[442]Mustafa Murad al-Dabagh' "Al-Talim fi Filastin fi A'hed Al-Intidab" (The Education in Palestine During the British Mandate), the *Palestinian encyclopedia*, second part (studies), third volume, p.68, Anis Saiegh (chief editor), the Palestinian Encyclopedia Society publishing, first edition, Beirut, 1990.

[443]The number of male students in 1942-1943 school year reached 461, and the number of teachers was 21. High school classes were up to tenth grade (at the end of the Mandate they reached twelfth grade). While the number of females was 442 students and 12 teachers, and the studies continued only to seventh grade. See more details on the education system in Dabagh's article, op.cit., p.68.

[444]Haron Hashem Rashid, *Madina Washa'er: Haifa walBuheri* (City and Songwriter-Haifa and al-Buheiri), Dar Al-Haiait publishing, Damascus, 1975, p. 79 and p. 81.

[445]Jamil al-Bahri mentions in his book: *Taarikh Haifa* (History of Haifa), National Library Publishing, Haifa, 1922, that the number of schools in Haifa was 30 that year (1922). Three Muslim schools, 17 Christian schools and 10 Jewish schools. He also mentions that the number of students in the Catholic schools was 300. p.26.

[446]We do not have detailed information about the schools. Their names were brought by Abd al-Latif Kanafani in his book:

15 Sharea' Al-Bourj Haifa (Al- Bourj st. no. 15 in Haifa), Bissan publishing, Beirut, 1992, p.48. This is the memory book of the writer, starting with his home which gave the book its title.

[447] Rashid, op.cit., pp. 305 - 306.

[448] Op.cit., p.279.

[449] Kanafani, op.cit., p. 49.

[450] Rashid, op.cit., p.286.

[451] Dabagh', op.cit., p.45.

[452] Ibid., p. 54.

[453] See note number 60 in Dabagh's article, p.77.

[454] The Selesian school is Carmel school nowadays, under the management of the Carmelite order.

[455] This school was established in Safad in the end of the Ottoman period. It was known for the "Scottish College," one of the well-known principals was Mr. Semple. It was moved to Haifa in the school year of 1936-7 after the Palestinian strike and mutiny in Palestine broke out. See Dabagh', op.cit., p.67.

[459] See Dabagh', ibid., note 60, p.77. This school became an institution for handicapped children.

[457] Dabagh' uses this table in his aforementioned article, p.68.

[458] Ya'akov Yehoshua refers to the connection between the newspaper and Zionist factors by the fact that the newspaper defends the Jews right for settlement. Yehoshua relies on stories and articles from the *Herut* newspaper. See Yehoshua's book: *Taarikh Al-Sahafa Al-Arafia fi Falestine fi Al-A'hed Al-Othmani (1908-1918)* (Arab Press History in Palestine During the Ottoman Period), Dar Al-Ma'araf printing house, Jerusalem, 1974, p. 134.

[459] See Philip de Tarazi's book, *Taarikh Al-Sahafa Al-Arabia* (The Arab Press History), Vol.3, Beirut, 1933, p. 70. Al-Matba'a Al-Adabia publishing, Beirut, 1933. Also Yehushua's book, op.cit., p.134. De Tarazi, Volume 4, p. 138 and p.140.

[460] Jamil al-Bahri stresses that the newspaper's approach is basically Zionist despite the editor Malul's attempts to bring the Palestinian Arabs and the Zionists closer. See Al-Bahri's book *Taarikh Haifa* (History of Haifa), National Library Publishing, Haifa, 1922, p.33

[461] There is an inaccuracy in establishing the date of the first

edition of the "Al-Yarmuk" newspaper. Yehoshua mentions the year 1930. See his book: *Al-Sahafa Al-Arabia Al-Filastinia fi Bedayat A'hed Al-Entidab Al-Barittani, 1919-1929* (The Palestinian Arab Press in the Beginning of the British Mandate in Palestine), Haifa University publishing, 1981, p.390. While Yosef Khoury notes in his book: *Al-Sahafa Al-Arabia fi Filastine 1876-1948* (The Arab Press in Palestine), Beirut, 1976, p.137 that the first publishing date was 1924.

[462] Yehoshua, op.cit., p. 334.

[463] Ibid., p. 418. De Tarazi, op.cit., vol. 4, p. 72.

[464] Yehoshua, ibid., p. 423. While Ahmad Khalil Al-A'kad mentions in his book: *Al Sahafa Al-Arabia fi-Filastine* (The Arab Press in Palestine), no mention of publisher, Damascus, 1966, p. 75, that the newspaper was established in September 1929 and ceased to appear that same year, that it was a religious newspaper.

[465] This newspaper-magazine is published today by the Ahmedian Community Council in Kababeer, which is a neighborhood close to Haifa, and edited by intellectuals of this group.

[466] Muneer Ibrahim Haddad, an active intellectual figure among the Arab citizens in Haifa, bought and activated the "Haddad" printing house in Wadi Nisnas.

[467] Kanafani gives a lot of details about the assembly of teams and the names of the players and what happened to some of them after they left the country due to the events of 1948. op.cit., pp. 109-116.

[468] For more details on al-Bahri see Hanna Abu Hanna's book: *Rehlat Al-Bahth a'n Al-Turath* (Tour Following the Heritage), Alwadi printing house, Haifa, 1994. pp. 71-84.

[469] Partial list of his publishing appears in 'Arfan Abu Hamad Al-Hawari, *A'lam min Ard' Al-Salam* (Personalities from the Peace Country), The Society of Scientific and Useful Research publishing, Haifa University, 1979, p. 270.

[470] The most famous one was *Al-Intidab Al-Filastini Batel Wamuhal* (The Palestinian Mandate is Invalid). The English edition:

Bustani, W.F, *The Palestine Mandate: Invalid and Impracticable*, A.U.B Press, Beirut, 1936.

[471]Al-Bustani, From Lebanese origin, moved to Lebanon after the events of 1948 and was appointed planning minister in the Lebanese government. He was killed in an aerial accident in 1958.

[472]*Dalil Al-Tijara Wal-Sina'a Wal-Hiraff Wal-Mihan Al-Arabia fi Filastine Washarq Al-Urdoun* (Commerce, Industry and Arab Professions in Palestine and the Trans-Jordan), 1935-1936, Jerusalem, Merchants' Union, p.62.

[473]For more details on Taha's life and his activities for the laborers and their rights see Ahmad al-Yamani, *Jameiat Al-Umal Al-Arabia Al-Filastinia fi Haifa*, (The Palestinian Arab Laborers' Union), Cana'an, Damascus publishing, 1993. The writer is one of the most prominent figures in the union and one of the members related to Taha. He suspects the Mufti's actions in anything having to do with the murder of Taha.

[474]To learn about the life and actions of Bishop Hajjar, see my book: *Roueya Jadida Lehayat Wa'mal Al-Mutran Gregorios Hajjar* (A New Perspective on the Life and Action of Bishop Gregorios Hajjar), Abu Rahmoun printing and publishing, Akka (Acre), 1985.

[475]Before the Mandate, more than 15 associations and unions that dealt mainly with humanitarian and educational assistance were established. Most of them were Christian. The reason lies within the influence of the different churches and foreign consulates which represented the European countries' interests, and in light of the increase in number of intellectuals towards the end of the Ottoman period. See Mahmud Zaid, "The Unions, Organizations, Clubs, Printing Houses and the Palestinian Research Institutions," in the *Palestinian Encyclopedia*, op.cit., the second part, volume 3, p. 182.

[476]In his article Klein brings a partial and minimized list of the unions and associations which operated among the Arab population in Haifa. He also refers to the increase of unions and to the ethnic-political social-economic division in the society.

This factor did in fact exist, however, there was cooperation in crucial matters such as strikes and rallies among all unions and associations in Haifa, op.cit., p. 114.

[477]See a detailed list of all the associations and unions in Palestine and particularly in Haifa, in Zaid's article, op.cit.

[478]Op.cit., p. 226, see in *Al-Carmel*, December 9th, 1920; *Palestine newspaper*, October 1st, 1929; and *Al-Sha'ab*, January 25th, 1945.

[479]Both unions, the Muslim and the Christian, played a wide social-political role among the Arabs of Haifa and outside it. Both prepared the grounds for the Palestinian Congress which debated the social-political situation in January 1920. At the same convention, representatives of a few of Haifa's associations and unions participated. See Al-Bahri, op.cit., p. 23 and 24.

[480]See note (1) in Al-Bahri's book, ibid., p.28.

[481]Zaid, op.cit., p. 232, *Al-Carmel*, November 30th, 1920; *Palestine newspaper*, December 28th, 1921.

[482]El-Bahri, op.cit., p. 29. Abd el-Rahman Yaghi, *The Life of the Palestinian Literature until the Nakba*, Dar Al-Afaq publishing, Beirut, 1981, p. 96 and p. 97.

[483]The location of the club is in a shack on Ein Dor street. The community built the Mar Elias Church in the 30's in replacement of it.

[484]Zaid, op.cit., p. 238; *Palestine newspaper*, May 1st 1929.

[485]Ibid.,p.224; *Palestine newspaper*, March 13th 1935.

[486]Ibid., p.226; *Palestine newspaper*, March 25th 1932.

[487]Ibid., p.229; *Palestine newspaper*, February 27th 1945.

[488]Ibid., p.231; *Palestine newspaper,* July 27th 1934.

[489]Ibid., p.262; *Palestine newspaper*, June 23rd 1944.

[490]Ibid., p.263; *Palestine newspaper*, April 10th 1930.

[491]Muhammad Al-Batrawi, "Malameh min Al-Masrah Al-Filastini Qabel Al-Nakba (Views from the Palestinian Theatre Before the Nakba), *Al-Zawiya* magazine (Ramallah), first issue, Summer of 2002, p. 95.

[492]For further detail on the plays in the 20's in Haifa see Yaghi's book, op.cit., p. 106.

[493]Salim Nassib claims in his book: *Umm* (The Umm Kulthum

Novel) (Hebrew), Asia publishing, Tel Aviv, 1999, that Umm Kulthum donated the profits of one of the concerts to the battle against the English conquest and the Jewish immigration to Palestine, and that she was recieved in victory applause, and was even given a new name: "The Star of the East," which she carried all over the world until her dying day, op.cit., p. 70.

[494]See A'dnan Mdanamat, "Al-Cinema Al-Filastinia" (The Palestinian Cinema), in the *Palestinian Encyclopedia*, op.cit., the second part, vol. 4, p.839.

[495]For a detailed list of the printing houses in Palestine, see Zaid's, op.cit., pp. 251-258.

[496]See the commercial guide of Palestine 1935-1936, op.cit., p. 200.

[497]This printing house was providing modern printing services such as silk, color and photograph printings, see op.cit., p. 201.

[498]For further detail on the organizing of the strike and the role of the Arab laborers union, see al-Yamani, op.cit., p. 69. He also brings forth opinions of different Palestinian historians about this stage.

[499]Ibid., p. 74.

[500]See the *Palestinian Encyclopedia*, op.cit., vol. 2, p. 325, for more information and details about the Palestinian Laborers' movement.

[501]The Governor of Jerusalem, Ahmad Hilmi, decided to outlaw the Communist group and the Laborers' Congress. See the general Palestinian Encyclopedia, ibid. But this decision was not executed because most of the members belonging to the two organizations remained in Israel after the 1948 war ended. Some of the Communist group's members were elected to the Israeli Knesset, like Tawfiq Toubi and Emil Habibi.

[502]Nader Aboud, *Haifa a'la Mar Al-O'usur* (Haifa throughout Periods), Kul Shai Library publishing, Haifa, 1985. Also Klein's article, op.cit., p. 114-115.

[503]Shimon Stern, "Haifa in the Mandate Period" (Hebrew), *Haifa and its Sites,* Ariel publishing, 37-39. Mars, 1985, pp. 79-84.

[504]Review of the dwelling arrangements of Haifa's Arabs by Ben-

Artzi: "The Formation of a Dwelling Models and the House Moving Characteristics of Haifa's Arabs," op.cit.

[505] In her book, Seikaly refers to the way in which the Palestinian Arab society in Haifa became an irrelevant society in anything that was happening in the city after the Jews took over the municipality, its institutions and other government institutes. In addition to managing the veteran Jewish neighborhood by way of establishing independent neighborhood committees, acting within the municipality's jurisdiction, Hadar HaCarmel committee for instance. At the same time, the Arab population of Haifa was shoved aside and was disconnected from the plans of developing it in the neighborhoods by the municipal authorities or in the general national plain. Op.cit., p. 84.

Epilogue: Coexistence - History, Myth, and Hope for the Future?

[506] Vashitz, op.cit., part 1, pp. 9, 17.

[507] Seikaly, op.cit., p.167.

[508] Vashitz, op.cit., p.18.

[509] Ibid., p.52.

[510] Ibid., p.195.

[511] Ibid., p.71-72. Records of the committee deliberations.

[512] Vashitz, Ibid., p.72.

[513] Ibid., p.79.

[514] Ibid., p.86-89. As an example, Victor Khayat, one of the senior businessmen in Haifa, asked the British government to release his Jewish lawyer, the Revisionist Vainshel from prison, so that Khayat would not lose a case worth one million pounds. With the increase of the rivalry between the Arab political parties, they preferred a Jewish lawyer at times, over an Arab lawyer from a rival party. The Jews did the same: When a group of house owners in Hadar HaCarmel tried to object the right of Hadar HaCarmel committee to collect taxes, they turned to the prominent Arab lawyer Abikrius.

[515] Ibid., p.91. This contradiction was discussed more than once in the national Jewish institutions, Moshe Sharett said after the

riots of 1929 that the Arab as an individual, felt that the Jews' presence was to his benefit, but as part of a group, he suffered and was even ashamed of these benefits.

[516]Ibid., p.94, article from 26.10.30.

[517]Ibid., pp.94-95.

[518]Declaration, 11.12.47, HCA, file 8615, 401/25.

[519]Letter by mayor Shabtai Levi to "Yehuda" publishing on September 8th 1946, Ibid., file 8342 394/14, list of municipality members, January 1949, Ibid., file 8342 394/14.

[520]Tamir Goren, *From Dependence to Integration* (Hebrew), The Jewish Arab Center, University of Haifa 1996, p. vii.

[521]Declaration, op.cit.

Illustrations

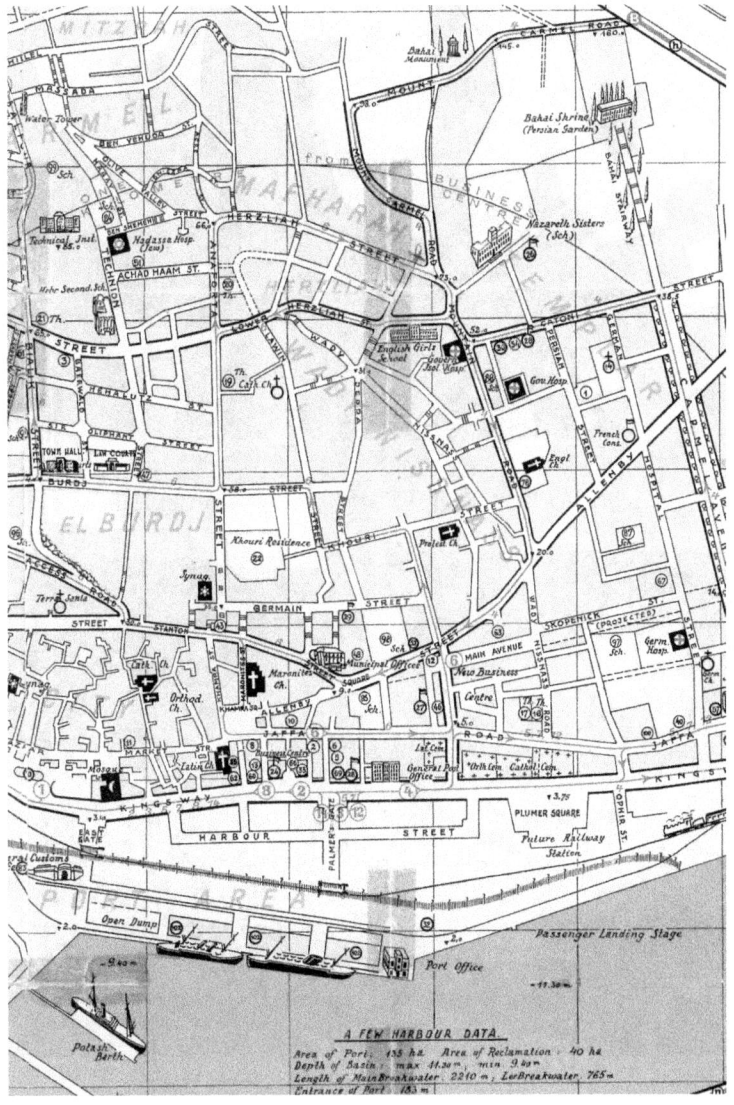

Haifa's downtown and port in a map from 1934

Arab workers on a 1st May celebration in Haifa

Haifa in the 20's, view from Mount Carmel

The city emblem during the Mandate

Joe Nadel's Swingers

Meggido Hotel in 1945 (Ya'akov Rosner, K.K.L Archives)

Café Jordan, 5 Nordau street (courtesy of Gideon Jordan and
Edna Blik Jordan)

The Selesian school football team, 1941

The bishop Hajjar's funeral procession, Hacarmel Avenue,
October 1940.

Graduates of the Selesian school (boys) and the Carmelite
school (girls), 1941